Caregiving AND Loss

Family Needs, Professional Responses

Edited by Kenneth J. Doka and Joyce D. Davidson

Foreword by Rosalynn Carter

Caregiving and Loss: Family Needs, Professional Responses

Edited by Kenneth J. Doka and Joyce D. Davidson

Foreword by Rosalynn Carter

This book is part of Hospice Foundation of America's
Living With Grief® series.

Support has been provided in part by the Foundation for End of Life Care.

This book is part of HFA's *Living With Grief* ® series

To order contact:
Hospice Foundation of America
2001 S Street, NW #300
Washington, DC 20009
(800) 854-3402
www.hospicefoundation.org
hfa@hospicefoundation.org

Managing Editor: Michon Lartigue
Typesetting and Design by Pam Page Cullen

Publisher's Catalog-in-Publication
(Provided by Quality Books, Inc.)
Caregiving and loss : family needs, professional responses
  / edited by Kenneth J. Doka and Joyce D. Davidson
  foreword by Rosalynn Carter. — 1st ed.
    p. cm.
    Includes bibliographical references.
    LCCN: 00-134618
    ISBN: 1-893349-02-0

  1. Caregivers. 2. Human services personnel. 3. Care
of the sick. I. Doka, Kenneth J. II. Davidson,
Joyce D.

HV40.C37 2001   362. 0425
                                 QBI00-1071

Dedication

*To my mother, Josephine (Jay) Doka
who, until her death this year,
modeled to her children
loving kindness and a generosity of spirit
stubborn independence
and
quiet strength*

KJD

*To Barbara and Joan
and to Anna Faye,
exquisite caregivers and examples of
"That best portion of one's life—
the nameless, unremembered acts
of kindness and of love."*

JDD

*And to all family and professionals
involved in caregiving
for the support and strength they give
to others and to one another
and for the strength and support they need
to get through another day*

KJD & JDD

Contents

Foreword

Rosalynn Carter

We are approaching a caregiving crisis in America. Thanks to the wonders of medicine and our knowledge about the causes of many health problems, we survive serious accidents and illnesses, live longer than our ancestors, and encounter problems associated with aging. Now in America, those 85 years old and older are the largest growing segment of our population.

With more people needing care, there are fewer people available to give it or to assist in its delivery. More women are working than ever before. Families are not as closely knit or as large as they once were. And yet family members continue to care for the vast majority of dependent people at home.

Sometimes family caregivers consider their responsibilities a rewarding mission. But for those who have been thrust into the role, it can also be an extremely lonely, stressful, and frustrating responsibility, with tasks that are always demanding. I know this personally, having helped care for my own gravely ill and aging family members.

I also know that being a professional caregiver can be quite stressful. Many are overwhelmed with their work and find themselves exhausted at the end of the day. Their tasks are demanding, too, and take much out of their personal lives.

At the Rosalynn Carter Institute (RCI) at Georgia Southwestern State University, whose mission is helping improve the lives of all caregivers, we have found that caring for a loved one is not an endeavor that should be undertaken alone. Almost all family caregivers, especially those providing the most intense levels of care, report significant physical and emotional stress. Many encounter serious loss of income and job opportunities. To offer the best to their loved ones and still stay strong and healthy, they need to be surrounded by compassionate, responsive assistance from the professionals who work with them. And these professionals must be willing to listen and respond to their needs.

Yet we have found in our research at the RCI that there are often difficulties in the family caregiver/professional relationship. Family caregivers sometimes feel that all the attention is on the ill family member, when they, the caregivers, need cooperation and respect — especially in the areas of communication and information-sharing. At the same time, professionals often feel that they don't have sufficient time to consult with families regarding how they might assist them. Physicians often don't realize that simply listening to their problems and concerns can be a huge relief for families in helping to alleviate some of their burdens.

There is much that our health care system should be doing to help caregivers through providing training, support services, and reimbursement for respite care. Local communities should also be providing more help, including spiritual counseling. Ample, carefully targeted supports are particularly crucial for family caregivers of people facing the end of life.

Caregiving at the end of life brings the distinctive responsibility of coping with many kinds of losses. Caregivers begin mourning losses while still helping their loved ones live their final days to the fullest. At the same time, the high economic toll that caring for terminally ill patients can take adds to their emotional as well as their physical stress. Their grief and loss absorb immense energy. And when the role of caregiver has ended, new issues may arise in balancing the challenges of forging a new identity while incorporating the loss.

Hospice plays a special role with caregivers during the end-of-life period, providing compassionate service at many levels—medical, emotional, and spiritual. Also, the hospice philosophy embodies the concept of continued support for the bereaved after the death.

It is fitting that the Hospice Foundation of America has chosen to focus on family needs and professional responses. We must all recognize and celebrate the crucial role of family caregivers in our society, and empower professionals to respond with increased awareness, compassion, and support.

Acknowledgments

As always, it is fitting to begin by acknowledging, collectively and individually, all those who make this book a reality. First, of course, is the staff and board of directors of the Hospice Foundation of America. Jack Gordon, the CEO and chairman of that board, has always provided an enlarged vision of the Foundation's mission. This year, he also contributed the topic. Foundation president David Abrams and vice-presidents Lisa McGahey Veglahn and Sophie Viteri Berman, as well as Bill Lamers, Jon Radulovic, Laura Spangler, and Katie Morgan offered valued time and varied talents. We both give special thanks to Michon Lartigue, our managing editor. In her quiet and gentle way, she kept us on track and on time. She even co-authored a chapter. And, of course, we both want to thank the authors, who contributed their chapters under impossibly tight deadlines. We both wish to thank Susan McVicker who, in the many roles she plays, greatly helped both of us. And we look forward to her continued contribution in the field of end-of-life care.

Individually, we both would like to acknowledge people who enrich our lives, enabling us to work and receive respite. They, too, are victims of deadlines.

K. Doka: In this year of my mother's death, I learned to once again appreciate the gift of family. My brother and sister and their spouses and families all came together in a difficult time. We were a model of mutual support. For that I am especially grateful. The terrible blessing of her death was that we came to reconnect and re-establish ties. As my nine-year-old great-nephew T.J. expressed it: "I didn't even know you were alive until the funeral." We now know we are all alive and family.

My own intimate network is an ongoing source of pride and support. For my son and his now wife, Angelina, and for my godson, Keith, and his family this has been a year of new transitions, experiences, and triumphs. And how could I fail to acknowledge Kathy.

I also need to acknowledge the College of New Rochelle. It is a wonderful place to work, made so by caring colleagues and a supportive administration, among them President Steven Sweeney, Academic Vice President Joan Bailey, and Dean Laura Ellis. My secretary Rosemary Strobel and faculty secretary Vera Mezzaucella all keep it running smoothly.

I would also like to acknowledge my colleagues in the Association for Death Education and Counseling, and the International Work Group on Death, Dying, and Bereavement, for all their stimulation and support. So many of them have become special and valued friends.

And finally I need to acknowledge my co-editor Joyce Davidson. I hope this is just a continuing chapter in a long collaboration.

J. Davidson: The topic of caregiving is dear to my heart, primarily because of the remarkable caregivers, both family and professional, whose journeys I have been, and still am, honored to share. Among the extraordinary professionals from whom I learn daily at University Hospital are first, of course, Pat Murphy, as well as George Blackwell, Gary Sabino-Benowitz, David Price, Anne Mosenthal, David Livingston, Lillian Pliner, Mary Brennan, Harriet Jernquist, and so many others. The staff at Broadway

House, under the exquisite guidance of Jeanine O'Reilly, have their "hearts in heaven and their hands upon the earth." All these people are truly noble and heroic in the face of others' suffering, and their work is an expression of reverence for life.

I want to thank the families who have been so generous in allowing me to bear witness to the miracle of their caregiving. I am humbled to be in their presence.

I am grateful to Ken Doka, both for the pivotal role he has had in my professional journey and for his friendship.

And to my husband, Rex, the primary victim of my deadlines: His quiet strength, profound integrity, and generosity of spirit are surpassed only by his patience. He is bedrock.

Finally, we both need to acknowledge Cokie Roberts for her ongoing, integral part in the Hospice Foundation of America Teleconference. And we give special thanks to former First Lady Rosalynn Carter, not only for the Foreword, but for all her pioneering, visionary efforts to support family and professional caregivers.

Part I

Caregiving as an Issue: Policy and Programs

The Baby Boom generation, driven by both its large numbers and its activist orientation, tends to focus policy and social concern on whatever problem it is dealing with at the moment. Baby Boomers focused social policies on their schools and colleges, they challenged and eliminated the military draft, they redefined gender roles, and they are restructuring workplaces. In short, their issues become social issues, driving debate and policy.

As Baby Boomers age, they have begun to face a new quandary: how to take care of aging parents who now make demands upon their limited time and resources. It is little wonder that caregiving is emerging as one of the key issues of this decade.

In truth, the issue of caregiving extends far beyond that of aging parents. Caregiving takes place in a variety of contexts and roles: Parents care for children with illnesses, injuries or developmental disabilities; spouses provide care for one another; and others in the intimate network, kin or non-kin, who care and matter, are also involved. For example, over 10% of grandmothers have, at least at one time, primary responsibility for raising a grandchild.

This book, like the teleconference it supports, is designed for professionals who support family caregivers as advocates or policy makers, as well as those who directly provide professional care or supervise those who do. It is important, then, to offer a variety of perspectives. The book includes substantive chapters on a range of issues, but it also provides two other features: first, *Programs That Work*, a review of programs that illustrate and model best practices; and second, *Voices*, in which caregivers speak candidly of their own experiences. These essays help to address concerns that statistics and theory can obscure the mixed realities of caregiving. In the discussion of policy, we may lose an authentic picture of the caregiving experience. We may see numbers and practices but lose the larger reality—the individuals who provide ongoing care. We run the risk of either emphasizing the ennobling aspects of caregiving or stressing that it can be emotionally and physically exhausting.

One choice of terminology needs to be addressed as well. Many people offer caregiving—professionals such as nurses, aides, or others as well as family members. Some people think that the term *caregiver* should always be reserved for members of the family, however family is defined. Other professionals, they claim, have their own title and are not as intimately involved. Yet that distinction can be difficult to maintain, as professional caregivers often experience strong emotional involvement. We have decided, however awkward, to use the term *caregiver* broadly, differentiating family and professional caregivers.

In this first section we begin defining caregiving as an issue. Levine begins this section with a powerful introduction that delineates the contexts and costs of caregiving. While the 'wear and tear' hypothesis—the notion that caregiving inevitably causes physical and mental strain—may be debated (see, for example, Lawton, Moss, Hoffman, & Parkinson, 2000), there is little question of its stresses and demands on time.

Lattanzi-Licht suggests that hospice can provide a broad model for programs that assist caregivers. The hospice paradigm of a community-based approach offering holistic care that integrates family, professionals, and volunteers has application far beyond care of the dying. Yet Halling's powerful personal story reminds us that even hospice has its limitations. Her voice is a testimony to the paradoxical nature of professional caregiving—it may be needed yet not always welcome.

Caregiving, as Levine points out, has significant economic costs. While family caregiving saves the government money, it costs employers in lost productivity, employee morale, and retention. Weinberg's piece explores this further, suggesting ways that the workplace can assist family caregivers. This is not merely altruistic; it is good practice, because it enhances morale and makes family-friendly firms more likely to attract and retain employees. Weinberg's piece is complemented by interviews with two companies, AT&T and Fannie Mae, that practice such policies. Both assess the mutual benefits of such programs and offer practical illustrations of family-friendly policies.

Gaventa also addresses the question of what helps. He stresses that professional caregivers can have a special role in creating and energizing caring communities to assist family caregivers.

Alexander adds his voice as well, in his moving story about the death of his father. Implicit in that story is the almost seamless integration of professional and family caregivers. The section ends with another Program That Works—CARE-NET, out of the pioneering Rosalynn Carter Institute—that leaves us with pointed advice: As we establish a knowledge base about caregiving, we need to develop models that offer case management, training, and information to those providing direct care. Only then can that seamless integration of family and professional caregivers take place. And only then can we advocate for policies, both in business and government, that provide a supportive context for caregiving.

Introduction:
Nature of Caregiving

Carol Levine

In his poem, "Dynasty," Robert Mazzocco (1996) writes of the "family voices"—his father's and his mother's—that he now hears in his own voice. "The older we get, the more you'll hear them, though no one else does," he says. These voices are accompanied by what no one else can or must see— the "family scars and family kisses" that each of us embodies. This phrase, "family scars and family kisses," eloquently captures both the pain and the love that epitomize family caregiving.

Family caregiving is often categorized as either one thing or another—burdensome or rewarding, exhausting or uplifting, a catalyst that brings families together or a wedge that drives them apart. Caregiving can be some or all of these things in the same family over time. Each family has its own scars and kisses—its unique history of relationships, shared experiences, private moments, debts incurred, and obligations both discharged and unfulfilled.

How, then, are we as family members, health care or social service professionals, pastoral counselors, community volunteers, and citizens to respond to family caregivers as they face the challenges brought on by illness or disability? This volume provides many answers to that question, because there is no single answer. This introduction provides some background about family caregiving as it is lived in the United States today. Statistics and policies frame the context of family caregiving yet they only hint at its human dimension. For that we need the stories and reflections of the participants (Strong, 1997; Lipsyte, 1998; Levine, 1998; Levine, ed., 2000), and the expertise of professionals, represented in this volume.

Caregiving: The Broad Picture

Several national surveys have data compiled on family caregivers, typically called "informal caregivers" to distinguish them from paid professional or paraprofessional providers of "formal care." (Although advocates for family caregivers dislike the term "informal care," which implies a casual, less-than-essential activity, it is ingrained in the research literature.) The number of family caregivers in the United States has been variously estimated at 7 million, 23.5 million, and as high as 27 million. The lower number comes from the National Long-Term Care Survey, a dataset that includes only care recipients over 65 receiving Medicare services (R.I. Stone, 2000). The higher estimates come from broad population-based surveys, which include care recipients of all ages. The 1996 National Alliance on Caregiving/AARP (NAC/AARP) random telephone survey of caregivers of people age 50 and older found that 23.5 million American adults—one in four—was providing some level of care (NAC/AARP, 1997). The 1998 survey conducted by the Harvard School of Public Health, the United Hospital Fund, and the Visiting Nurse Service of New York (Harvard-UHF-VNS) arrived at a similar estimate—from one in four to one in five adults providing care (Levine et al., 2000; Donelan, et al., forthcoming). Whether the definition of caregiving is broad (as in the NAC/AARP and Harvard-UHF-VNS studies) or narrow (as in the Long-Term-Care Survey), caregiving is an activity that engages most of us at some time in our lives, either as caregivers or care recipients.

In creating a profile of the typical caregiver, the parameters of the survey again determine the outcome. The typical caregiver in the National Long-Term Care Survey is a 60-year-old unemployed wife. In the AARP/NAC and Harvard-UHF-VNS surveys, the typical caregiver is younger, more likely to be employed, and more likely to be the adult child of the care recipient. More men are identified as caregivers in the population-based surveys than in the Long-Term Care Survey; in the New York City sample of the Harvard-UHF-VNS survey, women outnumbered men, but only by a margin of three to two. Although some men provided care at the most intense levels, by and large they were involved in less intimate tasks and for a shorter duration than were their female counterparts.

The Harvard-UHF-VNS survey asked potential participants whether they were currently caregiving or had cared for someone in the past 12 months. Many of the current caregivers had been providing care for five or more years. Of the people no longer providing care, the most common reason was that the person had died. Many caregivers are thus involved in the final illness of their relatives, which adds the prospect of death and bereavement to the caregiving burdens they carry.

All surveys agree that the need for care is greatest among the elderly, and within that large age range, among the oldest-old (those over 80). Two-thirds of the care recipients in the New York City sample were over 65 and 20% were over 80. A majority had serious health problems and over half had been hospitalized within the past year. The primary diseases included heart disease, cancer, diabetes, hypertension, arthritis, and Alzheimer's disease. Some of the caregivers simply said that the health problems of the person they cared for were due to "old age" and others gave only a vague diagnosis. It is true that, on the whole, disability rates are declining slightly among the elderly, but there is still a large reservoir of elderly people whose lives are constrained by chronic or terminal illness. Older people who are poor and from an ethnic minority group are particularly at risk for poor health.

While some caregiving involves only occasional help, for many caregiving is the equivalent of at least a half-time job. On average, the New York City caregivers in the Harvard-UHF-VNS study provided 20.5 hours a week of care. Some, of course, provided less, but others provided from 40 or more hours up to "constant care." The vast majority (85%) had not hired or arranged for a professional, such as a nurse, social worker, or a paraprofessional, such as a home-care aide.

The tasks caregivers undertake include personal Activities of Daily Living (ADLs) such as bathing, toileting, feeding, transferring from bed to chair, and helping the person walk. Instrumental Activities of Daily Living (IADLs)—dealing with the outside world—are another significant area of assistance. IADLs include shopping, housework, transportation, and telephone calls. These conventional descriptions of caregiving provide only the barest outline of the complexity of caregiving today. They do not capture the degree of difficulty in, for example, transferring a person from bed to chair, depending on whether the person is frail, paralyzed, cognitively impaired, or otherwise incapacitated. Bathing and toileting can be relatively simple or extremely difficult. Nor do the current measures take into account the amount of time the caregiver must spend dealing with insurance companies, government agencies, doctors' offices, transportation companies, and all the other vendors and suppliers of home-care services. Behavior management for a person with dementia is an emotionally draining and time-consuming part of caregiving, yet none of the large national surveys have measured this aspect of care. Many studies of Alzheimer's patients, however, do elicit this information from caregivers.

Family caregivers are increasingly involved in medical tasks as well. In the Harvard-UHF-VNS survey, 12% of the New York sample were operating medical equipment, such as feeding tubes,

IV infusions, or catheters. Larger percentages changed bandages or dressings (17%) or managed medications (35%). Training for these tasks was erratic at best: 18% of those operating medical equipment reported no training, as did 38% of those changing bandages, and 16% of those managing medications. When instruction was available, much of it came from outside the formal system, from friends and neighbors who may have had some medical background. Family caregivers, in this as in other areas, are often left to find their own help.

Economic Value of Family Caregiving

Despite the enormous attention to the costs of health care in the U.S., the contribution of "informal" or unpaid caregiving has generally been ignored. Peter Arno, Margaret Memmott, and I devised a method to estimate the annual economic value of caregiving—that is, what the system would have to pay should family caregivers all burn out at the same time (Arno, Levine, & Memmott, 1999). Using three large national datasets, we estimated the number of caregivers at 25.3 million. The hourly wage was set at $8.18 (the average of the minimum wage of $5.50 at the time and the U.S. Bureau of Labor Statistics' national wage of $11.20 an hour for home health aides). The weekly hours from the NAC/AARP survey, 17.9, was held constant for all calculations. This is clearly a conservative estimate.

We concluded that unpaid family caregivers contributed an estimated $196 billion a year in 1997 to the health care economy. This is not counted in the trillion-dollar health care enterprise. The figure is more than the annual amount spent on formal home care ($32 billion) and nursing home care ($83 billion) combined.

Financial Costs to Caregivers

On the micro level, studies of selected groups of caregivers have found a range of out-of-pocket costs, from under $1,000 a year to $10,000 or more. Privately paid home care or nursing-home care can cost upwards of $40,000 a year. In addition, caregivers also encounter financial problems related to employment. In the NAC/AARP survey, caregivers with annual household incomes under $15,000 (poverty level for a family of four) and those who had not graduated from college were more likely to report financial hardship (NAC/AARP, 1997). An earlier study of families of terminally ill patients with health care insurance found that a third had lost their homes, had gone bankrupt, or suffered serious financial losses (Covinsky, et al., 1994). In a 1999 national study of bankruptcies, 40% were related to illness in the family (Jacoby, Sullivan, & Warren, 2000). The elderly and single-woman-headed households were most vulnerable.

A qualitative study of an employed subgroup of the NAC/AARP survey reported that 40 percent suffered serious economic setbacks. They passed up job promotions, training, or assignments; rejected opportunities for transfer or relocation; were not able to acquire new job skills; or were not able to keep up with changes in job skills. In addition to loss of current income, their future economic security was jeopardized. On average, their lost Social Security benefits, which are calculated on the basis of wages, amounted to $2,160 annually or $25,494 over their expected retirement years. Those eligible for pensions estimated that their benefits fell by $5,339 annually, or $67,202 over the course of their retirement (MetLife, 1999).

The Impact of Caregiving on Health

Family caregiving can lead to serious health problems or exacerbate already existing ones. Stress—almost a *sine* qua non of caregiving—weakens the immune system, with resulting illnesses such as influenza and other infectious diseases. Poor technique in lifting a patient or in pushing a wheelchair can result in back strain and related problems. Elderly caregivers are most at risk for illness and even death. One study found that caregivers over the age of 65 who experienced stress were 63% more likely to die than their non-caregiving peers (Schulz and Beach, 1999). Sometimes the health impact of caregiving does not appear until the care recipient has died, making it particularly important that professionals provide or refer caregivers to bereavement services.

Mental health problems such as depression are also common, particularly among caregivers of patients with Alzheimer's disease or other cognitive problems. While some types of depression are incapacitating, caregivers often feel overwhelmed and sad, but are able to manage their responsibilities. Caregivers' feelings of this sort are not necessarily pathological; they may in fact be quite healthy reactions to very difficult and challenging situations. Certainly caregivers need understanding and support, in ways that help overcome depression without stigmatizing them. Caregivers may be reluctant to express their ambivalent emotions for fear of being judged "selfish" or "disloyal."

On the positive side, even those caregivers who experience depression and other negative emotions may also find some solace and reward in their tasks. Providing care to a loved one can create a powerful bond, even where none existed before. Many caregivers say that they have become more spiritual as a result of caregiving. This may mean becoming more religious, but it also may mean becoming more aware of life's fragility and the importance of close relationships and simple pleasures.

The Health Care System and Caregivers

Many caregivers are unable to appreciate these positive experiences because they spend so much of their time and energy dealing with a largely unresponsive health care system. It is hard to feel very spiritual when a loved one is crying out in pain, when each day's mail brings new bills, and each day's phone calls to insurance companies and vendors go unreturned.

Two facts about the American health care system are paramount: First, unless they are in prison or the military, Americans do not have a right to health care. Second, the most common sources of insurance—employer-based private insurance and Medicare for the elderly—do not cover long-term care.

Medicare, a federal program introduced in 1965, provides coverage for people over the age of 65 and for a few categories of disabled people. Medicare was specifically designed to cover acute care, not long-term care. Limited home care and nursing-home care are covered following a hospitalization. Prescription drugs are not covered. Although Medicare has uniform rules across the country, there are different patterns of interpretation. When coverage for home care became the fastest growing portion of Medicare a few years ago, raising Congressional worries, it was largely because for-profit home-care agencies in the South and Southwest were proliferating. The Balanced Budget Act of 1997 drastically reduced payments to home-care agencies, resulting in the loss of services for some of the neediest clients. A new prospective-payment system introduced in 2000 attempts to control costs through patient classification and "case-mix" adjustments. It is unlikely to make agencies more willing to take on clients with complex medical and social needs (Stone, 2000).

Medicaid is a federal-state program that provides coverage for poor people. Each of the 50 states determines its eligibility rules and level of benefits, as well as payments to hospitals and physicians, and may call the program by a different name (for example, Medi-Cal in California). Extreme differences between states are the result. Medicaid does pay for nursing-home care and, in some states, varying levels of home care. To become eligible for Medicaid, an individual or a married couple must be impoverished, and therefore many are forced to "spend down" their assets and become impoverished to obtain care. Even then, the entry process is generally described as difficult and demeaning. In New York City, spouses (generally elderly women) who legally refused to "spend down" their modest assets and whose husbands were then eligible for Medicaid are now being sued by the City for the costs of care.

Private insurance varies considerably according to the plan purchased by an employer. Increasingly, employers are choosing managed-care plans to control costs. Whether they are run for profit or are non-profit entities, these companies set up rules that govern access to specialists, hospitals, vendors of equipment, diagnostic tests, and other services. Private health care insurance does not cover long-term care, whether in the home or nursing home, and has very poor coverage of durable medical equipment (wheelchairs, shower aids, and the like) and disposable items such as incontinence aids.

Each of these broad categories has its own thicket of rules, regulations, and policies, which often work against each other and certainly make the caregiver's task of finding services incredibly difficult. None of the insurance mechanisms ensures that there will be an assessment of the caregiver's ability to provide services, the impact of caregiving on his or her own health and well-being, or any other characteristic beyond the legal or fiduciary relationship to the patient. Hospital social workers, who used to perform some level of assessment, now spend nearly all their time processing discharge papers.

Hospice, of course, is the one exception. Hospice care is covered by Medicare, as long as a physician certifies that the patient has six months or less to live, the patient agrees to forgo any curative treatment, and (for home hospice) there is a primary caregiver who is willing to take on the responsibility for most of the care. Hospice philosophy sees the family as the "unit of care" and provides emotional, spiritual, and other support. However, hospice care has been underutilized in the United States. "Operation Restore Trust," a federal anti-fraud inquiry into admission decisions, found that some patients did not meet eligibility criteria. This has had a chilling effect on entry into hospice. Even though a larger sample of reviews found that the majority of Medicare beneficiaries receiving hospice services were indeed eligible, many hospices became wary of taking patients who might exceed the six-month allowable stay. As a result of this, along with patient and family unwillingness to accept the philosophy and terms of care, and other attitudinal and access factors, patients in 1998 had a median length of stay of only 25 days in hospice before death, and far too many patients do not enter a hospice program until death is imminent. This is hardly an optimal arrangement for patients or families.

Policy Proposals Affecting Caregivers

Most research on caregiving took place in the 1970s and 1980s, an era in which the health care and social-service systems were relatively protected from economic constraints and in which there was a reasonably intact safety net. What has changed? Factors include the failure in 1994 of the Clinton Administration's health care reform plan to institute universal coverage, the advent of cost containment in all health care sectors, the dominance of corporate managed care, shorter hospital stays, and the growth of high-technology home care. Moreover, families are already feeling the impact of an aging population; most older persons have at least one chronic condition. The older the person, the greater the likelihood of serious disability.

The more aggressive stance of caregiving advocates comes primarily from families' experiences in these new conditions. Patients or families with "good" health care insurance have been shocked to discover how inadequate their coverage is to meet catastrophic or long-term needs. "Baby boomers" faced with long-term care needs for their aging parents have been dismayed to discover that Medicare does not provide them. Patients and families that welcomed managed care because it offered them "choice" have been unpleasantly surprised to discover how little choice they really have when it comes to doctors, hospitals, and services. Politicians and policy makers are eager to respond to their constituents but are wary of big-budget programs.

Federal initiatives

On the federal level, two main proposals have been advanced: a tax credit for caregivers and money for state governments to develop caregiver support and education programs, and a long-term care package introduced by the Clinton Administration in 1999 that included a $1,000 tax credit for caregivers. The bills had bipartisan support but only lukewarm reception from the policy community. The main objections were that the tax credit would benefit only some caregivers, not all. Those who owed no taxes because they were poor would not benefit, nor would those whose financial burden was far greater than $1,000. The definition of "caregiver" was also an issue, since most bills required the caregiver and care recipient to share a residence, which is often not the case. The most pervasive complaint, however, was that a tax credit is just a bandage on a gaping wound—the lack of a coherent, affordable long-term care policy in the U.S.

Those who advocated in favor of the tax credit argued that it would benefit many caregivers in the middle class, that its symbolic significance outweighed the negatives, and that it put caregiving on the national agenda. The tax credit bills were not passed the first time around, but in January 2000 President Clinton again proposed the idea, this time reaching a level of $3,000. As of November 2000 the 106th Congress had not acted on the bills, which were part of the budget deliberations.

The proposed money to state governments—$625 million over five years—had few detractors, but it also had few staunch supporters in Congress. This proposal was not funded in the final budget reconciliation in 1999, but was reintroduced in 2000 as part of a ten-year package. It was attached to reauthorization of the Older Americans Act, and in a last-minute action in October 2000, the bill was passed. The details of implementation and the amount of funds to be authorized remain unclear.

One other policy initiative had the potential to benefit caregivers. Under the 1993 Family and Medical Leave Act

(FMLA), employed family members can take up to 12 weeks unpaid leave when there is a new baby in the home or when there is a family or personal illness. They can be assured that their job will be held for them. This Act has been quite successfully implemented, without the disruption or costs predicted by employers. However, its application is severely limited because leave is unpaid. Most family caregivers cannot afford to take time off without pay, and many workers who used the FMLA ended up on welfare.

In November 1999, the Clinton Administration issued draft regulations that would allow states to use their burgeoning unemployment trust funds to pay workers who take parental leave. The debate about whether this is an appropriate use of unemployment trust funds has not addressed the inclusion of family caregivers. Under the current proposal, only new parents would be covered.

State initiatives

While the outlook for innovation on the federal level is uncertain, a recent survey showed that several states have taken initiatives to assist caregivers (Family Caregiving Alliance, 1999). The oldest and most-established programs focus on caregivers for people with developmental disabilities. California and Pennsylvania are two states with strong existing respite and information programs. Departments of Aging administer half of all state programs, although a range of other agencies may take the lead. Most state programs are small, and many place caps on services per client. Some states have Medicaid waivers, allowing them to use Medicaid funding in more flexible ways. A few pay family caregivers when this seems to be the only solution to a need.

Among the states with new initiatives, New Jersey stands out. In 1999, New Jersey allocated $50 million in state funds to developing caregiver programs. The initiative has several features, notably a "one-stop shopping" program called N.J. EASE (for New Jersey Easy Access Single Entry), which facilitates entry into different services such as adult day care, respite services, and home care. If federal money is allocated to the states, New Jersey's experience will be instructive (Report of the New Jersey Advisory Council on Elder Care, 1999).

Private initiatives

The private sector plays a significant role in health care policy development and innovation. The National Health Council, an umbrella organization of voluntary health care organizations and some corporations, convened a consensus conference on caregiving in 1998. The participants agreed that there is inadequate insurance coverage for caregiving necessities, inadequate financial support for long-term care, inflexible funding mechanisms, unsatisfactory relationships with health care providers, and inadequate support for transitions in care. The group's "Agenda for Change" focused on research, training, and advocacy in all the key areas (National Health Council, 1999).

Philanthropy is another avenue of policy development. The United Hospital Fund in New York City created the Family Caregiving Grant Initiative, awarding $1.5 million over three years to New York City hospitals to develop caregiver and staff training and support. Sixteen Phase I grantees received planning grants, from which seven received grants to develop their programs. These grantees will, it is hoped, provide some "best practices" for others to adopt. Other private foundations are funding specific programs and seeking ways to use their limited resources to stimulate change.

Finally, insurance companies (in a few states, with governmental support) are aggressively marketing private long-term-care insurance. The usefulness of this product is still unclear. It is very expensive for anyone nearing an age when it might be needed, and, at best, only a small segment of the population will be able to afford it.

Summary

Despite the hardships and sacrifices, families continue to take care of their sick and elderly relatives. They do so with little help from the health care system, policy makers, or paid help. As care has become more complex and demanding, the pressure on caregivers to take on more and more responsibilities continues unabated.

Most caregiving takes place in private, in the home of a family member, or the care recipient's own home. Within this realm, individual caregivers and families suffer the "family scars" and bask in the family love that Mazzocco evokes. Those who wish to assist family caregivers in their tasks should respect this privacy, while at the same time offering the benefits of professional and volunteer expertise and experience. The chapters in this volume offer some guideposts for that important role.

Carol Levine, MA, joined The United Hospital Fund in New York City in 1996 where she directs The Families and Health Care Project. This project focuses on developing partnerships between health care professionals and family caregivers. Ms. Levine continues to direct The Orphan Project: Families and Children in The HIV Epidemic, which she founded in 1991. She was director of The Citizens Commission on AIDS in New York City as well as a senior staff associate of The Hastings Center where she edited The Hastings Center Report. *In 1993 she was awarded a MacArthur Foundation Fellowship for her work in AIDS policy and ethics. Ms. Levine has written several books and numerous articles.*

1

Hospice as a Model for Caregiving

Marcia Lattanzi-Licht

It is necessary; therefore, it is possible.
—G. A. Borghese

As an approach to caring, hospice is a practical representation of traditional and symbolic practices. The term *hospice* comes from the Latin 'hospis' which refers to host and guest, and is also the root for the words hospitality, hospital, hotel, and hostel. Several historical threads wove hospice into its current form. From religious individuals and groups caring for the sick and dying to the establishment of places of rest and refuge for travelers during the Crusades, hospice has involved themes of journey, hospitality, rest and care.

The modern application of the word hospice began with Dame Cicely Saunders in her establishment of St. Christopher's Hospice outside London in 1967. Based upon the early work of Dr. Saunders and the growing attention to the needs of individuals facing the end of life, a distinct set of values has emerged to define hospice. Today, hospice is defined as a "caring community." Hospice offers a framework, not necessarily a place, for attention to important needs. Hospice is a return to a more human, family-oriented approach to care aimed at controlling symptoms and improving the quality of life for individuals at the end of life. Hospice values offer a foundation for caregiving in a wide variety of contexts.

Hospice Care: A Response to Unmet Needs

Hospice services are designed to attend to the needs of a population that has often been isolated, ignored, or abandoned. The grassroots involvement of volunteers was a key factor in the development of the hospice movement. The health care professionals and lay persons who established hospices in North America were aware of deficiencies in care of the dying. People who would rather spend their last days at home were not given that option. The spirit of caring and advocacy that was so much a part of the early delivery of hospice services continues today. Hospice staff and volunteers provide high quality care to dying persons and their family members in increasingly diverse circumstances and settings. The advocacy of today's hospice professionals focuses on access to services by more people, who are dealing with a broad range of chronic, life-limiting diseases.

There are ways the hospice model can be extended to other caregiving situations that need to be explored. The commitment to creating possibilities for quality of life and individual choices is an important dimension of all caregiving. People needing care and their families struggle to navigate systems with limited services, rigid guidelines, and high costs. Few families find the support they need without paying high out-of-pocket costs. Professional caregivers need to offer families guidance through the maze of caregiving challenges and potential resources.

Goals of Hospice Care

The partnership formed between a family and hospice personnel can ensure quality care for a person who is dying. Hospice supportive services are designed to offer information and back-up to family members so that they will be more able to care for their loved one. Hospice care focuses on addressing some central goals:

- To support individuals and families coping with dying

- To enhance quality of life through comfort care rather than treatment focused on cure

- To aggressively treat and expertly manage all pain and physical symptoms associated with an individual's dying

- To care for the whole person, addressing physical, emotional, psychological, spiritual, and social needs through an interdisciplinary team approach

- To confirm the individual's and family's sense of self-worth, individuality, autonomy, and security

- To acknowledge and offer support for individuals and their family members facing the losses and grief associated with dying and the death of a loved one

- To extend bereavement support for family members following the death of their loved one

- To be a positive influence upon the understanding, compassionate treatment, and care of the dying and bereaved (Lattanzi-Licht, Mahoney, & Miller, 1998).

These overall goals are the foundation for hospice and form the value base for its services and activities. When caregiving is offered in the context of these desirable approaches, the individual who is ill experiences an enhanced sense of security and worth. Caregiving that is grounded in a philosophy of caring that respects the wishes of the person who is ill and the family, and maximizes their functioning, represents the kind of support people appreciate most. While many are familiar with the principles of hospice, it is important to explore the application of these principles. The values of hospice represent universal approaches to caregiving and create a blueprint that advances the human experiences of caring.

Values of Hospice Care
Worth of the individual

In the commitment to address the unique needs and wishes of a person who is dying, hospice has an implicit belief in his or her worth. Regardless of progressive physical decline and the inability to be productive, hospice sees an individual as having significant value. Dame Cicely Saunders expresses this belief in her often-quoted statement: "You matter because you are you. You matter to the last moment of your life, and we will do all we can, not only to help you die in peace, but also to live until you die" (Saunders, 1978).

Choice and self-determination

Hospice care involves offering choices to people who are dying, then working to make those choices possible. Studies have consistently shown that people prefer to be cared for and die in their homes. A 1996 Gallup Poll found the numbers to be as high as nine out of ten people (National Hospice Organization, 1996). For example, a couple in their mid-eighties struggled to stay at home in spite of the wife's chronic congestive heart failure and her husband's progressive dementia. Their two children lived out of state and urged their parents to move to an assisted living facility. The parents insisted on staying in their home, and requested help from the parish nurse. She visited two to three times a week, helped the woman with showering and changing the beds, and monitored their needs. The parish nurse recognized that loneliness is often the greatest concern of elderly homebound people. A young neighbor did weekly grocery shopping, and friends visited occasionally. With a patchwork of support, the couple felt competent in their ability to manage and stay at home. Both the parish nurse and young neighbor utilized hospice values in their caregiving. The ability to be self-determining at the end of life, choosing where one would like to be, how one would like to spend time, and which people one would like to spend time with are all key components of quality of life. As a dying person faces diminishment and growing losses, the ability to communicate preferences and control one's personal environment becomes of great importance.

The hospice approach to care is captured in the recurring phrase at hospice training programs: "Meet people where they are." Acceptance of individuals, their lifestyle, beliefs, and choices is the foundation of effective caregiving. The inability to honor the ill person's wishes is an area of frequent conflict for families. For example, an adult son believes it would be best for his chronically ill parents to move to an assisted living center while the parents reject the idea, saying that they are comfortable in their own home and able to care for themselves with limited help. The belief that we know what is best or better for an ill person diminishes the person and tarnishes the relationship. Very few of us would allow someone else to make decisions for us that were counter to our wishes. What is important is not what the caregiver feels is best for the person who is ill, but what the person who is ill sees as best.

Allowing people choices, no matter how small, like the type of food preferred, or when to eat, communicates respect and confidence. The caregiver is wise to put opinion and judgment in the background and focus instead on deferring to the preferences of the person who is ill or dying. The only limitation to this approach involves safety and practical considerations.

At the end of life, making personal choices often involves small successes, not big outcomes. When a hospice nurse visited a 71-year-old man with major metastatic disease, his wife asked about his recent request for a steak dinner. For the past week, the husband had only been able to take in small amounts of soft food, and the wife thought it was not wise to even prepare the meal. The hospice nurse encouraged the wife to cook the meal, and she did. While her husband was only able to enjoy a few bites of the mashed potatoes and could chew but not swallow the steak, he thanked his wife as she sat next to his bed eating with him. "Now *that's* a meal," he said. "You are still the best cook around."

Whole person care

The hospice approach focuses on expert physical care and symptom management. The management of pain and other symptoms is essential and allows opportunity for attention to personal interests, making quality of life possible. Without vigilant attention to physical symptoms and pain, all other goals of care become secondary. A person in pain cannot communicate with loved ones in a meaningful way, or consider spiritual questions.

The dying process generates needs and responses in all areas of human life: physical, social, emotional, and spiritual. The recognition that dying is more than a physical event opens up possibilities for exploring the deep meaning of the experience. Through an interdisciplinary care approach, hospice attends to the full spectrum of human needs. Physicians, nurses, social workers, chaplains, other professionals, and volunteers bring together their different visions and knowledge to plan quality care for the person and the family. This collaboration results in mutual respect and attention to detail, enhancing care.

Another community example of services that mirror hospice values is found in a program sponsored by a local mental health center to support elderly persons experiencing depression. Senior citizen volunteers are trained and supervised in their home visits to elderly persons with depression. Family physicians, pastors, or health care professionals make referrals to the program. Often the elderly are widowed and isolated. The volunteers receive training in hospice principles and in coping with grief and loss. One volunteer stated after the hospice training session, "We are doing hospice, only the people we are working with are not actively dying. They need quality of life and support just as much, though."

Family-centered care

Illness and death impact families, not only individuals. The delivery of family-centered care, rather than care that focuses only on the dying person, is a major distinguishing element of hospice. At both ends of the life spectrum, the birthing and the dying processes, there is recognition of the family's preeminent place in these momentous life experiences.

Family members who care for their loved one live through a strenuous and stressful experience. On the other hand, there are significant rewards involved in caregiving, including the opportunity to redeem past relationship inadequacies. Caregiving offers opportunities for moments of closeness and intimacy that can diminish guilt and self-criticism after a loved one dies. This understanding of the value of caring for a loved one is an important dimension of hospice care. Hands-on care and family participation is possible in many settings. Even though Carol's mother was in a nursing home, when she visited twice a week Carol bathed her, fixed her hair, helped her with her dinner, and took her for a walk in her wheelchair. While Carol was not able to care for her mother at home, the nursing home staff wisely let her provide direct care for her mother during her visits.

Family members, along with the person who is dying, struggle with feelings of loss of control, loss of power, and an awareness of personal vulnerability. In addition, family members must contend with the physical demands of delivering and organizing the care of their loved one. Exhaustion, expectations and resentments, spiritual doubts, and the struggle to maintain quality in one's own life are all part of the caregiving experience. While family members have some unique concerns, in many ways the difficulties parallel those of the dying person.

Members of the hospice team can serve as buffers in the family situation. By supporting and occasionally relieving family members, the care of the person who is dying improves. The supportive activities that members of the hospice team offer to families include:

- Information
- Listening
- Guidance

- Specific instruction
- Respite care
- Stress management
- Modeling of effective caregiving techniques and approaches
- Advocacy
- Feedback
- Encouragement.

A goal of hospice includes accessing, involving, and supplementing the family's existing support, not replacing or supplanting it (Lattanzi-Licht, Mahoney, & Miller, 1998).

Family-centered care reflects the essence of hospice's approach. In the knowledge that human beings facing the end of life fear feeling alone or abandoned, hospice attempts to reassure both the person who is dying and the family members. The idea that hospice represents is 'I will journey with you.' This statement acknowledges the difficulty of the dying and caregiving experiences, and reassures families that they will not be alone as they face difficulties and uncertainties along the way. In addition, hospice's focus on family-centered care led to the development of bereavement services, perhaps one of the most distinguishing dimensions of hospice care.

Quality of Life and Time for Patients and Families

The intentional focus of hospice care is on living, not dying. This central point makes attention to quality of life critical. While each person defines the elements that give life quality, hospice staff and volunteers work with the family to create an environment of care where quality is possible.

Susan, a 60-year-old woman who was a successful administrative assistant at a major oil company, was dealing with end-stage lung cancer. When her birthday approached, she invited several close friends over to celebrate. After she finished a small piece of cake, Susan sat in her recliner and asked her husband to turn off her oxygen. She then proceeded to light up three cigarettes in a row and told friends that she might as well enjoy a smoke, since it didn't make much difference now. Quality of life involves people and activities that bring us enjoyment, affection, and meaning. Whether or not we agree with the elements that a person finds enjoyable, individuals facing the end of life deserve quality in their days.

There can be no quality of life or participation in meaningful activities when pain or debilitating symptoms are present. Mobility, nutrition, and elimination can all be consuming concerns for the person who is ill and for family members providing care. Only when physical symptoms and needs are sufficiently addressed can other important personal considerations emerge.

As illness progresses, small personal pleasures take on great significance. The comfort of being in one's own bed, of enjoying a favorite food, or of visiting with a grandchild are all examples of ways a dying person can enjoy life and time. For a person who is dying to be able to experience quality of life, it is necessary for caregivers to listen to his or her wishes and expressions of preference.

Elizabeth was in the end stages of metastatic breast cancer at 58. Her sister had come in from out of town to care for her and was struggling with numerous calls from colleagues and acquaintances requesting information on Elizabeth's condition or wishing to visit her. Elizabeth told her sister that she didn't have enough energy to deal with very many people. Her sister suggested that a friend help write a letter to the list of people who were concerned, giving them an update and requesting cards rather than phone calls. The office circulated a list for people who were interested in bringing an evening meal to Elizabeth and her sister. After the letters were sent, Elizabeth spent her limited time and energy with two close friends and her sister.

Bereavement care

Along with the principle of family-centered care, hospices maintain supportive contact with surviving family members for a year following the death of their loved one.

The bereavement services hospices offer may vary, but typically include:

- Initial contact by hospice staff to assess the individual's needs

- Written information about grief

- Periodic bereavement newsletters

- Invitations to bereavement classes, courses, support groups

- Periodic phone calls or visits from a hospice staff member or volunteer

- Retreats or camps for children, adolescents, and families

- Lending library of books, pamphlets, and films about grief

- Referral to a mental health professional if indicated or desired

- Opportunities to volunteer (typically after one year).

Hospices in the United States have typically developed services to meet the needs of their individual communities. In many communities, hospice staff are viewed as expert resources on death and grief. Almost all hospice programs offer bereavement services to members of the community, whether or not their loved one was cared for by hospice. Support groups and educational sessions and materials are made available to individuals upon request. In addition, almost all hospice programs (87%) report that they work with teachers and schools when a student death occurs. A smaller number of hospices (28%) respond to sudden, traumatic deaths and community disasters (Connor & Lattanzi-Licht, 1995). Numerous hospices act as resources for corporations and groups dealing with work-related losses. Finally, most hospices are involved to a greater or lesser degree in community education on death and grief.

In every community there are large numbers of people grieving losses. Hospices have begun to identify ways to address those needs in a more comprehensive manner. In general, hospice care has filled a gap by offering consumers needed services. The important lesson in hospice's success is rooted in its relationship to and concern for members of the community.

Applying Hospice in Other Contexts

Hospice principles of care and knowledge can be applied to a much broader segment of medical and community health needs. Corr and Corr (1985) stress that hospice care is a philosophy, not a facility, and that hospice principles can be applied in diverse ways. We have learned that hospice principles are applicable not only to terminally ill cancer patients, but also to individuals coping with chronic conditions in advanced stages, such as emphysema, congestive heart failure, and Amyotrophic Lateral Sclerosis. Much needs to be done to expand care and be more responsive to families struggling with chronic illnesses like Alzheimer's disease. One daughter, after caring for her mother suffering from Alzheimer's for four years, received hospice support during the last five weeks of her mother's life. She asked her physician why her mother had to be dying before they were able to receive such high quality care and services.

The countless families caring for loved ones with chronic diseases and the frail elderly could all benefit from hospice or hospice-like support. Efforts to balance the Federal budget result-ed in major cuts in home care services that left families without adequate support. Health care professionals need to advocate for the needs of these families and generate new models of caregiving and support that reflect the values and success of the hospice approach. Medicare regulations limit hospice care to the final six months of life, and physicians are often reluctant or unable to offer accurate prognostic information. While hospices struggle with the human and financial impact of a shortened length of stay for patients under hospice care, increasing numbers of people continue to seek hospice services. While a number of hospices offer bridge programs, or pre-hospice services, most communities still face deficits in services for caregiving families.

In addition, recent studies have shown that dying children are often denied hospice services and many die in significant pain (Wolfe et al., 2000). Finally, hospices need to make services more available to minority groups by recruiting and retaining staff that fully represent the community the hospice serves.

The growth in palliative care services and programs reflects an attempt to extend hospice principles of care to people prior to the last stages of life. The focus is on the broader group of people who need symptom relief in situations that are not necessarily terminal. The trend to palliative care is an important one, and it involves several areas of concern. Care is typically institutional and physician-directed, focusing on physical needs. It is important that palliative care services involve active participation of professionals representing psychosocial and spiritual care to ensure the delivery of full spectrum, high-quality care.

In the early development of hospice services in this country, one of the proposed goals was "to incorporate hospice care philosophies and principles into the fabric of the nation's health care system" (Rezendes & Abbot, 1979). Health care providers have begun to adopt many of hospice's principles by placing greater emphasis on family involvement and pain management. The philosophy of advocacy, as opposed to traditional medical paternalism, is now found in many settings, as well as an increasing recognition of the needs of persons facing the end of life.

Hospice offers a unique set of values that represent not just good care but an exemplary human effort. These values have a place in health care, and in services to grieving persons.

In addition, there is a challenge for communities to utilize their hospice programs well, and develop ways to expand and extend hospice-like services to those in need.

In today's health care environment, caregiving is almost the sole responsibility of families. Professionals offer back-up support and guidance, but families are primarily responsible for care delivery. Many families are struggling to provide care for a loved one without the benefit of adequate services. Hospice offers a broad and applicable model of response to family needs in caregiving situations. Communities, health care providers, and hospices are challenged to create ways to better apply the hospice model to a wide range of loss-related situations where needs are not adequately addressed.

Marcia Lattanzi-Licht, MA, RN, LPC, is a psychotherapist, educator, and author. An early voice for hospice care, Ms. Lattanzi-Licht was a co-founder of Hospice of Boulder County, Colorado. She is the principal author of The Hospice Choice *(Simon & Schuster, 1998) and publishes extensively in the areas of professional stress, loss, and bereavement care. She was the scriptwriter for the AMA-award-winning physician-education video, "Difficult Conversations."*

$\mathcal{V}$ o $\acute{\iota}$ c e s

Hoping This Could Be Somebody Else's Life

Elizabeth Halling

$\mathcal{I}$ pinched the phone between ear and shoulder as the social worker told me what she could do for us. She talked about counseling and finding community resources, both of which I had explored already on my own.

"Sorry," I said to her, "but I don't really get the big picture. You just kind of help people?"

"Well, yes," she acknowledged. "Mine is what you'd call a soft job."

Soft, I thought.

"How do you know when you're done?" I asked.

She paused. "Well, that would be when your son, um, dies. I sometimes help families after, you know, the death, but usually my responsibilities end at that point, or we'd try to refer you to bereavement services or something like that."

I didn't tell her that's not what I'd meant. I meant that, at the end of the day, how does she know she's done her job? How can she tell whether she's helped someone, or just rounded up a bunch of phone numbers? How can she tell if she's done any good?

My polite hostility towards our helpers increases daily, and it bothers me. The books say a lot of dying patients and their caregivers become angry with the professionals at one point or another, so this could just be a symptom. But it doesn't feel like a symptom. What it feels like is—and I know I'm angry, I know I'm not being fair—the people who are paid to participate in this marathon of suffering are the ones with the easy jobs ("soft"), while those of us in the trenches slog it out 24 -7 with no benefits and no vacation days. What it feels like is bad, bad luck for us and an office door that shuts at the end of the day for them. It reminds me of American missionaries in Third World countries who close their jungle clinic at 5 p.m. so the medical staff can take a break. Or the peace corps workers with their care packages of shampoo and treats. What about the starving natives? And how did I become one?

My son Gabriel had the first of many pneumonias at seven months. During that hospitalization he was diagnosed with cerebral palsy, followed later by cortical visual impairment (blindness), reactive airway disease (asthma), and seizure disorder (epilepsy). Now, at three, he has spent more time in hospitals than most people do their entire lives.

It's the respiratory stuff that brought us to hospice via a gentlemanly senior resident. Funny, I'm not mad at him, though he was the bearer of perhaps the worst news of my life. How kind of him, I thought, how respectful, to take a deep breath and tell us what all the other doctors were thinking: that a toddler with more than 20 hospitalizations for respiratory infections isn't going to last very long.

When Gabriel first went into hospice, I was simultaneously traumatized and relieved. Just the idea of it seemed so drastic, so hopeless; yet everyone kept telling me how wonderful the people were, how caring and committed. And since we were so used to scrabbling for any little bit of help we could get—allowing the church ladies to bring us dinners, sweet-talking and pleading with and roaring at the HMO—I could half-convince myself that it was just an extension of that, another set of services we could tap.

But it was at the same time an enormous shift and a relinquishing. Finally, I thought, we're going to be surrounded by people who know what to do and how to help. Finally we won't have to be the experts anymore. We'll have someone to share the burden, someone to show us the way. The big step we'd taken of putting ourselves in their hands meant that somebody else could take some big steps now, and big soft wings would enfold us, and we wouldn't have any more pain.

Turns out the hospice people are just people, not angels. They have opinions, which they tell us, and they fill out forms, which they don't show us. The nurse comes when we call, listens to Gabriel's chest, and usually suggests we have some serious discussions about his quality of life. The doctors know Gabriel's in hospice, but they tell us to take him to the hospital anyway, and the gears grind on around him and he is going to die and the gears grind on around him.

Pardon me, but this sucks. And pointing out that lots of dying patients don't get these services, that you could die in a lot more pain and with a lot less support than Gabriel, does not make me bow my head in appreciation. Gabriel only gets what hospice says he should get. Gabriel gets a nurse's visit once a week and a lot of people asking how we're doing and a long, lonesome valley that he has to walk all by himself. No amount of phone numbers from the social worker is going to take that lonesome valley away from him. He's three years old.

If I were interested in improving this situation, and not just mad about the whole thing, I would offer alternatives. I think a good alternative would be for somebody else's kid to die. I'd put Gabriel up against any other suffering kid and I have no doubt he'd win the suffering prize. Shouldn't he get to take his ribbons and trophies and go home? Can't we all please acknowledge that he's done his bit and now it's someone else's turn?

It would be fun someday to try out the other stages— denial, bargaining—but those just seem like detours. And the thing is, just because I'm angry and anger is a symptom doesn't mean there's nothing to be angry about. Let's quit talking about my feelings, let's talk about how hospice is failing me. When are they going to start easing the burden? How could they possibly think these few visits, these telephone calls, are sufficient? Who's with me here? Who's really with me?

Because it's not just Gabriel's turn—it's my turn, too. I was crushed and overwhelmed when he had to take three different medicines every day. It's now ten medicines, and I am still crushed. I was crushed when I had to do his IV infusions (the sterile water, the little alcohol pads). I'm crushed every time I feed him through his feeding tube (the enormous syringe, the sweet, clotted smell). He goes to sleep if you rock him and sing to him, but it's hard to sing when you are so crushed.

If I am very brave and think very hard about what we're doing and where we're going, I realize that I've been hoping the nurse and the social worker would take over for me. I've been hoping this would start being somebody else's life. But it's not somebody else's, it's mine: my boy, my pain, and my job, finally, to hold my son's hand, stroke his hair, and be with him as he dies.

But I'm not brave, I'm small and frightened, here at the edge of this darkness. Take this cup away from me. Take it away and give me back that sweet-smelling baby you promised.

The hospice chaplain wore a shapeless brown dress and told me over French fries that you can have God and you can also have really bad stuff happen to you. Look at the crucifixion, she said. Look how God didn't jump in and end it. I said, you know, I'm tired of this stuff, miracles for other people, septuplets on magazine covers, and for me a piercing lesson in Christian theology.

At this point, and to her credit, the chaplain didn't walk through the hospice brochure's bullet points on "best possible care" and "opportunities for growth." I should know better than to read the brochures, just as they should know better than to print them. Even though it seems preposterous, you can paint death as a fulfilling spiritual journey—and a mother will believe it, believing anything that promises to take away the pain. Well, I'm here to tell you, this isn't fulfilling. This is emptying. This is the spinning carnival ride where the floor drops out, you're splayed against the wall, and you can't even lift your head to turn away.

I often ask the hospice people if they feel they have a "calling." It's the only explanation that makes sense. Me, I wouldn't be here if I didn't have to, and it amazes me that someone would choose this. People who take on a hospice career, full of pain, death, and true emergencies (light-years truer than a flat tire or a crashed hard drive)—such people are remarkable. Someday I'll thank them. But it won't be any time soon.

These days, the salt of the earth and the milk of human kindness aren't enough for me. I want a hospice that provides encapsulated lightning bolts for smiting and coupons redeemable for time travel, ubiquity, and omniscience. I don't think that's asking for much.

In Memory of:
Gabriel Ricardo Marquez Uppman
May 15, 1997–November 17, 2000

Fannie Mae's Elder Care Initiative

◆

This interview was conducted by Dee Ellison,
National Health Council, with Susan Holik, Vice President
of Human Resources, Fannie Mae. Fannie Mae is a private,
share-holder owned company that works to make sure mortgage
money is available for people in communities all across America.
With approximately 3,800 dedicated employees, they are
also one of the world's most productive corporations.

Q: Please describe the Fannie Mae program that supports family caregivers dealing with end-of-life situations.

A: Fannie Mae offers its employees an extensive elder-care program, the Elder Care Initiative, which provides a broad range of services to family caregivers. The key component of Fannie Mae's Elder Care Initiative is a full-time, onsite elder-care manager. We contract for this person's services through a local senior-service agency, and therefore have access to a wide array of resources and services. The program includes referrals to resources throughout the community, appropriate in-house seminars, and group legal services.

We are extremely excited about the Elder Care Tool Kit, which is a new resource guide for employees to use in caring for an elderly relative. Along with reference materials, the kit includes a record book in which employees can track important financial, medical, and personal information related to their caregiving situation.

Another important component is our corporate-wide Flexible Work Options, which enables employees to request a schedule different from the one they normally follow, such as telecommuting, working part-time or following a compressed work schedule.

Q: What is the underlying philosophy or concern that led to the development of these programs?

A: This initiative is part of Fannie Mae's strong belief in work-life balance. We know our employees will confront important life issues, including the end of life. We believe it is important to help employees deal with the life issues that happen while they are doing their jobs.

Q: Has Fannie Mae done a cost/benefit analysis of this initiative?

A: It has, although we acknowledge the difficulty of attaching figures to intangibles such as employee commitment. The analysis found that, given our large size, the cost is relatively low. It also found the program to be extremely cost-effective in terms of productivity, morale, and employee retention. For example, it takes an employee who utilizes our case manager significantly less time to do research about needed services than if he or she had to start from scratch.

Q: How would you rate the success of this program?

A: We believe this program is extremely successful. It is convenient and helpful for employees at a difficult time, and it works well for the company from an institutional standpoint.

Q: What is the feedback from employees?

A: Employees report that they are exceptionally pleased with this program. Some use all of the available services, while others use only selected options. For example, the program enabled one woman to temporarily relocate to another city to help care for her mother. About six months after launching the program, Fannie Mae conducted a survey of employees who had used some aspect of program. One statistic is especially impressive: twenty-eight percent of those who responded said their caregiving situations were serious enough that, without the program's services, they would have had to quit their jobs.

Q: How does this program work in real life?

A: Not only do I see this program from the employer's side, I also used it as an employee when my dad was dying. The program was extremely helpful to me personally. I received a huge amount of information, as well as emotional support, from our care manager. She gave me the names of hospice organizations in New York and provided counseling about how to help my mother. We don't need this information until we're in the situation, and being able to tap into the case manager's resources eliminates the need for us to do our own research at an extremely difficult time. In addition, Fannie Mae's culture is such that it is an incredibly caring place, and my colleagues provided enormous support throughout.

Q: What are some of the program's elements that other companies could replicate?

A: Large companies could easily replicate this program, including providing a case manager and flexible work options. Smaller companies could tap into existing community resources and provide referral information to employees. They also could offer in-house seminars on relevant topics, such as advance directives.

Q: What would you have Fannie Mae do differently?

A: I really think this is an excellent program. One way it might be even better is if we could support employees in longer-term situations, such as caring for someone with a chronic condition. Those employees might need completely different work situations. We might need to allow them to go part-time for a year and then to come back into their job when the situation is resolved, or to rearrange schedules to let them take extended leave and then return to their jobs. Doing this might enable us to hold onto a valuable employee we might otherwise lose.

Q: Anything else?

A: When this program was being developed, the approval process involved four levels of managers, including Fannie Mae's president. During the time Fannie Mae was developing this program, four senior executives involved in the decision making process experienced some form of elder-care problem. Their experience helped cement the corporation's commitment to the program.

2

Family Caregiving and Loss: The Work/Family Dynamic

Myrl Weinberg & Dee Ellison

There is probably no more stressful time than when we are dealing with the end of life—whether it involves the terminal illness or death of a loved one, a friend, a colleague, or ourselves. We've all faced these situations, or know someone who has: an elderly mother who has terminal throat cancer, a child diagnosed with a rare but fatal disorder, a sister who has a severe stroke, a colleague diagnosed with ALS. As individuals face the end of their lives, family members, loved ones, and friends often provide ongoing care, both medical and non-medical, as well as emotional support.

Yet many of these family caregivers are also employees who must meet work obligations while dealing with caregiver responsibilities. For many family caregivers, working outside the home is a financial necessity. In addition, working outside the home often provides needed respite, as well as professional and personal satisfaction. The workplace is frequently the only place family caregivers feel they have any control.

Nevertheless, these employees face the challenge of managing the competing demands of caregiving and employment. Family caregivers understandably feel stress and fatigue, which can affect their mood and performance and cause them to have trouble concentrating. Many need to take more time off than usual for the tasks of caregiving. However, despite these distractions, employees want to continue to be productive and do well at work.

Employers have a stake in helping their caregiving employees manage this balancing act successfully because they too want to maximize the employee's productivity. However, for employers to be willing to adopt policies and programs that support family caregivers, they must see bottom-line benefits, including cost savings to the organization, increased productivity, better employee retention levels, and increased employee morale.

Policies, both corporate and governmental, can help or hinder workplaces in becoming more sensitive to the needs of family caregivers. For example, there are limits on who may take advantage of the Family and Medical Leave Act; it does not currently apply to workplaces with fewer than 50 employees or those who have worked less than 1,250 hours during the previous 12 months. At the present time, insurance often does not cover the costs of community- and home-based care. Because many Americans receive health benefits through the workplace, employers could play a pivotal role in encouraging insurers to cover these costs.

The good news is that family caregiving is on the national radar screen today more than ever. Traditional broadcast and print media are covering this issue, as are "new media," such as the Internet.

In addition, as our population ages, policymakers are finding themselves in the role of family caregivers, and legislative proposals are beginning to address this issue. President Clinton signed a bill in November 2000 to renew and expand the Older Americans Act, the measure that provides senior-assistance programs. Among other things, the Act creates a new $125 million family caregiver program to counsel and train families who care for elderly relatives.

At the time of signing President Clinton said, "Enactment of this legislation, extending and improving the Older Americans Act and establishing the National Family Caregiver Support Programs, reflects our continued commitment to our older population and represents a victory for all Americans." He added, "This program will help hundreds of thousands of family—spouses, adult children and others—who are struggling to care for their frail older loved ones who are ill or disabled."

Objectives for the Workplace

Increased awareness of working caregivers' needs, along with a demonstration of bottom-line benefits, should result in an increase in the number of:

- employers offering benefits that support employees facing end-of-life situations;

- "family friendly" workplace environments in which employees feel comfortable accessing available benefits and requesting the support they need; and

- health care professionals who have the information they need to act as advocates for working family caregivers when appropriate.

Clearly there are no single or simple solutions, but important steps can and must be taken now to aid this valuable but vulnerable population of Americans in the workplace. This chapter will review: the existing situation for working family caregivers and employers; newly developed model activities identified by the *Last Acts'* Workplace Committee that employers can offer; and a National Health Council report that sets a new vision—and specific action steps—for family caregiving.

The information in this chapter can provide guidance for health care professionals, employee-assistance professionals, funeral directors, and others working with individuals with chronic conditions and their families. It will help them understand what family caregivers must contend with in the workplace and enable these professionals to serve as advocates with employers when appropriate.

The Situation Today: The Working Caregiver

The U.S. Department of Labor estimated, in 1998, that 30% of the workforce had some responsibility for an elderly relative and that this number is expected to increase by the year 2008 to 54%—more than half the nation's workforce. The strains of caregiving, especially in crisis situations, may create conflicts for some employees. Beyond the struggle of "working two jobs," their caregiving role can result in lost employment opportunities in terms of promotions, wages, and personal reward. The increased absenteeism and lower productivity of some caregivers can also work against them when they receive their performance evaluations.

The culture of the workplace is critical. Not only must companies offer benefits, but employees must be assured that they will not be penalized for accessing them. Employees' comfort level in using these benefits is often tied directly to managerial encouragement and support.

When these benefits are available to family caregivers, they do make a difference. For example, Fannie Mae offers its employees extensive family caregiving benefits through its Elder Care Initiative. About six months after the launch of the program, Fannie Mae conducted a survey of employees who had used some aspect of the program. One statistic stands out: Twenty-eight percent of those who responded said their caregiving situation was serious enough that, without the program's services, they might have had to quit their job.

The Situation Today: The Employer

From the perspective of employers, it is important to see family caregiving as a business issue. It is estimated that $11.4 billion is lost in productivity each year due to family caregiving responsibilities, and that number will continue to grow as the population ages (MetLife, 1997).

Employers are, of course, concerned about the bottom line. It is thus important for employers to help employees maintain their productivity and avoid having to leave the organization.

Many companies do have formal or informal policies that help their employees meet the challenges of caregiving. Research (*Last Acts*, 1999) has found that basic benefits today are common—including bereavement leave, family and medical leave, or an employee-assistance program. Eighty-eight percent of the employers in the Workplace Committee study offered bereavement leave. Sixty percent of employers offered family and medical leave or an employee-assistance program. Yet when employers were asked about other kinds of employee programs, the reported numbers dropped sharply. Only 6% of the employers studied offered any comprehensive programs beyond the basics, such as training managers about appropriate responses and providing helpful company policies for end-of-life situations (*Last Acts*, 1999).

Research also found—no surprise here—that companies will be more likely to adopt activities and policies that benefit family caregivers if they are low-cost and easy to implement (*Last Acts*, 1999).

Model Workplace Programs
FANNIE MAE'S ELDER CARE INITIATIVE
The key component of Fannie Mae's family caregiving program is a full-time, onsite professional elder-care manager, who helps caregiving employees research elder-care services and develop an appropriate plan of action. Fannie Mae also offers other services, including an optional group legal service for employees and onsite elder-care seminars on various topics, such as caring for someone with Alzheimer's, preparing advance directives, caring for the caregiver, and estate planning for elderly relatives (see interview on page 39).

AT&T's Life Tracks Program

AT&T also has adopted a program that works, using the Intranet as the primary method of communicating to its employees. Its Life Tracks program covers major events in life, including those relating to family caregiving and end of life. Life Tracks refers employees or their relatives to appropriate resources, such as hospice (which AT&T's health insurance covers) and other end-of-life programs (see interview on page 53).

Both Fannie Mae and AT&T believe their programs are an effective and important benefit for employees. Fannie Mae has conducted a formal cost/benefit analysis, which found that the cost of the program is comparatively low and that it is extremely effective in terms of improved productivity, morale, and employee retention.

It is clear that no one model exists for employers to use in supporting employees who also have family caregiving responsibilities. Large companies obviously have more resources for establishing support and referral programs than do medium or small companies, but steps can and should be taken by companies of all sizes. The culture and values of each organization may be the best predictor of "caregiver-friendly" workplaces. It is encouraging to note that more than four out of five caregivers who work report that their employer's attitudes toward the demands of caregiving are "understanding" (NAC/AARP, 1997).

But there is much more to be done.

Last Acts' Workplace Committee

Last Acts, funded by The Robert Wood Johnson Foundation, is a national campaign to improve care and caring near the end of life. To understand and to help improve the current work/family situation for caregivers, *Last Acts* is examining the ways in which employers can support their employees who face caregiving and end-of-life situations, such as the terminal illness of a loved one.

Last Acts' Workplace Committee (formerly called the Workplace Task Force) advocates for workplaces that are supportive of employees dealing with end-of-life situations, including terminal illness, family caregiving, and death. The National Health Council and Fannie Mae serve as co-conveners of the Workplace Committee.

To help move the country forward on end-of-life issues, the Workplace Committee developed a set of model activities for employers to use in helping employees plan for, and cope with, end-of-life situations, including family caregiving. These model activities cover, among other things:

- Providing end-of-life decision making resources and company benefits, such as flexible work options and referral to community services;

- Establishing a culture of support and sensitivity for employees who encounter caregiving and end-of-life situations; and

- Training managers (often the first people to hear about employees' concerns) to deal with these issues consistently, sensitively, and confidentially, including helping them identify ways to access benefits and resources and facilitating schedule changes.

To learn employers' and family caregivers' reactions to its model activities, the Workplace Committee commissioned Mathew Greenwald & Associates, a Washington, D.C.-based research firm, to conduct extensive research. The research revealed that working caregivers who deal with end-of-life situations need more support but often don't know where to go for assistance. Many caregivers say they talk with their supervisors and colleagues, but only one-fourth of family caregivers interviewed reported that they spoke to someone in the human resources department about their situation. As a result, the human resources department often was unaware of the employee's concerns and thus could not provide assistance.

In vetting the model activities with employers, the Workplace Committee discovered that workplace programs for the terminally ill, family caregivers, and the bereaved are only beginning to emerge as a work-life issue. Employers who participated in focus groups for the Workplace Committee research identified key benefits to the organization of offering caregiving and end-of-life support services, including boosting morale, helping employees work more effectively, and positioning the organization as "family-friendly." At the same time, employers said that, for such a program to be successful, it must be cost effective, easy to implement, carried out by professionals, and voluntary.

A New Vision and Possible Actions

Along with other organizations, the National Health Council is also active in the area of family caregiving. The Council, a private, nonprofit umbrella organization of 120 national health-related organizations, works to bring quality health care to all people, with a focus on those with chronic diseases and/or disabilities.

The Council has played an active role for several years in helping to raise awareness of, and generate action supporting, family caregivers. The Council's report, *Family Caregiving: Agenda for Action*, grew out of its Consensus Conference on Caregiving in December, 1998. The *Agenda for Action* provides a new vision of a supportive environment for family caregivers and identifies specific actions that would benefit them in several areas, including research, advocacy, financial support, and training.

One of the specific areas addressed during the conference was "Increasing Support for Balancing Work and Family Commitments." The Council's *Agenda for Action* identifies three objectives related to the workplace:

- Employers should offer company benefits and services that help caregivers balance work and family commitments;

- Family and medical leave should be more widely available to working caregivers; and

- Public policy should provide financial incentives to employers who offer benefits and support to employee caregivers across the life span.

The Council's *Agenda for Action* identifies numerous specific actions to help reach these objectives, including the development of a cost/benefit analysis and model programs for employers interested in providing caregiver support, as well as the development and dissemination of education programs for corporate managers and supervisors on ways they can work constructively both to support caregivers and to meet company objectives.

Some of these efforts already are underway. For example, the National Alliance for Caregiving has established a national clearinghouse of materials on family caregiving (www.caregiving.org). In addition, as of this writing, the National Health Council is compiling information on what has been accomplished in its *Family Caregiving: Agenda for Action* and plans to publish a *Progress Report* identifying actions that have not yet been completed and setting new targets.

Conclusion

There is an inevitable impact at the workplace as working caregivers try to meet both their caregiving and employee responsibilities. It is important for those in the health professions who assist working caregivers to be aware of the additional stress these individuals face, and to serve as their advocates with employers whenever appropriate.

It also is critical that employers understand the bottom-line benefits of these programs. With such understanding, employers will be more likely to implement critically important family caregiving support activities. Even if an employer can't do it all, he or she can still do something to provide support for employees who are also family caregivers, resulting in both bottom-line and goodwill benefits.

Myrl Weinberg, CAE, serves as President of The National Health Council, an umbrella organization that works to bring quality health care to all people, with a focus on individuals with chronic diseases and/or disabilities. The Council has long been involved in end-of-life and family caregiving issues, and held a national consensus conference on family caregiving with top experts in the country. The conference resulted in a report, Family Caregiving: Agenda for Action, *which identifies specific actions that can be accomplished within three to five years. Ms. Weinberg's career has focused on issues affecting persons with chronic conditions, including medical research, health care delivery, long-term care, social security, and end-of-life and family caregiving.*

Dee Ellison serves as Director of Communications for the National Health Council and oversees the Council's communications efforts. She also manages several program initiatives, including family caregiving, designed to advance the Council's goals and objectives.

AT&T's Life Tracks Program

◆

This interview was conducted by Dee Ellison, National Health Council with Skip Schlenk, Director, AT&T Work and Family Program. AT&T Corporation is among the world's premier voice and data communications companies, serving consumers, businesses, and government. With 160,000 employees, AT&T provides services to consumers worldwide.

Q: Can you tell me about AT&T's program that supports family caregivers dealing with end-of-life situations?

A: AT&T has a program that uses the company's Intranet as the primary method of providing information to its employees. The Life Tracks system covers major life events, including family caregiving and end-of-life issues. Life Tracks refers employees or their relatives to appropriate resources, including hospice (which AT&T's health insurance covers) and other end-of-life programs.

As part of its program, AT&T also offers accelerated benefit options for individuals diagnosed as terminal, that is, with a life expectancy of six months or less. For example, these employees may be able to receive a lump sum payment of up to 50% of their life insurance coverage, with the balance paid to the beneficiary upon death.

AT&T also offers a generous package of benefits for its employees, including bereavement leave. For example, it offers family-care leave that covers up to 12 months of leave, with benefits, over a 24-month period. The company also has a gradual-return-to-work policy, under which employees can work part–time (25 hours a week), with full benefits, for six months following family leave.

AT&T also offers flexible work schedules, compressed work weeks, and telecommuting. Another interesting benefit is three personal days of leave that can be taken in two-hour increments, enabling family caregivers to leave work for a home or hospital visit.

Q: What is the underlying philosophy or concern that led AT&T to develop this program?

A: AT&T has always been focused on its employees and believes it is important to provide assistance to employees during life's transitions.

Q: How would you rate the success of the program?

A: AT&T feels these are very effective benefits and that it is important to offer them.

Q: What is the feedback from employees?

A: The National Council on Aging did a survey for AT&T of employees taking care of elderly family members, including domestic partners. The survey, released in 2000, found that AT&T's employees greatly appreciated the information and the benefits the company offers.

According to the survey, employees felt they could work better during this difficult period because of the flexible work arrangements and the ability to briefly leave work during the day to take care of their relative. They indicated that these benefits help diminish their stress levels. Employees self-report that these benefits make them feel positive about the company and that, in some cases, the benefits enable them to continue working when they might otherwise not be able to do so.

USA Today featured two employees, one from Syracuse and the other from Kansas City, in an article about family caregiving. Both said that AT&T's flexible work arrangements made it possible for them to continue working.

Q: What are some of the elements of AT&T's program that other companies could replicate?

A: Companies could replicate AT&T's flexible work arrangements. Small companies may be even better positioned to offer this benefit just because they are small and less bureaucratic. It would be quite easy for companies to offer personal leave days that employees can use in two-hour increments. In addition, family resource and referral programs are now fairly affordable for a business of any size. Thus, companies could offer family resource programs that provide consultations, information and referral, as well as seminars and employee support groups.

Q: What would you have AT&T change or do differently?

A: Death is difficult to talk about. Right now, we often don't even use the word. We use euphemisms like 'passed away,' or 'we lost her.' People often don't know what to say to colleagues when they return to work after a loved one has died, making it uncomfortable for everyone. It would be extremely useful if there were a way AT&T could help facilitate that discussion among employees. It would be helpful if there were a better way to ease that transition.

3

Creating and Energizing Caring Communities

Bill Gaventa

Introduction

Loss can come in many forms for family caregivers: loss of life or abilities, loss of dreams, loss of money and home, loss of a loved one. Caregivers and professionals alike know, however, that one of the hardest losses for many in acute or chronic caregiving situations is the loss of connections with others, the loss of support from a caring community, in whatever form that takes for a family.

In the face of loss caused by acute crisis or long-term chronic illness and/or disability, the tasks of family caregivers are often compounded by a dual challenge. First, they have to find appropriate and effective professional services, or 'formal' support. Second, there is the task of maintaining or strengthening the 'informal' support they receive from friends, extended family members, neighbors, colleagues, acquaintances, and members of community organizations of which they are a part.

When I was a chaplain at a residential center for people with developmental disabilities, I often felt that the biggest tragedy was not the disability that led to institutionalization, but the loss of connections and relationships. The questions are basic: Who shows up in a crisis? Who comes to visit me? Who calls? Who stands by me and us over the long haul? Where are the people I was counting on?

If families are lucky, their professional services and supports are excellent. But the question of caring communities and networks still remains. It is not a question of either/or, a family needs both good professional services and good informal supports. One does not supplant the other. So the question becomes, how can caregivers, and especially professionals, assist in maintaining or strengthening the community ties that people have? Or, in their absence, how can professionals assist in the creation and energizing of caring networks and communities to support those who are the primary caregivers in extraordinary situations?

It is far too easy for professionals and caregivers alike to get caught up in the common refrain of grieving the loss of caregiving communities and networks like "we used to have." Where are the communities of yesteryear, the kind we had when I was growing up, where people knew their neighbor, cared for one another, supported one another, when families stuck together? You, the reader, can add your own verse or version. At some level, that analysis may be right, but there are fundamental problems with it. First, it adds to the sense of loss and disempowerment. Second, it may keep caregivers and professionals from seeing the communities people do have. Third, the issue of developing new informal supports is still there. And fourth, it can become a basic assumption that defeats the task of creating and energizing caring communities before you even begin.

In the "Green Bible" of community building, *Creating Communities from the Inside Out*, authors John McKnight and John Kreztman say it succinctly. Community is built on assets, not deficits. The fundamental question is whether you look at the glass as half full or half empty. Community is built, as they say, with "capacity vision."

Exploring that basic assumption leads to others, including assumptions that caregivers and professionals alike make about the communities in which they live and their own roles in caregiving. For professionals, that exploration leads to some fundamental challenges to traditional understandings of what it means to be professional, as well as to new roles through which they can assist in the creation of caring communities. There are a number of exciting and promising tools, resources, and strategies that await professionals. The key is new partnerships between caregivers, professional service providers, and the communities in which they live—partnerships that not only support the 'supporters,' but also create communities that are better and stronger for everyone.

Assumptions and Challenges

The implications and necessity of 'capacity vision' for creating and energizing caring communities will be a constant thread in this discussion, but for a moment let's think of some basic assumptions that all of us make about community, based on our own experiences.

Assumption #1: Community is about place, but it is also about people, times, and relationships. It is about relationships with people we have known for a long time, and also about new relationships, such as connections with others who are going through the same kind of caregiving struggle or journey with loss. The tools of mass media, internet, and e-mail have made the latter form of community much more visible and accessible to any number of caregivers.

Assumption #2: Communities respond to others in need. We know that. We hear and read about it. It happens most often in a crisis, like a flood, fire, or snowstorm, when you hear people say, "It was terrible, but it pulled us all together and people helped each other in ways they usually do not." It happens in an extraordinary event or opportunity, e.g., a visit by a famous person, a celebration of hometown hero, or people organizing to fight a perceived threat. (The latter can, of course, be negative in relation to community when manifested in the "not-in-my-backyard" syndrome.) Community also happens with good leadership— people who unite others in a common vision and help to organize and mobilize a community to work on a goal together.

Assumption #3: Common to all those experiences of community are the ways that crises, opportunities, and visions lead people to reach beyond their anxiety, fear, helplessness, embarrassment, routines and habits, or cultural customs that may have gotten in the way. A fundamental assumption about community building around people in need follows, and that is that people who know others who are struggling with caregiving demands often would like to help but do not know what to do, or how to do it. They look, for example, at a parent caring for a child with multiple disabilities or a parent with chronic illness and say things like, "I wish I could help but don't know how," or, "That mother and father are incredible and special in their love. I could never do that." Both beg the question of what they could do to help, i.e., the huge number of possible responses on the continuum between doing nothing and taking over the role of the primary caregiver.

Thus, a related assumption about community is that people want to help but often do not know how. Not knowing how may also involve the fear of a disease, illness, or chronic condition that overpowers one's sense of ability and capacity. We who wish to create and energize caring communities have to believe that people are looking for a way to make a difference in the lives of others and in their communities but may not know how to do so. As John McKnight says, community is about helping people find and use their gifts (McKnight, 1996 video).

For professional caregivers who have spent years of education and training honing their own gifts and skills, that assumption may be counterintuitive. A vast system of professional health and human services has been built on the notion that specialized professional caregivers are necessary to assist those with particular or unique needs. Advocates have secured public funding by saying, "We need these specialized services. Only professionally trained people can really do this." Professional caregivers often have an identity and livelihood that depends upon having people come to them for help because of their special skills and gifts.

One of the challenges of creating caring communities is for professionals to recognize that others also have useful gifts—gifts which professionals cannot possibly give within the usual "boundaries" of their professional roles. They must then be willing to give some of their expertise and power away to informal supporters, empowering them and enhancing their gifts. Said another way, a professional may be the best doctor, nurse, social worker or counselor around but he or she cannot make up for the lack of response from others in the community.

The challenge goes deeper, though, as John McKnight aptly outlines in his classic essay "John Deere and the Bereavement Counselor" (McKnight, 1995). Professionals, policy makers, and communities must look at the ways that our drive to create professional services for almost every kind of caregiving need has unintentionally taught communities and sources of informal support that they do not have the skills or capacity to support others in crisis. For example, in how many arenas of caregiving have we said, "Oh, you really have to have special training to do this." The challenge is determining how professional caregivers can best empower, rather than disempower, community members and organizations to provide direct support to caregivers.

Professional Roles in Creating and Energizing Caring Communities

The task facing professional caregivers to assist in the creation and energizing of caring communities is one that sometimes gets assigned to a particular professional, e.g., the social worker, the chaplain, a 'community bridge builder,' or case manager. That may be a first step, but too often these roles in community building become roles of trying to find or build other professional services and supports for a caregiving family. The broader challenge is one that faces all professional caregivers: How do we integrate the assumptions outlined above, as well as new skills, into the professional skills that we offer people under our care?

There are at least four major roles and skill sets that can be developed: consultation, collaboration, competition, and coaching (Gaventa, 1996).

Consultation

First, do professional caregivers know who the 'community' is for the people in our care? Do we ask? We often ask about immediate and extended family, but the question should be wider. Where are the sources of support? What organizations or associations are important to the individual? What are the relationships already present that can be supported and encouraged by professional roles?

Consultation is not a skill that comes easily for some professionals who feel it is their obligation to prescribe the answers to others. For many professionals, 'consultation' has often meant contacting another even more knowledgeable or specialized professional. But in a broader, more useful context, 'consultation' means stepping back and finding out who and where a given person's or family's other sources of support are, and recognizing that they have gifts and strengths to offer, too. It means acknowledging that others may know better. It means involving those people in planning supports early on, not calling them with a pre-determined plan of care and trying to dictate roles.

The key preposition is "with" not "for." Who is around that table where the plans are made? There is a huge difference between a doctor or psychologist saying to a pastor and congregation, "Mr. Smith has indicated that you are important sources of support for him, and we would like to involve you and others in figuring out how we can best support him and his family" and saying to

Mr. Smith or the pastor, "This is what you need. Now if only your church would provide it, things would be better."

This kind of effective consultation flows naturally from good assessment and evaluation, and the resources and models already exist. There are many helpful forms of 'spiritual assessments,' for example, which include not only attitudes and beliefs, but also sources of support and meaning for individuals and their families (Fitchett, 1994). Good psychosocial assessments also include environment, community context, and cultural supports.

Collaboration

Good consultation then calls for ongoing cooperation and collaboration. If the basic attitude in consultation is to share knowledge because we recognize that we do not know it all, the root of good collaboration is sharing power, responsibility, and control. Collaboration calls for new alliances between 'formal' and 'informal' organizations in communities to support caregiving families. Examples include health services and congregations, schools and community-based after-school programs with recreational groups, service agencies, and neighborhood associations.

One of the basic challenges is that formal service organizations and informal community associations have very different structures for mobilizing care and action. McKnight and Kretzmann (1996) illustrate that difference with two organizational charts—one a pyramid and the other a circle. David Schwartz, in his excellent book *Who Cares? Rediscovering Caring Communities*, describes the difference between the "caregiving machine" and the "vernacular" in ordinary communities.

The point is that effective collaboration does not come easily to many professional caregivers. Its crucial importance is perhaps nowhere more evident than when professionals of one culture confront the task of consulting and collaborating with sources of community support in ethnic and cultural communities different from their own. Then, the importance of finding out with whom one should consult and how responsibility must be shared with those sources within that other cultural community becomes clearly evident. It does, indeed, "take a village to raise a child" or a community to really support a caregiving family in chronic crisis.

Competition

At first glance, the term 'competition' may appear to be the opposite of good community-building skills. In reality, it is the recognition that communities and organizations of all sorts can be mobilized when someone says, for example, "You know, such-and-such a community has organized a new respite care program for families with parents with Alzheimer's that involves all kinds of community groups." Or, perhaps, "You're a member of First Baptist Church. I heard of another Baptist church in such-and-such a town that organized a wonderful Saturday respite program for families with children with disabilities, in which the youth groups and others not only watch the kids but participate in learning activities together."

Competition, then, can be friendly and inspiring. In professional services, we often call it 'state of the art' or 'model' services. It involves knowing enough about creative community initiatives around the country to be able to say, "They did it there. Why can't we do it here—maybe even better?"

Coaching

The role of 'coach' is perhaps the most significant one for professionals who want to develop new skills in creating and energizing caring communities. Think about the role: A coach is not the one playing the game, but the one on the sidelines teaching, encouraging, demonstrating, supporting, motivating, and celebrating. A good coach gives away what he or she knows, while also finding and supporting the particular gifts and skills of the players. Why not expand that role to think of 'coaching' potential caregivers and sources of support?

There are at least four important skills for 'community coaching':

THE POET

First, a coach is a poet, or artist, philosopher, theologian, or musician. Common to all those roles is the capacity to listen to the groups within a particular community, discover the images, symbols, and values that define the heart of a community, and illuminate its own identity and dreams. For professionals, that means listening to feelings, beliefs, and other sources of commitment and imagination. It means being able to set aside the jargon of particular professional service systems, and translate caregiving issues into words that people use and understand. If a professional in the area of disability who believes in 'mainstreaming' or 'inclusion' collaborates with a congregation, it is important to discern which of the congregation's spiritual traditions define and support that concept (e.g., hospitality to the stranger), rather than using jargon from a service system. We must look for visions, values, and traditions that would support a new caregiving initiative in a community or organization—ones that would guide and energize a commitment from within, not from the professional who stands on the sidelines.

How might a doctor or nurse work with the congregation of the Jones family, who are caring for their mother with a terminal disease, in order to find the people who would like to support them but are unsure how, and then provide the specific training and back-up support? As 'theologian' in this situation, how might the professional listen and encourage the congregation to see that this is not an extraordinary situation, but one that allows the congregation to become the community of support it believes itself to be?

THE WITNESS

A coach not only knows the theories and facts, a coach is also able to motivate others by telling stories and sharing personal experiences that reveal something of his or her own value system. This isn't easy for professional service providers. Too often the professional role values objectivity and professional distance. That distance has been increased by professional cultures and language that are difficult for common folks or communities to understand.

The key skill as witness is to realize that communities are energized not so much through professional theory and ideology as through story and example. When professional service providers talk with community members, leaders, and organizations, they must be willing to tell stories, not cite cases, and to talk about individuals and families in ways that reveal the depth of their understanding and appreciation of them as people. In other words, the challenge here is professional vulnerability, i.e., being willing to share the ways in which you as doctor, nurse, psychologist, case manager, etc. really care about the individual or family, including the ways in which your relationship with them has touched, impacted, or taught you.

Why do that? The primary reason is that you are inviting community members into a relationship as support-giver that builds on the depth and foundation of human relationships, not on professional skills. We remember, as Parker Palmer so profoundly outlines, the teachers who had the courage to teach with their heart as well as their minds (Palmer, 1998). To expand Palmer's premise, one of the major reasons people do not learn or get involved is fear. That is certainly true when professional service providers ask communities to get involved in caring for people who they have historically said need "specialized professional services." To help people overcome that fear, a professional leader not only must impart skills but also reveal the ways in which he or she has found promise, opportunity, and reward in situations that feel threatening to others. People come back to the stories that define a community, congregation, family, or individual. They remember the coach who lets them in on his or her story, and makes frightening situations real, manageable, and even promising.

THE GUIDE

A coach motivates, teaches, and then guides, but it is a different kind of guide than we find in most human service systems. There, we professionals 'guide' others through our specialized programs and services, showing others the excellent work we believe we do. We are too often more like a tour guide, or one who demonstrates and justifies to funding sources the importance of what we do.

Professional caregivers are often the fix-it guides—the ones with the answers, the ones who write the how-to books that fix relationships, health problems, and human needs in the same way others fix an old house or landscape a yard. In community, though, we seek out people with not only the answers but also with wisdom.

The guide in community building is more like a 'spiritual guide' or a guide on an Outward Bound expedition. The coach as guide invites people into a new world and then models new abilities and skills. This kind of guide is patient, listens to questions, and helps people learn their own skills, gifts and capacity to meet the challenges in front of them. It is crucial that professionals who seek to energize caring communities around individuals and families with particular needs recognize that they are often inviting people into a land that seems foreign and strange. It means learning to empower others to recognize their capacity as friends and supporters in that land, which is very different from the message that says you have to have specialized, professional training to deal with the situation. A guide works with the questions and gifts that people bring, and is prepared to learn from others. A professional provider may guide others into a world of illness and disability and support their caregiving skills, but it will be the others who guide the professional into the dynamics of a particular association, congregation, organization, or community. Indeed, one of the key skills of a guide is knowing where to find the other guides. Who knows this community, and how can I enlist them in helping to organize a new caregiving initiative? (Schwartz, 1996).

THE CELEBRANT

The fourth coaching role is that of the celebrant, who celebrates the gifts and skills and strengths and efforts made by others. A good coach helps a team find things to celebrate when they have tried hard, even in a loss, even when progress is slow, even when we cannot find the fix or cure. Celebration has many dimensions. It means seeing gifts and strengths in others where others may not see them, including the gifts and strengths of people who are in need of support or care. It means seeing capacity where others see deficit. For professional caregivers, so often focused on assessing needs, limitations, or illness, that means another set of eyes, a new vision. It means assuming there is abundance in community rather than scarcity (Palmer, 1992). It means an unexpected expression of gratitude.

Celebration in community caregiving often takes the forms of volunteer recognition. Such recognition is important, but it is also important to realize that the foundation of celebration is based on mutuality and shared story. We are celebrating not just what you or we have done for others, but what they have done for us. What have we learned? One of the many moving scenes in the Bill Moyers series *On Our Own Terms* took place in a volunteer hospice in San Francisco. One of its ritual celebrations was to gather volunteers in the room of a person who had just died and share stories and feelings about the strengths and gifts of that person. A celebrant helps others to find and celebrate individual and shared gifts, and recognizes the importance of finding traditional rituals or creating new ones that give community caregiving initiatives a way to celebrate commitment, vision, learning, and gifts.

From Roles to Strategies: Resources for Creating and Energizing Community Caregiving

Community building with "capacity vision" recognizes the challenges inherent to many professional roles, and as discussed earlier, has to take into account the assumptions that many make about community in a new century. That vision, while acknowledging the longing for the way communities used to be, must recognize and celebrate the strategies and resources that people in many disciplines and roles bring to the creation of new forms of community. These new communities are ones where people feel valued, connected, and supportive.

There are significant initiatives in many areas of the country that are attempting to create and revive community life. They have come from efforts to address the questions of how we create and energize caring communities to meet the visions and needs for community participation and support that are part of what it means to be healthy, both as a person and a citizen. In my role as a clergy person and community builder I work toward inclusive supports with and for people with developmental disabilities and their families. One of the exciting aspects of the last ten years has been discovering ways in which people are asking the same questions and developing similar strategies in other areas of human need and support. This chapter does not outline all of them, but I do want to point to some of what constitutes, for me, a small but important canon of community-building strategies and resources. There may well be similar resources and strategies in many other areas of support for caregiving families and communities.

Assessment and Planning that Draws People In

Two of the key strategies, consultation and collaboration, can happen in many ways, but let's look at a few models:

In the field of disabilities, a whole body of literature, planning strategies, and resources focuses on the theme of 'person-centered planning' (O'Brien, 1998). Rather than 'professional-centered' or 'service-system-centered,' person-centered planning explores the assets and dreams of an individual and his family rather than focusing on the limitations or deficits. The primary question is how others can assist an individual in living the kind of life he wants to live—a life built on connections, relationships, and personal dreams—while also taking into account the kinds of formal supports or therapies an individual may need.

There are a variety of models for person-centered planning. One is called the PATH process (Planning Alternative Tomorrows with Hope), which uses a personal strategic planning process and graphic recording techniques to help people visualize and articulate their dreams, then explores how relationships and support can be organized to help them move toward those dreams (O'Brien, Forest, & Pearpoint, 1998). Others are the McGill Action Planning System (MAPS) process, personal futures planning outlined in a number of publications, one of which is Capacity Works (1995), Essential Life Style Planning, (1996) and others.

If done well, person-centered planning involves anyone the person wants; it draws others in to help figure out a vision and a plan of support. Person-centered planning assumes that community support is both formal and informal. It is not a plan developed by a professional interdisciplinary team and then presented to patient, family, and potential supporters. It is not a prescription. Rather, it is a process that assumes that the more heads and hearts you have the more creative people can be, that people may be more willing to take on specific pieces of a plan they have figured out together rather than shying away from taking on the whole thing. It is also a form of planning that builds on what we now know as the 'six degrees of separation.' In other words, who knows whom, and how can we build on the network of contacts and relationships to help find answers and supports?

More recently, the movement known as 'self determination' or, in some countries, 'individualized funding,' gives even more potential and power to this form of planning. Rather than regarding someone as a 'client' or 'resident' of a formal support agency, the model of self determination allows an individual, along with his or her family and network of formal and informal support givers, to develop a plan of support. This plan is based on the assumption that people need freedom and choice, supports at individualized levels, the authority to control (including hire and fire) paid support providers, and the responsibility to give back to the community in the form of volunteer service and responsible use of public funds. The plan is then budgeted, and public support funds that previously went to pay for a slot or bed in a facility are instead made available to the individual and her caregiving community (Shumway & Nerney, 1994). Self determination/individualized funding has the promise of helping people to stay in, draw upon, and contribute to their communities and relationships.

Helping the Plan Come Alive: Circles of Support

In good person-centered planning, the group that comes together with an individual and his family may then constitute itself into a 'circle of support' to which others can be invited. The circle will probably change over time, like all relationships, and can have varying forms of organization and facilitation. One of the first circles of support was organized by Judith Snow and her friends, and was initially called her Joshua Committee—a group dedicated to helping her move from isolation in a rehabilitation system into her 'promised land,' her vision of living in and contributing to community life (Pearpoint, 1990). Circles of support have been used in inclusive school settings with peers and playmates of children with disabilities, with adults in community settings, and with many others (Communitas publications, 1995).

One model for a circle of support based on congregations is outlined in a Mennonite publication called *Supportive Care in the Congregation* (Preheim-Bartel, 1986). This model builds on the fact that, for many people, the congregation is the most stable form of community support and has traditionally mobilized supports for members in crisis.

The circle of support model provides a strategy for organizing support for the long term, not simply an acute-care crisis, and for mobilizing a network of both formal and informal support providers around an individual and family. It advances the community beyond the dilemma of wanting to help but not knowing how, as well as freeing individuals and families who need support from the dilemma of wanting help but not being sure how to ask (or who are tired of asking). The circle of support model draws upon the willingness of others to do something specific once they have had a part in hearing and defining the needs. It also helps them realize they are part of a support circle, that it is not all up to them. They have a valued part that makes a difference, but it is not solely their responsibility.

Another advantage of this model is that, while it provides a concrete process for creating and energizing a caring community, it does not have to be formalized. Many people are involved in all kinds of associations, clubs, classes, and groups that can organize a circle of support without calling it that, simply because that is what they would do for any member in need. Thus, it is important for professionals to help identify those groups in a person's life, and then perhaps to serve as their 'coach.'

Let me give an example. Bill Van Dyken is a chaplain at a facility for people with developmental disabilities in Iowa. The agency had a number of respite beds, but they had more requests than openings. Bill developed a strategy for talking with families, getting their permission to call their congregations, and then going with them to tell their story to the Board of Deacons, the Outreach Committee, etc. Bill would help outline some ways in which the congregation could help. Often, one of the first strategies was to find a group of individuals willing to take turns being 'volunteer respite providers,' as the system would call it, but which the congregation saw as simply helping a member in need. Bill and the family arranged ways for this circle of friends or volunteers to receive whatever training and back-up they needed. What he discovered was that people would often step forward in response to a specific need when they knew they would be involved with a group of others.

Jody Kretzmann, John McKnight, and others involved in the Asset Based Community Development Institute and network have taken this model to another level by identifying the myriad forms of community associations and networks in any given community. They then work with them to identify what they do, what they would like to do, and if they would be willing to do something similar, or new, to address an individual or community support need (Kretzmann, 2000).

Learning to Be Askers and Connectors

David Schwartz used to be the executive director of the Pennsylvania Developmental Disabilities Council, which provided funds for a variety of community building and community support initiatives. His book *Who Cares? Rediscovering Community* (1996), is much more than a description of some of those initiatives; it is his testament to his own journey as a professional learning about the new skills professionals must develop if they want to discover, create, and energize caring communities.

One of the key roles he identifies is that of the 'asker,' which Bill Van Dyken illustrated in the example above. The key here is that the person knows (or gets to know) the community and has the ability and chutzpah to ask others to be involved. They know who will respond and how a particular organization, congregation, association, or community works. The asker breaks through some of the major assumption barriers identified earlier in this chapter. One is that people who need support are often reluctant, for a number of reasons, to ask others. A second is that people who could give support often want to but do not know how.

Schwartz states in a fresh way a major tenet of community building—that askers and connectors have the most success when they connect capacity to capacity, interest to interest, strength to strength. In other words, if an asker is seeking people to support an individual or family with a caregiving need, the best way to connect with others may not be through the need but through the interests and gifts of each individual.

For example, if a family with a teenage son with autism is burned out by the struggle to find appropriate support, the role of an asker may be to discover the particular interests of the son— for instance, his fascination with car racing—and then to find others who share those interests. Instead of recruiting volunteers to help a family care for its son with autism, community builders look for people whose hobbies are car racing and who could be invited to share that interest with someone. Thus, the asker appeals to someone's sense of strength rather than to his or her limitation ("I don't know anything about autism") and offers to find or provide all the help that person may need. The hope, of course, is that a shared interest may lead to a real friendship, and eventually create all kinds of support for that teenager and his family. Thus, the counterintuitive challenge for professionals who want to be community builders is that we must learn to work from strengths and capacity in spite of the traditional caregiving focus on limitation and need.

Community Building to Community Organizing: What Can We Do Together?

The final strategy for caregivers, whether professionals or others, is to explore how community organizations and associations might be challenged to take on new caregiving initiatives that build partnerships between formal care provider systems and informal sources of support. This strategy moves beyond the individual responses and strategies that have been the focus of this chapter to more structured ways of responding to needs in a given community.

Addressing this area last is meant not to diminish its importance but rather to avoid the trap for many professionals and caregivers that community building cannot happen without new organizations, major new funding, or action from the powers

that be. The first challenge is to work with what we have, what
we can do, and what our church, club, organization, network, etc.
can do to help.

Numerous initiatives focus on building partnerships and collab-
orations between formal and informal caregivers. The Amherst
Wilder Foundation in St. Paul, MN has become one of the
reporters on these initiatives, publishing an excellent series of
books that assist the development of non-profit organizations and
chronicle some of the lessons being learned: *Community Building:
What Makes It Work?*; *Collaboration: What Makes It Work?*; and
The Collaboration Handbook. The resources from the Asset Based
Community Development Institute, including the training video
based on the book *Building Communities from the Inside Out*,
are also excellent resources for any collaborative initiative to build
community supports by tapping the power of existing associations
or seeking to build new partnerships.

One of the exciting national models in the last two decades
has been the development of interfaith volunteer caregiver initiatives, many started with initial funding from the Faith in Action
program of the Robert Wood Johnson Foundation. In this model,
coalitions of congregations or congregations and human service
agencies join together to address the informal support needs of
people with an identified need—for example, people living at home
who are frail because of age or disability, people with mental illness
or disability whose major need is to have a friend (the Compeer
model in mental illness supports), people with HIV/AIDS, etc.
The human service providers in these initiatives often become the
sources of referral and training, while the interfaith caregiving
project works with congregations in the community to recruit
individuals willing to put their faith in action by reaching out, with
others, to address specific needs. New projects can be funded
through the Faith in Action program of the Robert Wood Johnson
Foundation. Existing projects are networked and allied through
the Interfaith Caregiving Alliance (see Resource Section).

The Circle Comes Round: It's About All of Us

Community building is about reaching out to others for their sakes, but it also is about reaching in, way in, to our own hearts. Working on the boundaries between professional and friend, formal agencies and informal supports, needs and hopes, involves risk. It is not just about creating and energizing caring communities for others, it is also about the vision we have for our own community and the networks that support us, both in our personal lives and in our work.

As such, community building involves our core identities as well as our skills. It is about who we are as individuals and a people together as much as it is about what we can do, and how we can support and build networks, associations, and communities that care.

This kind of work goes to the heart of what it means to be professional service providers and caregivers, a discussion that is beyond the scope of this chapter (Gaventa, 1993, 1999; Palmer, 1999). But it is crucial to note briefly that creating and energizing caring communities means training and education that make room for both the skills one needs and the growth that community building makes possible. Parker Palmer's wonderful new book, *The Courage To Teach*, comes out of this kind of reflection and learning for teachers, which is very different from simply learning about teaching objectives. Clinical pastoral education and other forms of professional training involve opportunities for learning new skills while reflecting on the values, beliefs, dreams, and histories that make up our personal and professional identities.

As you begin or renew your own work in community building and seek to teach it to others, be sure to find and design training that makes room for the many personal dimensions of community building. That can include recognizing that people are already connected, or dealing with feelings of isolation and disconnection.

It can include talking about what we are learning about ourselves as we reach out to others with more obvious caregiving needs, and the ways they are teaching and helping us. It may be reflecting on the spiritual journey of community building and caregiving. However you do it, it is crucial. Expanding circles of care and support brings us all back to the center of who we are, the sources of our commitment and vision, and ways we all need to be supported and energized as we seek to energize and support others.

Bill Gaventa serves as Coordinator of Community and Congregational Supports at the Elizabeth M. Boggs Center on Developmental Disabilities, part of the Robert Wood Johnson Medical School of the University of Medicine and Dentistry of New Jersey. He works on community supports, training for community services staff, and supervision of a program in Clinical Pastoral Education. He also coordinates a training and technical assistance team for the New Jersey Self Determination Initiative, a statewide process now supporting more than 200 individuals and their families.

Voices

Jitterbug

Brian Alexander

You should have seen my dad jitterbug. You should have seen him go. Go Dad, go.

This memory comes from the time I saw him jitterbug, maybe 15 years ago at a country club dance in the small Ohio town where I grew up. My dad had grabbed a young woman about 25 years old, and had begun to jitterbug. I could not take my eyes off him or his undulating trousers and the way he moved and smiled, and the way the young woman mostly stood there, wide-eyed at what dancing used to be. She made only occasional contact with my father's hand as she tried, and failed, to plot his next move. She was adornment, a pretty magician's assistant, more spectator than dancer. She giggled. People watched. They smiled, too. That was a sight to see.

So is this. I am staring down at his bare feet, my brother and I facing him, each of us holding one of his arms on our shoulders, our arms around his waist, doing our own sad jitterbug. My brother and I wear swim trunks because we are dancing Dad to the shower.

We have to help him because the bone marrow cancer has made a mockery of his all-too-visible skeleton. His vertebrae are crumbling. His hip is Swiss cheese. His skull a sieve. His femur is dissolving like Alka-Seltzer. It could snap, we have been told. So my brother and I are very, very careful. We do not really think this dance is a good idea, but my father wants a shower. He hasn't had a shower in a long time, probably the longest period of time since the closing days of World War II and, though we cannot, he can still smell the hospital smell and he wants it gone. And so my brother, my father and I are going to take a shower. Dad can have anything he wants. He is about to die.

Here are some things I know about my father, some things I want you to know, too: I know my father was raised in Cleveland, poor but not desperate, in the Depression. He lived in the immigrant part of town with Poles and Czechs and Hungarians. Mrs. Hanebeck made *potica*, a honey-and-walnut pastry, on cold winter weekends, and she used to give my dad some.

I know my father saw Bob Feller pitch his first game. I know my father was a pretty good baseball player, too, and that a scout saw him play while Dad was in the army and told Dad to look him up after the war, but Dad never did because he had met Mom—a nurse—and was not about to look up a scout he met three years earlier. And I knew, really, that though Dad was probably pretty good, he liked telling this story and that over the decades the scout's interest had bloomed.

Here is another thing I know, too: My father is the golden boy of retired men, the avatar of the new era of retired healthy oldsters. He flirts with young women at his gym, then tools off in his 300Z sports car and his leather pants. Three months ago, he came home hurt from Wales, where he played in a golf tournament. He thought he had ruptured a disk lifting my mother's luggage. "God forbid your mother would pack light," he had told me over the phone when I called to ask how the trip went.

Because he is the envy of other men his age, he did not think he had cancer. But then he kept not feeling better. He kept not eating. He said he did not eat because his shoulder and back hurt so much and he was irritable because they hurt. So you see, it was a shock to get the phone call from my mother and to hear her say, "It's cancer," and then a day later to hear my father, who doesn't want to talk to me on the phone, who sounds utterly unlike my father, say, "We'll have to get this cancer taken care of."

Damn right. We'll get it taken care of. A cut here, a snip, a blast of radioactivity and that'll be that. But I know. And by the time my father is admitted to the hospital two days later, his kidneys have failed. His blood is loaded with poisons of all kinds. His clavicle is falling apart. I am sure and so I buy an airplane ticket, even as he is telling me not to come.

When I walk into my father's hospital room that first day, I do not want there to be any more days. I am tired, probably overwrought, but sleep would not have mattered. He is an insubstantial skeleton sinking into a bed with stainless steel railings. He is so pale I almost fail to recognize him. He is unshaven. He can barely speak. I feel my knees start to buckle.

I walk to the bedside and lean over the railing and do what I never do—kiss him on the forehead. This alarms him, so I make a crack, "What a pain in the ass, Dad." He likes this guy talk and his eyes apologize as if to say, "Look's what become of me."

And he is crying to boot. My father always gets angry when something bad happens to him, even if it's medical, but he is not angry now. He is scared. I have never seen my father scared. Have you ever seen yours scared? I mean really frightened the way facing death can make you frightened?

Soon after I arrive an oncologist enters. He says "okay?" after every sentence as in "We need to get those kidneys working again, okay? That's important, okay?" He flips through charts as he speaks, not really looking my father in the eye. And worst of all, he says this: "Your femur is showing some weakness, okay? And it's going to be fragile so we might want to think about putting a steel rod in there, okay?"

He says this like a mechanic tells you it's time for new brake shoes and the thing is, I know my father is dying. I have only been in his hospital room for an hour and I know he will die soon. My mother knows this. I suspect my father does, too, and I wish somebody would just tell him, not make ridiculous statements about putting steel rods in his bones. I want them to treat my father like a man.

I keep staring at him, thinking how much like a helpless child he seems, until finally I say, "Dad, how about a shave?"

He likes this idea, so now I want to give him the shave of his life. My mother and I struggle to slide him out of bed. We turn off the fan that inflates the air mattress meant to prevent bedsores, and then we swing his legs over the edge. This is the first time I have seen his legs since I have arrived. I am stunned by the exposure of his bones.

He puts his weight on my shoulders as we transfer him to the chair by the bed. He thuds into the chair and puts his hands on his knees. "Gee-awd!" He moans this as a way of saying that he's been lying down too damn long and it feels good to sit up like a man and put his hands on his knees. He's not a bed guy and he does not want anybody to think he is.

I find a pump bottle of no-rinse soap that does not require water, and I pump it into his hair, massage in the foam. His body melts under my hands. It occurs to me that aside from my mother holding his hand, nobody has touched my father in a week except to give him a shot or take a temperature or draw blood, and it also occurs to me that this is the longest span of time I have touched him, ever. And so I stand rubbing my father's head like a puppy's and I know that it has come to this, that my father really is dying, that he has been dying, but not knowing it, for a while now, and I have never been sadder in my life.

I wash his armpits and his back and then take a towel I have soaked in hot water and I place it on his face. He exhales so heavily I am startled. "Oh, God!" It feels good.

I lather him up and start with the sideburns. He orders me around: "Over here, now." "Don't go back and forth so much." I smile at the brief return of my father.

My mother has been staying at the hospital until late these past three nights, going home, and then returning first thing in the morning. My father, it seems, hates being alone even for a few minutes. He is afraid he is going to die alone in the night, so I ask a nurse to move a cot into his room. At the end of the day, I drive my mother back to the house and we stop for a quick meal and then I gather up some clothes and a pillow and toothbrush and hustle back to the hospital where my father says, "Where the hell have you been?"

It's not that my father wants to talk or even really wants company in the usual sense of the word. He wants a witness. He is clearly not interested in sleeping and it seems to me he might be *afraid* to sleep. I lie next to him on a cot as he aimlessly pushes buttons on the TV remote control.

Every twenty minutes or so, my father has to pee. It is hard for him to manage the plastic jug and the strain to urinate and his aim and "these goddamn tubes!" So I hold the jug under his penis as he sighs over and over but manages to dribble just a few drops. I empty the container into the toilet each time. He likes the fact that I am here to do this because I am a man and can understand.

We do not talk much. We watch *60 Minutes* and make comments. He switches on the History Channel. Hours tick by and he tries to pee and switches channels and I try to think of something to say.

What do you say to a dying man who is your father and who is not known for wanting to engage in long meaningful conversations about your lives and who, in any case, does not really want to talk about dying, a notion that is new to us, a topic that sits quietly in the room like a very large gorilla? What do sons and fathers say in times like this? How does it work?

I'm not sure if he sleeps at all. I doze off a few times. Finally, at sunrise, I give up and raise the blinds. Dad turns on *The Today Show*. This becomes our routine as the next four days blur together. I stay at the hospital until after the doctor makes his five-minute morning visit and then I go back to the house to once again fail at sleeping.

The red blood cells, at least, are working, making him seem flush, and the nephrologist has managed to jump start his kidneys, enough at least to avoid dialysis and we all seem to be very happy about this, but I can't help wondering what the point is.

Still, I root for his kidneys. My father's kidneys become the most important things in my life because if his kidneys work again, he will be released from the hospital to die at home and as much as I want my father to die, I do not want him to die here.

It's not that the hospital is a terrible place. It's nice as far as hospitals go. The floor he is on is named after a golfer who had cancer and gave a lot of money. But people die in cancer centers and though one of the nurses wears a defiant button that says "No, it's not depressing on the cancer ward," it sure seems pretty goddamn depressing to me. One night there is violent sobbing, followed by an empty room in the morning. Relatives walk around bleary-eyed and dazed, holding cups of coffee they never seem to sip from. The woman across the hall, the one whose 50-something husband has brain cancer, sits hour after hour in a chair trying to read, and every time I walk out of my father's room, we exchange glances, weak smiles, unsaid words. How's yours? Not good. How's yours?

I begin to think of this floor as a charnel house and I want my father out. *I* want out. But don't mind me. I'm sleep-deprived and overwrought.

One morning—the second? the third? they all haze over—the doctor announces he is prescribing chemotherapy, okay? and I blurt out "What's it going to do for him?" which irritates the doctor and makes him nervous, too, I imagine. "Really," I continue. "What will it do? Buy time? How much? What are the side effects? Is he going to be throwing up?"

This is not going to get any better. I am not a doctor, but I know this anyway and I know my father and how precious his sense of self is, and so I want my father to die while he still has a little of it left. I only want him to take the pills if they are mild and do not rob him of his hair or make him throw up and if they help him die easier. But the doctor refuses to talk about death. He talks about how the drugs will kill some of the cancer cells popping up all over my father's bone marrow and he promises me this is the mildest form of chemotherapy possible. And then he also orders a series of shots to stimulate production of my father's red blood cells. The shots are a miracle of genetic engineering called EPO, a miracle that costs $300 per syringe.

Another day—the next day? or the day after that?—a lay minister friend comes again with her Bible and Book of Common Prayer and Communion. I have already gone back to the house but my mother tells me later that there were some prayers and some talk of God. There were tears. My father is scared out of his wits about what will happen when he dies and the unanswered questions about heaven and hell and oblivion. Finally, though, I guess my father was tired of being scared and said, "I think that's enough emotion for one day."

One of the mornings I open the blinds in his room to wait for the sun and my father says, "Did you ever see *The English Patient?*" I saw *The English Patient*. I read the book. I know my father is referring to the Canadian nurse's act of mercy in breaking open the vials of morphine to end the English Patient's life. I say "Too bad we don't have any pretty Canadian nurses for you, Dad." He smiles at my deflection. We know what we mean.

One evening I come in for my shift, to spend the night, and find that a nurse has slid a rubber hose up his penis, a catheter. At the moment that rubber hose hit paydirt, a full liter of pee came rushing out of my father's bladder. He must have been in pain for days but did not want to have a rubber tube shoved up his penis and so kept trying to pee. He points to the tube running out of his penis, raises a hand and shakes his head. Another indignity.

The oncologist will note my father's catheter and say, "You know, if you continue to have problems urinating, we might want to think about doing a little prostate surgery, okay?"

I am pleased that when the doctor says this, my father, despite barely being able to register any reaction since I have been here, displays the most complete look of contempt I have ever witnessed. You see, I reckon that a guy has a right now that he's gonna die awfully damn soon, and seeing as how my father's body is literally disintegrating under his skin, I figure he's going to die very soon indeed and somebody ought to just come out and tell him instead of leaving him to wonder when.

Another night—there are only five nights, but they are like a continuous groggy stream so I'm not sure which night this is—I fall asleep at some point and then wake to hear groaning and to see my father trying to get up, to stand up, to hurdle the railing that has been raised, crib-like, along the sides of his bed. He is about to pull the tubes from his arm, to topple the IV stand, to rip out the catheter. He wants out. Out of bed, out of this hospital. Out.

I rush to his bedside. "I've got to get out of here," I think he says, though it's hard to tell because he is drugged and panicky and confused. Though I agree with the sentiment, he has gotten himself tangled in his tubes. I cannot fight him and unravel the tubes, too, and prevent him from trying to stand and maybe breaking a leg, so I push the nurse call button.

This is not my father, I think, as we perform our sad jitterbug, arm in arm, me pushing him back against the mattress so he cannot move, he flailing, jabbering. He is like I was so many years ago when I was a small child having a nightmare, fearing death and vague terror and he used to wake me and tell me that everything is okay and it was, too, except not for him, not now. The terror is real and it's really going to get him and I think how unfair it is that a man has to go backwards into his little boy nightmares.

Thirty seconds later, nurse Amy, one of my favorites, is there. She knows exactly what to do, somehow managing to calm him. "What the hell?" says my dad.

"It's okay, dad," I say. "You just got a little tangled up here." I am talking down to him now, too, and I hate myself for doing it. Amy works to figure out the mess of lines and I lean over my father's chest, put my arms around his shoulders, hugging him to keep him still while Amy works, and he rattles on, making semi-sense about "damn tubes" and "what a mess, what a mess, why me. . ." I feel hot tears pushing out of my eyes. I hug my father to keep him from tumbling backwards but also because now I have an excuse to hug my father and I catch the drops on my forearm before they hit his skin because we sure as hell have had enough emotion.

Amy notices, though, and touches my hand and keeps on working, and her empathy only makes me cry more. She mouths the words "Are you okay?" behind my father's back and I feel a little shame.

The next morning, as I raise the blinds, my brother and my mother walk into the room and my father gives my brother the same reaction he gave me, that look of humiliation, of a man brought low. It is a look almost apologetically humble. My brother makes a crack, something like "You look like hell," just as I did—we all know what we mean—and then he touches my father tenderly.

A few minutes later the oncologist, the "okay?" man, walks in and he says my father's kidneys have come back enough. He can go home tomorrow. And let's take out that catheter, okay? Yes, let's.

And those kidneys are looking good, and he says this as some sort of victory as if everything is good again because doctors have brought my father from the brink of death by kidney failure so that he can wait to die of death by bone marrow cancer.

My mother tells the doctor that she and Dad have airplane tickets for the Dominican Republic in a few months and could he write a note explaining that they cannot go now so she can get the tickets refunded? "You might want to wait on that," he says. "Mr. Alexander is not going to be playing golf, but you might be able to go and enjoy the vacation."

We laugh again. We just can't help it. The doctor looks hurt.

I walk out of my father's room to get my mother's car for the trip home. I feel liberated. When I leave the room, I cannot help noticing that the woman across the hall is not sitting in her chair. She is not reading, and she is not watching TV and she is not talking to her husband with the brain cancer. She is not there. The room is empty.

We, at least, are getting out alive.

Once home, my father, with our help, sits his bony hips down onto his bed and closes his eyes, then releases a deep sigh. My mother leaves the bedroom for a moment and my father looks at my brother and me and rasps, "Give me the vial of morphine." He's not joking. He's home, now. Now he can die. But we don't have any morphine.

A few hours later, we do. The "Hospice Assessment Team" arrives. There are two nurses and a social worker, and I hope the social worker does not tell my father she is a social worker because if he knew somebody thought he needed a social worker, well, it would kill him. Just kidding.

They walk to the bedroom and say hello and my father shuts down. He hates strangers observing his humiliation. My mother speaks for him. They outline how hospice works and what will happen and give numbers and ask questions. There are forms to sign, lots and lots of forms, until my father who has not spoken, says "Jesus Christ, you can't even die without paperwork." He is both joking and not joking and my brother and mother and I know what he means, but the social worker, who is young and earnest, believes this is a signal to explain why all the forms are necessary. "It's okay," I say, "he's just kidding."

The hospice workers also supply a very detailed booklet about procedures and how the system works, and the social worker makes a point of flipping to the back pages to explain the information on hurricane preparedness. This makes us laugh out loud and I fear she has taken offense, but I say to my father "God forbid you would die in a hurricane, Dad." Hurricane season ended a month before and we're not waiting for next year. He wants to die as quickly as possible and we want him to die as quickly as possible, too. I'm pretty sure the hospice team has no idea how sick my father really is. I wonder why nobody told them.

After the hospice workers leave we try to give dad some time to sleep. My brother and I go to Denny's for pancakes and omelets and then we go to a liquor store. This is not for my father, though we would give him whatever single malt he wanted no matter what a doctor said. It is for us.

Soon after we return, a van pulls up to the house and a young man begins unloading a hospital bed, and a potty chair and other odds and ends like a walker, and he wants to know if there is anything, anything at all he can get for us. We cannot think of anything so he begins to put the bed together in my parents' bedroom. We get my father up and out of bed and walk him onto the back patio, the lanai, as they say in Florida, and he sits down in a patio chair and glances over his shoulder at the young man assembling the hospital bed.

My brother is alone with my father for a moment, but as I walk towards the lanai, I hear my father say, "Did you ever see *The English Patient*?"

The next day, my father declares that he must have a shower, and so my brother and I do our little dance with him. He feels heavy, though he is positively skeletal. With every step I imagine the snap of his femur but after about a minute we have traversed the 15 feet from his bed to the shower and we set him on a shower seat and turn on the water. He groans with pleasure and when we start to suds up the washcloth and scrub him down like a car in a suburban driveway, he groans even more. We shampoo his hair and massage his scalp. We stand in our trunks and dance around like the little boys we once were, when we would dance in hot summer rainstorms.

This would be a good time, I think. Right now. This would be a good time to die.

We dance him back to the hospital bed. He has been spending the nights in his and Mom's bed. I know for a fact that he does not want to die in the hospital bed. I know for a fact that my mother does not want him to die in *their* bed. She could not bear it. My mother wrestles him into his pajamas. We comb his hair and I shave him again. I am amazed at how wiry his beard is. My dad has always had a tough beard and now it seems as if his whiskers are the toughest part of his body, the only things left that are living up to their reputation.

He rests for a few hours and then we walk him back to the chair on the lanai. He is alone with my brother again and he says this: "You can't kill me. It would hurt your mother too much," referring to my mother's ardent Catholic beliefs and then, "I wish you could."

Later that day my other brother arrives, so all three of "the boys" are here now. We watch part of the Ohio State-

Michigan football game. My father does not pay attention. He's busy dying. We pretend he is not busy dying. We say things like "How about that?" and "Whoa!" and then look at him to see if this has registered and it hasn't. He's too busy dying, and I want to know so badly what it is he is thinking about. I do not want him to be afraid, a hopeless sentiment, I know, like asking a man in the desert to not crave water.

A friend who knows about this sort of thing through her own work with hospice calls me from New York, and we talk about the drugs my father has been prescribed. One is an anti-depressant, which now seems hilariously absurd, and there are pain pills. She warns me that my father may not be able to swallow pain pills much longer and she recommends a liquid morphine that we can slide under his tongue. I call the hospice to request it.

It gets to be Sunday morning, so my father says he'd like to sit on the lanai again. We struggle to walk him out and then position the chair under him. He takes the newspaper and reads a little, or maybe just acts as if he is reading while the rest of us really do read. He observes us being a normal family reading the Sunday paper and drinking coffee, not a family in which somebody is about to die. I wonder what it is like to be such an observer from such a vantage point. Does he look back on his sons as tots opening presents at Christmas? Does he wonder if he should say something?

I wonder this, too: I wonder if I should say something, arrive at a summing up, a profound statement. I feel I should. I feel there should be something said, but for the life of me I cannot think of a single appropriate thing. Earlier, a day or two, I guess, I sat by his side and asked if there was anything he would like to talk about. He said, "There doesn't seem to be much to say."

I was a little disappointed, but then I thought, well, no, there *doesn't* seem to be much to say. I wanted some sort of movie death scene, but movie death scenes only happen in movies.

A nurse is scheduled to come every other day, but because nobody has realized, I think, how close my father really is to dying, and because the days are rapidly approaching Thanksgiving, there is always a new nurse who asks the same questions and tries to get my father to talk. I want them to know who my father is, the dancer, the traveling salesman, the golfer, the dad. I feel compelled to sit them down and tell them but then I think they have a job to do and so I let them do it.

Actually, they are here more often than every other day because we keep having to call them to stop by. We have questions. We want answers. We want to know what we should do. We want instructions.

What to do, for example, when my father has not pooped in days? This worries not just my mother, but even the nurse. She said my father should most definitely poop soon. To me the pooping angst seems misplaced. The man is clearly going to die sometime very soon. Why are we bothering him about pooping? Besides he has barely eaten in days, so it's not like there's a Caesar salad and a nice ribeye wending their way through his alimentary canal. Why can't we just leave him alone?

Apparently, the reason has something to do with block-ages in his colon which, I am given to understand, can be painful, though I still wonder how much more painful a colon blockage can be than having your bones fizz away. Still, we rouse my father from his hospital bed yet again to sit on the potty chair and we gather round like Greeks at Delphi hoping for a revelation. There he sits, naked on a plastic seat with a hose sticking out of his penis, with the facial cheeks of a dieting supermodel staring out at us. I decide to empty his catheter bag while we wait.

This amuses him because emptying that bag has become something of an obsession to me, and he mutters, "God, that kid loves to fiddle with that bag." I am 40 years old and I am "that kid" because I have always been that kid and, frankly, I have always fiddled with things and often broken them, too, which gave me the family nickname of "Fingers." But draining the bag is something I can do and I want to do something. I want to take some action and this is all I can think of.

I drain the deep yellow urine, which is now almost viscous with white particles—particles I imagine to be calcium from his bones—into the plastic jug. I pour the contents of the jug into the toilet and then rinse it with a little bleach.

Finally, my father gives up and my mother decides to call hospice. By the time yet another nurse arrives it is dark out and I wonder why this can't wait until the next day, if there is one, and I hope that my father dies that night so he will not have to suffer the indignity of an enema. But it can't

wait. First the nurse shoves a gloved finger into my father's
rectum and feels nothing abnormal. Then she presses
against his belly, then she has me fill a very large plastic bag
with water and an oily, soapy material she has brought. My
brothers and I roll dad over onto his side and are shocked
to see that the lowest bony knob on his spine has broken
through the parched vellum of his skin, something my
mother feared would happen with so much time in bed.

Just as I have been so concerned about emptying his
catheter bag, she has been worried about bedsores. These
are two things we feel we can control and so we try obses-
sively to do so and now my mother feels she has failed in
some way. This is all very, very important to us. Salve is
brought, a pillow is arranged to keep my father slightly on
his side, not just for the impending enema but also to keep
the bedsore from hurting. My father lies there, helpless, as
the nurse slides in the enema and drains the entire contents
of the bag into my father's guts.

I suppose this nurse has seen her share of dying people
and has no doubt given her share of enemas. I admire her.
She perspires a little with the effort and manages to seem
both professional and caring, which must be a tough line to
walk when you are surrounded by staring family members
who have had little sleep and who have spent those sleep-
less days and nights watching a loved one disintegrate.

My father, meanwhile, lies sullen and silent, angry that
he has to lie with his ass exposed to the world, helpless
and weak and dying without a shred of anything that made
him who he thought he was. He started giving the nurses

the silent treatment a day or two ago and he still refuses to speak.

Within half an hour, my father declares he needs to sit on the potty chair again and so we help him up and wrestle him onto the chair. He releases vile gasses and tiny streams of poisonous oils as if all the chemicals and cancer and corruption in his body are trying to drain out. It proves to be a tiny amount, though, and he does not poop. I, however, wash that potty chair and bleach it, and disinfect it until I would eat a vichyssoise out of it.

With Dad back in bed, my mother and my brothers and I talk with the nurse. We tell her that my father will not go to see the urologist, an appointment my father's oncologist had insisted on making before Dad left the hospital, an appointment to check on that "little prostate problem, okay?" and my father will not take any more $300 syringes full of bioengineered red blood cell fertilizer, and he will not have another enema nor any more of the chemotherapy pills. The hospice nurse says that's fine. She says this as if she has been waiting for us to say this, as if she would have advised us to say this but could not.

My father's speech has been raspy and weak since I arrived in Florida but now it has become slurred, as if he cannot move his jaw properly. He is much worse, much worse than I thought it was possible to be and still be alive. My middle brother has left to go to work because we have no idea how long our father will take to die, and if this drags on for weeks he will be needed back here later. There is talk of my oldest brother going, too, because he has only so much vacation, whereas I am self-employed and can stay. But today, seeing him now, my oldest brother thinks he will remain for awhile longer.

My father watches the stock market roundup on CNBC. His eyes, which never really close, now, and which lose focus entirely and roll in his head for long intervals, manage to follow the tracking ticker at the bottom of the screen, tick, tick, ticking the movement of shares up and down.

He sleeps. We give him the liquid morphine now, because my friend was right. My father cannot swallow a pill.

My father's mind frequently leaves his body. With every hour that passes his eyes roll more precipitously into his head. If we listen carefully, we can hear a faint sound deep inside my father's chest. My mother, who was a nurse in wartime, knows what this is. "The death rattle," she tells us.

That night, my father wants out of the hospital bed for his transition to the big bed. We can barely sit him upright and it takes all his strength. He sits, still and breathing, from the effort. My brother and I sit on either side of him, and my mother tries to convince him to stay where he is. He shakes his head no. "Give me a minute."

I know my father wants to die in his own bed. I want him to die in his own bed. "It's okay, Mom," I say. "We'll just sit here for awhile."

We sit for a very long time. My father looks down and stares at his thighs, two sticks of bone wrapped in skin. He shakes his head back and forth. I can hear his mind say 'God! Would you look at that?' He looks at my brother's thighs. Then he turns his head and looks at my thighs. We are thick and meaty compared to him, thick and meaty as he was once but is not now, and he sees his thighs in his mind as they once were.

We sit like this for half an hour. My brother and I have put our arms behind my father's back to support him, to keep him upright. We want this effort to seem casual, to go unnoticed, but now our arms are burning. I vow, and I guess my brother does, too, to keep my arm there forever if need be.

"I'm okay," Dad says. "Just let me alone for a second."

We stand up and stare at him sitting there on a bed he wants to escape. He looks for all the world like a boxer slammed to the canvas, who is hearing the count run past eight but cannot get up. Get up, Dad. Get up. His getting up out of that bed becomes the most important thing in my life, the most important thing there ever was. Just get up.

We consider lifting him out of it, but we are worried about snapping what's left of his bones in the process. And so we wait.

Suddenly my father leans forward precipitously and we jump up at him, startled, startling him, because we think he has just died. He looks up at us, amused at our thinking he has died. He rolls his eyes. "Sheesh!"

We laugh. We laugh so hard tears get squeezed out of our eyes and we keep on laughing, and though my father is not literally laughing, he thinks this is very funny, too.

And then he says he wants us to help him lay back down in the hospital bed. He'll die right here. My brother and I lean him back and tuck pillows around his body and mess with the height of the head and foot until we think he's comfortable.

On Tuesday, November 23, my mother wakes us up at dawn just the way she used to do for school, but now she says, "I think this might be it." She has called the Episcopal lay minister again. My mother wants my father to have last rites. I wish she would skip it. The very idea of one last prayer to God to forgive and forget seems ridiculously desperate.

But there she is, the very nice lady who believes, as my mother does, that this is a good idea and they lean over my father and they say the words and my father tries, vainly, to say some of the words, too, because he is terrified and he wants to say words, and he hopes God will forgive his sins and take him someplace nice after all this living and dying is over with. My father leaks out a couple of tears and he wants to say the words and the nice woman tells him it's okay, she'll say the words for him, and he seems grateful and I want my dad to die right there, boom, just like that, because this seems pathetic and horrible and not like my dad at all. I do not want him to beg and be afraid.

I cannot watch any longer, so I take a cup of coffee my mother brewed—amazing how she manages her morning routine—and I go stand in the driveway in early morning fog and I watch and listen to birds waking up and think how much my dad liked watching animals.

My father does not die. By now, I know you are wishing he would die and believe me, I have been wishing it too.

There have been tiny, wonderful moments I will always remember, but they will exist so strongly in my memory because they are stark counterpoints to the horror I have witnessed. If I had to choose, I would have spared my father all of it and skipped the moments. I do not think he has any dance steps left to perform. His disease is only a painful reminder that he could perform them once and now cannot.

And I feel guilty because I have not helped my father die. So I eye that bottle with the eyedropper and I wonder about it. And I think about how my father told my brother that killing him might hurt my mother. I dither.

Sometime around noon I walk into the bedroom and say, "Is there anything I can get you, Dad?"

"I wish there was something you could give me."

There is, of course. But I dither.

An hour later, for no apparent reason, my father begins to try to sit up. I call my brother and we help him sit up, doing all the work now, because my dad is virtually inert, but once we get him up, he rolls his head into the crook of my neck and my heart breaks.

We lay him back down. This, I know, is his last effort.

Over the past two days, my father's mouth has accumulated flakes of dried saliva and skin, and we have tried, lamely, to clean this off his teeth. He has gnashed at it, licked his lips, rolled his tongue to get rid of it, but it clings and now his mouth is full of it. We try to use a toothbrush but fail to make much headway. It is grotesque. When I call my New York friend and tell her this, she explains that "mouth care" is very important and she chides the hospice workers for not leaving tools and instructions for how to clean out my father's mouth.

This evening when the nurse arrives I tell her about my father's mouth, and it turns out there are special tools and swabs that taste minty fresh for this very purpose. She wets the swabs, little pink sponges at the end of sticks, and wipes out the inside of my father's mouth. I would not have thought he would be able to open his mouth like this, but he does. He opens it wide like a baby bird waiting for food.

"Oh, you like that, huh?" the nurse coos, as if talking to a pet. My father does not make any sign he has heard, but he opens his mouth again and again as she wipes the gunk out, and strokes the surface of his teeth.

I feel awful. My father has always loved his teeth. He brushed with brio, foaming huge masses of toothpaste into a sink and brushing as hard as a guy detailing a hubcap. And now I have let him down and allowed his teeth to be covered with goo, his tongue and his cheeks to accumulate trash. So I apologize. I apologize irrationally, frantically and I'm not even sure if he can hear me.

My friend in New York tells me that the death my father is enjoying right now is about as good as it gets unless you die like Nelson Rockefeller in the middle of sex with a younger woman. The scary part is, I believe her. We are a white, upper-middle-class family in the U.S. and we have drugs and my father is going to die any minute and though that seems like a very long time to me, the fact is, he has not lingered for months on end. He wants to die, and I think he is making himself die sooner, even, than scheduled because there is not a damn thing left to do. And this is as good as it gets.

Most of us are stripped bare, eaten alive, degraded. This is certainly true of my father, but most of us will have it harder. This has gone quickly, really. A formal diagnosis of cancer just three weeks ago. It seems much, much longer.

We are up all night, which is how I come to blame lack of sleep for these ravings. We try to take shifts, my mother retiring to the couch for a couple of hours while my brother sits with my father, and then I take over, and then Mom, but the system breaks down and for much of the night we sit watching him breathe. At one point, he stops breathing and we hold our own breath as if in sympathy, and then with a gasp he breathes again. His eyes do not focus at all now. The rattling in his chest grows louder and louder so it sounds very much like the rattle of a rattlesnake.

I am with him at daybreak and just before the light of dawn penetrates the fog, I open the shutter so Dad can see out if his eyes could focus, and then there they are—focused, alert, questioning. Light outlines the trees and I say, "How about that, Dad? Another day."

I have never seen a man look more disappointed.

Indeed, my father now seems to regain some strength. We were going to call my middle brother and ask him to come, hurry, today, but now we put it off. This could go on for awhile, this torture, and my brother is having Thanksgiving with some friends and we want to let him have that. There is talk of my oldest brother going home.

At some point during the day we all stand around my father's bed and my mother grabs his arm and says, "Do you know we all love you," and there is some recognition in his eyes, a tiny nod.

I take a walk that day and watch a bald eagle steal a fish from an egret, and I think how much my dad would have liked to have seen that. Then, that evening, I take another walk with a very large glass of Scotch, and I look at the stars and I speak to them and I imagine a Milky Way full of whirling spirits and I ask them to please hurry up and come get him because this has stopped being useful.

And when I come in, my mother makes us promise we will go to bed, we will not wait up in a vigil. And so we do.

I lie on the fold-out sleeper, feeling the steel bar under the thin mattress, and I think about how much I want my father to die. I gave him a big dose with the eye dropper before I went to bed, and I have made my mother promise to give him a big dose in four hours because I know that, contrary to her instructions, my mother will not sleep. I wonder if I am a weenie for not giving him a very, very big dose. I wonder if he would be a weenie if it were me.

And then the strangest thing happens. I know it happens in my mind's eye, and that it is not real, but as I lie there half asleep I feel a wisp, a streak of white vapor, touch my cheek and tell me that everything's okay now, and I see my dad float up through the ceiling and begin to whirl around the Milky Way.

Go Dad, go.

Then, seconds later, though it is really five hours later and 4:00 am, my mother bursts through the door and says

"It's time." Just like another school day, "Come on boys, it's time. Get up!" and I know what she means and slip on my shorts and rush to the bedroom. My brother joins me and we listen as dad's gullet rattles and his eyes stare blankly and roll and roll and his body lies motionless and his hand curls up under his neck, cocked at what must be an uncomfortable position except we don't think he can feel it, and his fingertips are slightly blue and I know for a fact that my father has already left and that there's nothing in there any more.

I ask my mother if she gave my father the drops and she says she did. I say, "Well, let's give him some more. He can't tell us if he hurts." She can accept this rationalization. She does not want him to have pain. And so I fill the eyedropper and I slip it into his mouth and drain it out under his tongue and it makes a slight burbling noise as the air flows in and out of his mouth.

It is very foggy and so we are reluctant to call my other brother. He is across the state and, knowing him, he would drive way too fast to get here in the fog and we picture his car wrapped around a cypress in the Everglades and so we wait. But then we can wait no longer and make the call.

We all wait as the rattle becomes louder and louder and the breathing becomes slower and slower. Half an hour later the rattle and the gasping fill the room. He breathes once every 15 seconds or so. We surround his bed, hoping my other brother can make it in time. I take hold of my father's hand and feel his pulse racing. My brother strokes his forehead. My mother places both her hands on his chest. This is impulsive, this touching. We have not said a word but we are all compelled to touch him at vital points and to feel it and so we sit and stand and lay our hands on his body and a large breath enters my father's mouth and then nothing happens for a very long time.

His pulse races. His heart is panicky. It has gone on without him for hours already and now it wonders where the air is. It pumps harder and harder and faster and faster, a 78-year-old heart at the end of the century, a heart that survived the jazz age and the Depression and a World War, and a couple million miles of highway in a Chevrolet Impala and the disappointments of his children. It races and panics, searching everywhere for a little air. It pounds out its last beats like a 19-year-old sprinter's and then the body gasps shockingly, alarmingly gasps, and the pulse goes away and my father begins to turn blue and cold and that's the end of that.

My mother leans into his body and bows her head and allows herself a small tear but that's all for now because there's work to be done and arrangements to be made and it occurs to me this is Thanksgiving morning, and now I have something to be thankful for.

In an hour a nurse from hospice will come by and wash my father's body, wipe it down and prepare it for pick-up by two men who will take it to a crematorium.

Eventually, my brother and I will take my father's ashes surfing and distribute them among the waves. But right now, while I wait for the young men and the hearse, I stand out in the driveway with my morning coffee and think of the law of the conservation of matter. All the matter that ever was in the universe is still in the universe, says the law. It will always be there. Forever. My father will exist as smoke and ash and bits of bone and teeth and then those will be broken into elements and the carbon will find its way into more organic matter, maybe a bird, and the calcium will seep into rock or maybe an animal or perhaps a glass of chocolate milk a kid will drink after school before he sits down with his mother and spells the words for tomorrow's spelling tests, and maybe it will be the week for double-letter words like "stubbornness" and "happiness" and "jitterbug."

In Memory of:
Robert Alexander
April 17, 1921–November 25, 1999

programs · that · work

CARE-NET

◆

Why It Works – *From the Editor*
*The Rosalynn Carter Institute (RCI) for Human Development
was established to honor former First Lady Rosalynn Carter
by enhancing her long-standing commitments to human
development and mental health. Dedicated to focusing on
the difficulties and rewards experienced by caregivers, RCI,
like many states and communities, seeks to address the needs
of caregiving families and professionals with innovative
techniques. It emphasizes two major themes—
expanding the knowledge base for caregiving and offering
ongoing training, as well as bringing together family and
professional caregivers for mutual education and support.*

In 1990 the Rosalynn Carter Institute (RCI) for Human Development created a model program, the CARE-NET (Caregivers' Network)—a coalition of agencies, organizations, and individuals in West Central Georgia—which addresses concerns of family and professional caregivers in a mostly rural, sixteen-county region.

Implemented through a leadership council composed of distinguished representatives from a variety of agencies and organizations, the CARE-NET promotes opportunities for linking professional and family caregivers for collaborative endeavors. The CARE-NET develops service and educational programs to meet the needs of caregivers and provides recognition and support for caregivers. The organization operates under the auspices of, and is staffed by, the Rosalynn Carter Institute for Human Development of Georgia Southwestern State University.

The West Central Georgia CARE-NET has had several notable accomplishments. First, in 1993, a comprehensive two-year study of caregivers and caregiving in the region was completed and published in a report entitled *Characteristics, Concerns, and Concrete Needs of Formal and Informal Caregivers—Understanding Their Marathon Existence.* A summary version of the report was published for public distribution in the region. Using quantitative findings and anecdotal information from the study, along with her own personal caregiving experience, Rosalynn Carter (with Susan Golant) wrote *Helping Yourself Help Others: A Book for Caregivers*, published by Times Books in 1994.

Next, from 1994 through 1996, the CARE-NET embarked upon a comprehensive education and support project for caregivers in the region funded by The Pew Charitable Trusts of Philadelphia. The centerpiece of the project was a five-week program called *Caring for You, Caring for Me: Education and Support for Caregivers*, which brought together family and professional caregivers for persons with any illness or disability across the life span for education and mutual support. After conducting the program for over 400 caregivers in West Central Georgia, *Caring for You, Caring for Me* was published in the form of a *Leader's Guide* and *Participant's Manual* by the University of Georgia Press and distributed throughout the U.S..

A third major accomplishment of the CARE-NET has been the recent development of a new service model called 'care managers for caregivers.' Funded by a grant from the Robert Wood Johnson Foundation, professionals in case management and social service are trained to focus on and offer supportive services directly to family caregivers. To date, more than 70 family caregivers have received such services as strength and needs assessment, counseling and emotional support, and assistance in navigating the complex health care and social service system.

The network has also helped caregivers in the region in numerous other ways. The CARE-NET and RCI sponsor an annual conference that brings nationally recognized experts to the region to share their expertise with caregivers. Additionally, the CARE-NET and RCI have developed an educational resource center that contains books, videotapes, pamphlets, and audiotapes for use by caregivers in the region. With its focus on the well-accepted concerns of caregivers, the CARE-NET has served as a unifying force for agencies in the region. Through the network, the RCI has offered consultation to agencies and organizations that have been instrumental in bringing new services to the community, including hospice and respite care for families caring for children with disabilities.

Through a grant from the Robert Wood Johnson Foundation, the CARE-NET model was replicated in 18 adjacent counties in South Georgia in 1998. The South Georgia CARE-NET operates under the auspices of the Division of Social Work at Valdosta State University. Though both networks offer similar programs and services, differences in the two organizations reflect the character of their respective leadership councils and the unique strengths and needs of caregivers in each region.

An important next step for the RCI is to implement the CARE-NET model in states and communities across the nation. An additional priority is to assist in the development of a caregiving knowledge base that has as its core the evaluation and dissemination of successful caregiving practices.

For more information about the CARE-NET concept or the RCI, visit the institute's website at rci.gsw.edu or write to the Rosalynn Carter Institute for Human Development, Georgia Southwestern State University, 800 Wheatley Street, Americus, Georgia 31709.

Contributed by David Haigler, Rosalynn Carter Institute

Part II

The Caregiving Experience: Implications for Professionals

As we stated earlier, there is a tendency to typify family caregivers in two ways—either as selfless saints who receive great rewards from the tasks of caregiving or as individuals on the verge of collapse from the demands, stresses, and wear and tear of caregiving. The reality, of course, is more complex and multidimensional. For professional caregivers to be effective, they need to understand all the dimensions of the caregiving experience.

Chichin begins by reminding us of some often-forgotten caregivers: Paraprofessionals such as home-care or nursing-home aides are in the nether land of caregiving. They provide direct, daily care. They often become very close to the patient and to the family. Yet their assessments or advice are rarely sought. They have no role in decisions. And when a death occurs, they are often simply dismissed or asked to move on to a new case. I remember when my father died; no one had thought to call his home-health aide. She arrived, planning to take care of him, as she had for the past three months. It turned out to be a fortunate oversight; we advocated successfully that she be paid for the day. And she stayed and grieved with the rest of the family. We all needed that to happen. But that happens far too rarely. Chichin aptly calls our attention to the needs of these paraprofessional caregivers, offering sound suggestions for support. And the theme is echoed by Karen, a home-health aide who voices both the frustration and pride of this type of caregiving. She makes a personal plea for the needs that Chichin addresses—teamwork and support.

The caregiving experience is affected by the caregiver's cultural experience. Harper, Lartigue, and Doka emphasize that culture defines the family system, mutual obligations, norms of caregiving responsibilities, family patterns of communications, beliefs about the roles of professionals, and values that influence caregiving decisions. Implicit in their call for professionals to be sensitive toward culture is a caution that the professional's own cultural background may influence judgments about family caregivers. I remember, for example, a nursing home staffed primarily by nurses from Jamaica, a culture in which the elderly are rarely institutionalized. The nurses' immediate assumption was that the families of nursing home patients were derelict in their caregiving duties. The importance of culturally sensitive interventions is also illustrated by the Synagogue HOPE Project. This program works because it builds upon the unique spiritual strengths and values of Judaism. Other spiritual traditions can relate this model to their own spiritual perspectives.

Jacobs' chapter on the selfless caregiver is a critical one. The selfless caregiver often draws two responses—either unbridled admiration or concern that the person has lost himself in the process. Jacobs reminds us that we have to begin where family caregivers are. We need to understand and respect the values that motivate them, gently supporting them in their own caregiving journey. Skofield's voice offers one such perspective. He reminds us of the many relationships that frame family caregiving. Moreover, he portrays the many conflicts even the most devoted caregivers experience.

And an entire chapter could be added on the reluctant caregiver. Not every caregiver is selfless. Even more frustrating for professional caregivers are those family members who seem reluctant to assume even the smallest of caregiving tasks. Perhaps Jacobs' comments can be applied here as well. Professional caregivers need to understand their perspectives—their culture, prior relationships, and present demands, in order to assist them as they face the challenges of caregiving. And in such cases it is important to be able to accept imperfection, ambiguity, and diminished expectation.

The remaining sections reinforce two critical concepts. The first is that family caregivers, reluctant or selfless, need not labor alone. Reinhard's chapter reminds us that nurses have a critical role in offering support to family caregivers, both on an individual level and in being advocates for shaping public policy. She provides sage and practical advice as to how that is best done. She also offers a practical suggestion of a program that can ease isolation: Caregiver Fairs. Such fairs can be easily presented by a variety of organizations, such as churches, synagogues, departments of aging, even support groups. These fairs offer more than useful information on available services; they raise awareness about such services. Sometimes, people do not recognize a need until they know a service is available. And the caregiver fairs provide reassurance that one is not alone. A Program That Works—Talbot Hospice Foundation—reminds us of what committed volunteers can accomplish. Lamers, too, contributes a helpful sidebar here. Physicians can ease isolation when they are sensitive to the needs of family caregivers.

Witrogen McLeod's chapter amplifies the second critical point, though it is reflected in Chichin's, Jacobs' and Reinhard's chapters as well. Self-care is a critical component of caregiving. Professionals have a role in assisting families in incorporating that into the caregiving experience. But they should not only educate about self-care. They must model it.

4

Paraprofessional Workers in Long-Term Care: Dealing with Loss and Bereavement

Eileen R. Chichin, Orah R. Burack, & John M. Carter

Health care professionals often experience feelings of grief and bereavement, particularly when employed in settings in which death is commonplace (e.g., Lerea & LiMauro, 1982; Lev, 1989), such as institutional or community-based long-term-care programs. Here, professionals who regularly care for the dying are faced daily with loss, often losing an individual to whom they have become emotionally close or with whom they identify strongly.

Increasingly, we recognize that health care *paraprofessionals* are also strongly impacted by the constant caring for the dying in the long-term-care setting. Frail, elderly individuals, many of whom are relatively near death, constitute the majority of the patient population. Their primary caregivers, who form the foundation of both the institutional and community-based long-term-care industry, are members of the paraprofessional work force. To date, their issues and needs have been inadequately addressed, although this trend is changing.

What is Long-Term Care and Who Uses it?

Long-term care encompasses a broad range of services for individuals who cannot function totally on their own. These services address health, personal care, and social needs, and can be delivered in institutions or in the community. For the purposes of this chapter, we will focus on both institutional and community-based long-term care; however, discussion of community-based long-term care will be limited to home care provided to an individual in his or her own home, and will exclude other community programs (e.g., day care, meal programs, etc.).

Generally, those who access long-term care suffer from chronic physical or mental illness or severe functional or mental disabilities. There are growing numbers of "high-tech" home-care programs around the country, serving those individuals with very complex, often acute, care needs. However, most home-care clients have chronic care needs described as "custodial," including bathing, dressing, toileting, and feeding. Long-term-care clients cared for at home range from those in infancy to those in advanced old age, the vast majority falling into the latter group.

A key factor in determining whether one lives at home or in a nursing home is the ability and willingness of family members or friends to provide care. Nursing home residents bear a strong resemblance to home-care clients; in both home and institutional settings, significant numbers of individuals suffer from Alzheimer's disease and other dementia, as well as numerous co-morbid chronic afflictions such as arthritis, cardiovascular disease, and diabetes.

Not surprisingly, with the exception of those residing in veterans' facilities, the majority of those accessing long-term care are women. In both community and institutional settings, many have at least one person remaining involved in their care, even after placement in a nursing home. Although they are in the minority, some individuals truly have no support system at all. Often, when these people are able to describe their situations, they report that every relative and friend in their lives has predeceased them.

Who Is the Long-Term-Care Paraprofessional?

The person who provides the majority of care to those in both community-based and institutional long-term care is generally a paraprofessional. In the home setting, the paraprofessional worker can have any one of a number of titles, including personal care worker, home-health aide, or home attendant. While none of these are professional workers, the training they receive varies, and some are qualified to perform more complex tasks than others. What they are able to do varies by training and title, as well as state to state. The nursing home caregiving paraprofessional generally holds the title of certified nursing assistant (CNA).

One key factor differentiating the long-term-care paraprofessional from his (or more likely her) acute-care counterpart is the longevity of the relationship between worker and patient. (The patient in home care is generally referred to as the 'client,' while in nursing homes he or she is called a 'resident.') Often a worker cares for the same person for months or years, performing the most private of personal tasks. As a result of this longevity and intimacy, an emotional closeness often develops between these two members of the caregiving dyad. This is both the best and the worst thing about long-term care: Workers become very attached to those for whom they care, but the decline and eventual death of the individual is then a particularly sad experience for the worker.

Both home-care workers and CNAs are drawn from an unskilled workforce pool. They tend to be women, and often heads of single parent households. The pay is relatively low, given the physical and emotional strain of the work. Some are unionized, and those who are not tend to be paid even less. A number are from minority backgrounds, generally from a different ethnic or cultural background from those for whom they care. Turnover in the long-term-care industry is high (Waxman, Carner & Berkenstock, 1984), although some do stay in the field for many years. Those with prolonged tenure on the job seem to believe they have job security, although others may stay for what they see as the intrinsic rewards of the work—forming close relationships and helping others.

The Home-Care Worker

While home-care workers and nursing-home workers are drawn from the same pool and care for the same type of patient, those working in the home tend to work in isolation. Supervision is minimal (which may be perceived as either good or bad by the worker), and thus social support is unavailable as well. Very often the worker is alone for his or her entire shift, with no one to talk to but the client. While some clients can carry on conversations, often they have diminished cognitive capacity, and their level of confusion prevents them from normal verbal interaction. Sometimes, clients are verbally or physically abusive (although there are also reports of workers abusing clients). In Kaye's (1985) work with paraprofessional home-care workers, he describes the "emotionally needy" client (one who is depressed, suspicious, or anxious) as being most demanding of the worker. Compounding the difficulty for the worker is the system's failure to teach them the skills of social support or crisis intervention, or how to identify problems in the home.

Sometimes clients and workers are poorly matched. While this situation may also occur in an institutional setting, it is more difficult to resolve in the home where one worker is assigned to one client, and other workers are not nearby to pitch in or change assignments (although home-care assignment changes can and do occur).

Fischer and Eustis (1988) have noted that the relationships between home-care clients and their workers can provide great rewards while simultaneously presenting great hazards. Those in close relationships feel wanted and needed; on the other hand, one party can make extensive emotional demands on the other and it is difficult to distance oneself. As Collopy, Dubler, and Zuckerman

(1990) remind us, "home care is vulnerable to the mutabilities of strained relationships."

Family/worker relationships can also assume prominence in the home setting. While some families are helpful and accept the home-care worker as a kind of extended family member, others take advantage of the worker. Other feelings may also come into play; for example, family members may feel guilty when they can no longer provide care alone and must engage the services of a home-care worker.

In a study of paraprofessional home-care workers in New York City (Cantor & Chichin, 1990), 487 workers were asked about their relationships with clients. For the most part, client/worker relationships were rated very highly. More than four-fifths chose the 'frequently' response when asked if their clients accept and trust them, and whether clients say they are grateful for the workers' help. Similar proportions stated that clients frequently made them feel needed and showed concern for them. In small group discussions conducted during the study, workers described situations in which the client and worker became so close that the client became upset when the worker took a day off, even if a relief worker was supplied. One worker described her client as having become like her mother. Several workers said they feel their clients truly love them, and expressions of affection between worker and client are the norm.

In summary, workers in this study reported feeling good about their relationships with clients. They repeatedly made statements such as "when you do something for (the clients) they appreciate it." One worker described home care as including both good and bad, but "there are more good parts than bad." Most stated that they planned to remain in the work for a long time. However, they emphasized; "I am not in this for the money—you have to do it for love" (Chichin, 1992).

The Certified Nursing Assistant

The certified nursing assistant spends his or her working hours in a nursing home, and, like her home-care counterpart, cares for some of the oldest and frailest individuals in our society. Similar to the home-care worker, the paraprofessional in the nursing home is relatively low-paid. They work in nursing homes ranging in size from fewer than 50 beds to several hundred beds, approximately 75% of which are for-profit.

It is estimated that nursing assistants perform 80-100% of the hands-on care delivered in nursing homes (Institute of Medicine, 1986). In the eyes of many, according to Aroskar, Urv-Wong, and Kane (1990), CNAs are "often incorrectly viewed as the ones who clean up incontinent residents, clean up vomit and generally just clean up." However, they clearly do much more. Like their home-care counterparts, they perform a variety of physically challenging tasks, such as bathing, toileting, feeding, positioning, and transferring residents from bed to chair. And, just as in home care, they provide a good deal of emotional support to their residents. Unlike home care, the nursing home paraprofessional is responsible for a significant amount of paperwork. In addition, the patient load is significantly higher than that of the home-care worker, who logistically can only be assigned to one patient at a time.

Yet despite their workload and their low rung on the pay scale, most CNAs really like what they do. In a study exploring nursing assistants' attitudes toward limiting life-sustaining treatment (Chichin & Olson, 1997), CNAs were asked their feelings about their work. They made such statements as the following:

> [My work] is meaningful...(and) I love to do it and I
> love the residents assigned to me. The care I give them
> is the same care I would give if it were my own mother
> or father. It's not 40% or 60%; it's 100 %. I do this
> because I want to. I don't do this because I want praise.

What I try to do is, if I see somebody who is not going to be here long, I go into their room and if they are unresponsive I try to hold their hand for a while and let them know somebody is there, and I know what's going on. If they're responsive and alert, I sit down and talk to them for a while to be a friend so that they can have somebody and they don't feel they are by themselves... I let them feel somebody is there.

We're like a family [to the residents]. We're there eight hours a day, five days a week and I think at times I feel the staff is more attached than the family.

Some CNAs spoke of situations in which the resident had bonded so closely with the nursing assistant that they preferred to stay with her even when the family came to visit. This emotional attachment to the residents is one of the most appealing aspects of the job for CNAs.

What Happens When Death Occurs in Long-Term Care?

Whether in the home or the nursing home, paraprofessional workers provide the bulk of hands-on care, often describing themselves as surrogate family members. As such, they are profoundly affected by the decline and death of their client or resident. Doing this kind of work for love, not money, clearly has emotional implications for both worker and client/resident. But since the worker will almost always outlive the person for whom she is caring, the worker is the one who will repeatedly be faced with loss and bereavement.

In work done with nursing assistants in a project funded by the Greenwall Foundation (Chichin, Burack, Olson, and Likourezos, 2000), CNAs spoke repeatedly of the difficulties of caring for people to whom they become attached and who subsequently die. And often, when the death occurred while or immediately after nursing assistants provided care, they wondered if something they did caused the death.

It has been suggested that, like our society in general, many CNAs fear death. This was reflected in a study of staff feelings about residents' requests to withhold or withdraw life-sustaining treatment (Chichin & Olson, 1997). In the Greenwall nursing assistant project (Chichin et al., 2000), a nursing home administrator told us that she encountered many CNAs, particularly from other cultures, who were especially fearful of caring for the dying. To allay their fears, she said, she often told them the following: "You have nothing to fear from those who are dying. You have more to fear from those who are living. When you are caring for someone who is dying, yours is the last face they will see before they stand before the throne of God. They can only do you good" (personal communication, Sr. M. Bernadette Therese, O. Carm., Oct. 4, 1996).

One issue encountered with relative frequency in the nursing home occurs when a resident's death is associated with his or her decision to withhold or withdraw life-sustaining treatment. The extensive use of technology in health care has enabled us to prolong dying for an extended period of time. Increasingly, individuals are opting to limit the use of such technologies in certain situations, particularly through the use of advance directives. While these instruments, which outline treatment preferences in advance of cognitive decline, have not gained universal acceptance, more and more people are beginning to outline their wishes for treatment via a living will, durable power of attorney for health care, or health care proxy. Thus, in the nursing home, when many residents become unable to swallow, they are offered whatever small amounts of food and fluid they may be able to take, but generally are able to swallow only tiny amounts, if anything. As a result of the patient's inability to take food or fluids, death may occur in a relatively short period of time.

This may be very difficult for nursing assistants, especially when it occurs with a resident to whom they are particularly attached. The impending death of the resident is difficult enough for the nursing assistant; when he or she believes death could have been "prevented" with a feeding tube, the situation is even more distressing. While some CNAs say, "When God is ready for her, she'll go, whether she has a tube or not," others express a strong desire to keep the resident alive, no matter what. They may know of other residents who do receive feeding tubes and who remain alive for a prolonged period of time. While the quality of life they experience may be questionable to some, to many of the CNAs (like many of their professional counterparts) simply keeping someone alive is viewed as a success.

As part of the end-of-life ethics project for CNAs mentioned above (Chichin et al., 2000), a series of support groups were held to allow CNAs to share their experiences in caring for dying residents to whom they had become attached (Burack & Chichin, in preparation, 2000). For the most part, CNAs felt they did not receive a great deal of emotional support, despite the difficult nature of the work they do. Although peer support was often available, administrative support was not the norm. Some CNAs said they were made to believe that caring for dying people is just part of the job and there was no reason for any management-level staff to provide support. More often than not, CNAs expressed the view that their needs were rarely addressed.

Issues of close attachment to residents were discussed at length. A relatively small minority said they made a conscious effort to remain emotionally disengaged from residents, thus preventing distress when the resident died. The majority, however, felt close attachments were inevitable. Furthermore, they felt they gained a great deal from the attachment; they felt as if residents were members of their families and they felt cared about and respected by the resident. Nonetheless, they recognized that this attachment was a double-edged sword, and that forming a close attachment with a resident essentially guaranteed that the worker would experience profound sadness when the resident died.

Some of the anecdotes reported by CNAs in the support groups (Burack & Chichin, in press, 2000) clearly illustrate the close aspects of their relationships and the intense sorrow they feel when the resident dies:

> One nursing assistant said she found out her favorite resident died while she was on vacation. When she returned, the head nurse told her, 'Your baby died.' The nursing assistant said she was so upset she cried for two days.

> ...another nursing assistant said he was at home when one of his residents died unexpectedly and a co-worker called to let him know. The nursing assistant said that when he got off the phone he said to his wife, 'One of my friends died.'

> ...another nursing assistant said he had cried earlier in the day when one of his residents had died unexpectedly. This was a resident he had felt close to and would often go to for advice. The nursing assistant described this resident as having been his mentor and the loss was considerable.

Dealing with the death of a patient is difficult in and of itself. Other issues may compound this loss. One of the more distressing for many nursing assistants is care of the body after death, especially in the beginning of one's career. One nursing assistant said that the first time she had to clean the body of one of her residents, she hid in the bathroom. Fortunately, the nurse in charge was understanding and had another nursing assistant prepare the body. Another nursing assistant said that the first body she had to prepare bore a strong resemblance to her son. Every time she looked at his face, she saw the face of her son, and she said she will "never forget the name of that boy."

Intensifying the distress associated with a patient's death in the home setting is the absence of peer support when a death occurs.

The home-care worker is, for all intents and purposes, left to grieve alone. Because she does not come into regular contact with other workers, she cannot share her feelings of loss. While she may turn to her family or friends for support, often they may see this loss as part of her job and they cannot understand why she has such intense feelings.

Compounding the loss for both CNAs and home-health aides is the fact that immediately after the death they are assigned to another patient. Very often the cycle begins again: become close to a patient, the patient dies; become close to another patient, that patient dies. And so it goes, and the worker is expected to carry on. Over and over again.

Workers' Feelings of Loss and Bereavement: What Can We Do To Help?

Reports of certified nursing assistants, paraprofessional home-care workers, and the literature on the emotional component of caring for the dying (e.g., Lev, 1989; Vachon, 1994) seem to indicate that those who regularly care for dying patients benefit from support. And they also agree on what is helpful to workers: Essentially, what seems to be most useful falls into the categories of formal and informal emotional support, occasional instrumental support, and the use of rituals.

Vachon (1994), in writing on emotional problems in palliative care, notes, "Not only do patients and their families suffer distress, so too do those who care for them." To begin, then, we must be cognizant that CNAs and home-care workers who regularly care for dying patients will naturally be stressed and distressed by their experience. Recognizing this is the first step toward effectively dealing with it. Patients who are cared for in both community-based and institutional long-term care settings will be better served if those in administrative and management positions address this issue.

An overarching issue that impacts paraprofessional workers who care for frail elderly and other chronically ill individuals in both the home and in institutional settings, is the guilt they experience when, no matter how conscientiously they care for their patients, the patients continue to decline. These patients are often suffering from conditions for which there is no cure, and despite aggressive treatment, death will be the outcome. Nursing assistants and home-care workers need constant support and reassurance from professionals that they are doing good work and providing excellent care (assuming this is the case), even though their patient is clearly failing.

Sometimes the decline is relatively quick; more often it is gradual. No matter how long it takes, it wears on the worker. Constantly reiterating to these workers that death is not a failure can be very helpful. Philosophical changes are needed throughout our health care system to reinforce the belief that helping patients achieve a comfortable, dignified death is a worthwhile goal and one of the greatest gifts we can give to another.

CNAs "are as much on the front lines as cops, firemen, and rescue workers" (Karioth, 1998). This clearly applies to paraprofessional home-care workers as well. However, in contrast to these workers, CNAs and home-care workers do not regularly (or often even infrequently) receive a "debriefing" after someone dies. In her work on loss and bereavement for paraprofessional health care workers, Karioth notes that nursing home staffing precludes giving CNAs time off in which to grieve. Clearly, this is also true in the home-care setting. In place of that, it would be very useful if nursing leadership were aware of the possibility that CNAs and home-care workers are distressed when death occurs. Paying them a visit and making a statement to the effect that "this must be very hard for you" is most beneficial. If this can be done in combination with short breaks when workers feel overwhelmed, it would make the nursing assistant or the home-care worker feel at least somewhat supported and valued.

It is also important to remember that, particularly in the institutional setting, there are paraprofessional workers caring for dying patients around the clock. Often when a patient dies we remember to acknowledge the nursing assistant on the day shift, when more management staff is in place who may remember the importance of noting the good work and the loss the workers experience. It is perhaps even more important to ensure that support is also given to those working on the evening and night shifts—workers who form the same attachments to residents and who do the same physically and emotionally draining work but who often feel forgotten.

Other more concrete things can also be useful. Education about care of the dying is helpful to paraprofessional workers. While this is included in training sessions for both institutional and community-based workers, more detailed training is desirable. Such education is useful before a worker even gets to the bedside. Ongoing in-services are invaluable, as well as informal educational support given to the worker by nurses while care is being delivered to someone who is dying.

Paraprofessionals need to see that the work they do with the dying is perhaps more important to the patient's physical and emotional comfort than that done by any other worker. Non-technical care is paramount in ensuring the patient's maximum level of comfort. Stressing to home-care workers and nursing assistants that their work is key to a dying person's comfort and dignity increases the satisfaction they derive from their work. In conjunction with appropriate pain and symptom control, meticulous mouth care, turning and positioning as appropriate, and simply holding a dying person's hand are the bailiwick of the paraprofessional worker, and are among the most important things anyone can do for the dying.

Another useful intervention is to simply let workers know what to anticipate when someone is actively dying. Hospices often give information to families about what to expect when someone is close to death. An understanding that changes in alertness, changes in skin color, changes in breathing, etc. may all signal that the end is imminent may make it less shocking to workers when it occurs.

Workers in the home-care setting in particular need not only greater education and ongoing support about caring for the dying, but also clear procedures on what to do when someone dies. Anecdotal evidence from paraprofessional home-care workers, as well as their professional supervisors, describes horrifying scenes— for example, when someone panics and calls 911 at the time of death, and the body of a terminal patient who did not have a "do not resuscitate" order in place is subjected to cardiopulmonary resuscitation. Thus, the worker—perhaps alone in the home— is confronted not only with the emotional component of losing a patient to whom he or she has become close, but also must view the violent CPR procedure, which may be the equivalent of desecrating a dead body.

Care of the body after death is also a difficult issue for paraprofessional workers. In the home setting such care cannot always be done with another person because the home health worker works alone. However, it generally can be done by two people in the nursing home. As noted in the ethics workbook for CNAs developed in the Greenwall project (Burack, Chichin, and Olson, 2000), when residents die, nurses are supportive of the nursing assistants and give them time to adjust to the death before asking them to clean the body. Nursing assistants find this to be beneficial, as well as having nursing assistants work in pairs to care for the body.

Another area of which long-term care administrators should be aware is the relatively high degree of religiosity of many individuals who do this type of work. Often, when asked where they turn for support when distressed over repeated losses of patients, workers note that religion is helpful to them. In studies of both paraprofessional home-care workers (Cantor & Chichin, 1990) and nursing assistants in nursing homes (Chichin et al., 2000), the majority of workers described themselves as very religious. An awareness of this can be useful in developing rituals to memorialize the lives of nursing home residents or home-care clients who have died.

Integrating a religious component into these rituals may be helpful to all survivors—families as well as staff. In fact, the development of any kind of ritual when someone dies is most helpful. Some nursing homes hold an immediate memorial service around the bed of someone who has died, with staff on the unit gathering for a moment of silence. In other nursing homes, a rose may be placed on the bed of the deceased after the body is removed and the bed made up with new sheets. While it is helpful to staff if the facility is able to keep the bed vacant for 24 hours, this is not always financially feasible.

Both home-care workers and CNAs express the desire to attend funerals of patients for whom they have cared. If the home-care worker is not assigned to another case, she is often able to go. In some nursing homes, arrangements are made to provide coverage so that the nursing assistant may attend the funeral. In most facilities, however, staffing levels and cost often do not allow this to happen.

Workers, however, still would like to find some way to express their own grief and extend their condolences to families. One relatively simple way to facilitate this is to encourage CNAs to write condolence letters to families by keeping writing paper and stamps on the nursing units specifically for that purpose. They should be given a brief "special" time at work to do this—time that is outside of their assigned break time.

Some workers in the Greenwall Foundation nursing assistant study (Burack et al., 2000; Chichin et al., 2000) even said they would like to do something for the family, such as going to the home and preparing a meal. While this may seem a little above and beyond the call of duty, it nonetheless illustrates the intensity of feelings that CNAs can have for the resident who died and the family who survives.

Support groups for paraprofessional workers are most useful, albeit rather expensive if conducted on work time. Support groups enable workers not only to verbalize their experiences, but also to derive support from their peers and group leader in a formalized setting. A number of the CNAs who participated in the Greenwall project (Burack & Chichin, 2000) took part in a five-session support group where they were encouraged to talk about their feelings about caring for dying residents. The response to these sessions was overwhelmingly positive. While they appreciated the opportunity to discuss their feelings about their work, they also were most grateful for being given the sense that their opinions were valued and that the work they did was important.

Summary and Conclusions

We entrust the care of the most vulnerable segment of our society to individuals with relatively little education, very little money, and even less support. Nonetheless, a surprising number of caring workers are drawn to both community-based and institutional long-term care. It is unlikely that their incomes will increase significantly while so employed, but if we want those in need of their services to be well served we need to do a better job of supporting these workers.

Educating them more intensively in care of the dying, and providing support and positive reinforcement, is of paramount importance. Thus, we need to develop and implement ongoing educational programs for paraprofessionals on caring long term for people who are likely to die. We also need to provide both formal and informal emotional support to these workers and to take time to recognize their good work. We must create a variety of rituals, in which these workers can participate, that celebrate the lives of those for whom they have cared and that also acknowledge their fine work along the way.

And finally, we need to work together to help everyone involved in our health care system recognize that death is not always a failure. Unfortunately, those who are employed in this system—professional and paraprofessional alike—have long embraced a cure orientation. But we are slowly, too slowly perhaps, moving toward an orientation of care. The sooner we can educate those who care for the dying that a comfortable, dignified death is a worthy goal, the more all health care workers will find greater meaning in care of the dying. If we want to maximize the quality of the last years and final days of our frail elderly, it is imperative that this philosophy be communicated to the paraprofessionals who care for them.

Eileen R. Chichin, PhD, RN, is the Co-Director of the Center on Ethics at The Jewish Home and Hospital of New York, an Adjunct Assistant Professor in the Department of Geriatrics and Adult Development at Mount Sinai Medical Center, and a member of the Hertzberg Palliative Care Institute at Mount Sinai.

Orah R. Burack, MA, received her Master of Arts in Psychology from Brandeis University. Since 1996, Ms. Burack has served as Project Coordinator for a number of research studies undertaken by The Jewish Home and Hospital of New York, focusing primarily on end-of-life care.

John M. Carter, MD, is the Co-Director of the Center on Ethics at The Jewish Home and Hospital of New York, an Assistant Professor in the Department of Geriatrics and Adult Development at Mount Sinai Medical Center, and a member of the Hertzberg Palliative Care Institute at Mount Sinai.

Voices

No Fame or Fortune

Karen

My name is Karen and I am a home health aide. I would like you to see through my eyes for a moment. When I tell people that I care for the sick, the elderly, and the terminally ill their first remark is usually, "Boy, you must have a lot of patience!" And yes, patience is a very important quality to have in order to do this job. So are courage, wisdom, and mental and physical strength. But most of all, you have to love what you do, because there is no fame or fortune in being a home health aide.

Fortunately for me, it's always rewarding and fulfilling— to the very end. I feel so blessed that I can meet a family and become a source of support to them in their difficult time of caring for their loved one. It's almost impossible to care for a seriously ill or dying loved one alone. And it's also terribly difficult when people are not together in their feelings and their goals. In my ten years of doing this job I've seen what chaos can come about when there is no teamwork. Teamwork is so very important in dealing with the complicated needs of the patient and family, and it's so important to communicate with all the team members— the patient, family, friends, doctors, RN's, LPN's, CNA's and others. There is such a great need for everyone involved to pull together. It's so much easier to have a plan in place so that if plan A fails you can go to plan B. In my mind, the greatest team of all is hospice. I think whoever came up with the concept of hospice deserves the Nobel Peace Prize.

I think it's very important for any caregiver, including a home health aide, to have a support system, because, believe me, we too at times need someone to talk to or to turn to, for it can get pretty overwhelming. I often have to deal with my patients' taking their anger and frustration out on me. Sometimes I can turn to the patient's family members for some help, but they too may be angry, so then I am left to deal with it alone.

I often wonder what keeps me going, but then I get to work and know that I can give my patients some needed security and comfort, or calm their fears, or keep them from being alone. The family member who was angry with me yesterday may today say, "I don't know what we would do without you." And I may get a big smile and a hug and apology from the patient who yelled at me yesterday and told me not to come back.

My job often impacts my personal life—for instance, when I'm too tired after a twelve-, twenty-four-, or forty-eight-hour shift, and I have no energy left for my husband or to do something with my daughter that she really, really wants to do. I tell my family that they have me forever, and that my patients and their families are depending on me to help them through this difficult time, but I feel guilty about shortchanging my own family. My husband once told me that he feels like my job is coming between us, and he wondered if he needed to make an appointment to see me or get in line and wait his turn. I have cancelled dates with friends because of work, and not being able to socialize can be very hard on my friends and family. Even when I do have time off, I often get calls from work, so in a way my job comes home with me. There is also the physical strain of my job—the back pains and muscle aches from lifting my patient, or the physical exhaustion and lack of sleep, when I'm too tired to even eat a proper meal, much less prepare one.

Things so often go unsaid and undone, and then everyone is left shattered, trying to pick up the pieces and move on. Even we as caregivers are left with grief and sadness, because no matter how hard you try not to get emotionally involved, it's impossible not to when you spend so much time with someone. The agency I used to work for instructed us not to get emotionally involved with our patients. The reason I quit doing agency work and now work as a private aide was that the agency sometimes pulled me off a case and sent me to another one where they needed me more. I often didn't have a chance to tell the patient and family goodbye, and I was not supposed to keep in touch with them after I left. That wouldn't be a problem if I didn't care about them, but it was very hard for me because I did care very much about them and wanted to be with them on their final journey.

So the challenges keep coming, but I am determined never to leave a situation unresolved. For me the most important thing is knowing that there is always something I can do to help, no matter how small it is—whether it's reading to the patient, singing a favorite song, giving a massage, helping to relieve the pain, or encouraging their family and friends. The way I see it, no one should die alone. When we came into this world we had someone, so why should we have to be afraid and alone when we leave? For me, birth is sunrise and death sunset.

My job has taught me to appreciate the simple things. Knowing that someone cares makes a big difference. If you happen to have a little love to spare, please give it away— it's the greatest medicine of all, and it's free.

Contributed by Karen, who asked that her last name not be used.

5

Cultural Differences: Sensitivities Required for Effective Caring

Bernice Catherine Harper, Michon Lartigue, & Kenneth J. Doka

> In a changing world, the challenge for professionals
> in the hospice movement is to build upon that which
> has successfully served our patients and families and to
> embrace with enthusiasm the opportunity to create
> innovative new programs that serve and support
> diverse and culturally expanding populations
> (Harper, 1997).

Introduction

One reality of caregiving is that the burden is subjectively perceived. In other words, different people, when faced with the same burdens and tasks, will view these responsibilities differently. One person may find caregiving exceedingly painful or tedious; another may view the opportunity to provide care for a loved one as a rewarding gift.

Numerous factors affect a caregiver's perception or sense of burden. Prior relationships and history, the nature of the caregiving duties, and the extent of professional and family supports are all influential. Culture continues to be a critical element as well, because it often defines expectations about an individual's responsibility to family members and is a key parameter of a familial experience.

Professional caregivers can be truly helpful only if they understand the importance of these cultural dimensions. Their advice and counsel will be accepted only so far as they are sensitive to both the general and cultural needs of the family caregiver. If professional caregivers wish to render effective assistance, they will need to offer it in ways that are professionally and culturally competent. This is critical in any caregiving context, and it is especially important in caring for the terminally ill, for this represents a last opportunity to influence not only the experience of dying, but also the surviving family's continuing journey with grief.

This chapter seeks to provide a basic understanding of the importance of culture. Primarily it addresses three questions: What is culture? How does it affect caregiving? How can professionals increase their cultural sensitivity in assisting family caregivers?

What Is Culture?

Culture, simply put, is a way of life. It emerges from a shared identity, at any given time, and is all-inclusive. It is often reflected through material items such as clothes, foods, or other tangibles, but it also includes non-material aspects of everyday life, including beliefs, ideals, values, and attitudes. It defines our worldview and shapes the assumptions by which we live. The truth is, culture is far more extensive than the customary identification with ethnicity. Of course, our ethnic background is often the most influential foundation from which our cultural perceptions are based, but there are varying methods and ways of identifying with a particular group.

We can speak of the culture or subculture of specific ethnic groups such as Japanese-Americans or Latino/Hispanic-Americans. But religious affiliations or groupings, such as Jehovah's Witnesses, may also share a common way of living. Culture can also be defined by social class, physical challenges (e.g., deaf subculture), or any factor that leads to a sharing of common values, perspectives, and a way of life (e.g., gay subculture). All of these share, within a group identity, a related way of life.

There is, of course, one caveat that must be mentioned: Culture is a continuum, which means that individuals identify with a culture to varying degrees. That realization is a critical point of assessment for formal caregivers. Just because someone is ethnically Latino/Hispanic-American does not necessarily mean that the person identifies with Spanish culture. The degree to which they share in a culture should be determined, not assumed. This determination can be done through candid communication as well as observation.

Furthermore, cultures tend to be internally diverse. Even when an individual identifies with a culture, it does not mean that every aspect of that culture is embraced or can automatically be applied to an individual. The difference between a cultural generalization and a stereotype is that the former becomes a basis for questions while in the latter the answers are assumed.

How Does Culture Affect Caregiving?

Because culture is a way of life—one that includes values, beliefs, and attitudes—its effects on the caregiving experience are extensive. Culture affects not only the norms and expectations that frame caregiving responsibilities, but it also defines who is expected to be involved in the process of providing quality care.

Each cultural group defines the family system in its own way. For some, there may be a strong historical sense of an extended system of kinship. In other cultures, this extended system may include non-kin. For example, in many traditional Italian and Latino/Hispanic families, godparents may play an extremely important role in handling or taking on family responsibilities. Yet in other cultures there may be limited interaction, even among kin. There may be contact around holidays or family rituals and anniversaries, but there may be little expectation of assistance from the extended family in a time of crisis.

And just as culture defines the family system, it also defines normative expectations about relationships within the particular system. This has many implications. Critical values, such as autonomy, which define the weight of comparative caregiving claims, can be defined by culture. For example, in some cultures, individual autonomy is prized. A person may assess his caregiving responsibility to a loved one with a primary concern of how those duties will first affect his own life. In other cultures, family comes first without question or hesitation. These types of values frame the sense of caregiving obligation or claim on time and resources.

In some cultures, individual family members are expected to make considerable sacrifices to care for another. In other cultures there is a decreased sense of obligation and caregiving demands will be negotiated within the family system. Culture may define whether these obligations are different for men and women, or by familial role, status, or birth order. The oldest child, in many cultures, holds primary responsibility for caring for an aging or ill parent. In others, the youngest daughter, an unmarried child, or non-working child may be the assumed responsible party. Naturally, these obligations may not be shared or accepted either across or within generations. Or, they may not be accepted by spouses or significant others, especially if these individuals do not share the same cultural beliefs or values.

Cultural norms also affect communication patterns within a family. For example, some cultures can openly and noisily express their concerns and feelings (McGoldrick, Pierce & Giordano, 1982). But in other cultures, feelings are rarely shared. McGoldrick (1982) notes that in many traditional Irish families feelings are repressed. Even in situations of tension and anger, individuals are more likely to cease contact and emotionally cut off family members than to address fundamental issues.

Cultural values and beliefs affect willingness to seek outside assistance, as well as openness to address pertinent caregiving issues. In some cultures, seeking help is acceptable. In others, it is cause for shame, indicating a lack of self-sufficiency on the part of the family. One African-American woman, insulted by a home-health aide's presence, insisted that she already knew what to do and was perfectly capable of taking care of her own mother. Some cultures may be reluctant to seek help for particular problems. Among traditional Chinese families, Alzheimer's or other forms of dementia are a source of embarrassment to the family (Yeo & Gallagher-Thompson, 1996). In other cultures, hereditary conditions or disabilities may have implications for the family, such as affecting abilities to arrange suitable marriages. And each person's cultural norms and values will create unique sources of tension with the values and cultures of the helping profession (Sue & Sue, 1999).

And finally, cultural values will frame treatment decisions. There are unique cultural norms about what types of decisions and options are within the range of acceptability. For example, Jehovah's Witnesses feel that the use of blood or blood products, whatever the medical rationale, is incongruent with their religious beliefs.

Since culture is all-inclusive, the above delineations are not complete. While they represent some major ways in which culture affects the caregiving process, keep in mind that there are many others as well. Again, an example from the Jehovah's Witnesses may illustrate this: They do not celebrate birthdays or holidays. In one instance, a family of Jehovah's Witnesses was reluctant to let their mother continue in an Alzheimer's day program since the recognition and celebration of special events was used as a significant means to stimulate and connect participants. Again, the point is that culture will influence the caregiving process in many subtle and unique ways.

Selected Examples: Culture and Caregiving

Many of the ways in which culture affects caregiving can be illustrated by an examination of particular ethnic cultural examples. The following examples are meant to be illustrative, not comprehensive.

African-Americans

Barrett (1998) makes a critical distinction between Blacks and African-Americans. To Barrett (1998), Black is a statement of racial identity. Included among Blacks are African-Americans whose roots in the U.S. go back to the enslavement experience, as well as waves of immigrants from the Caribbean, South America, and Africa.

Pinderhughes (1982) reminds us that African-American identity is influenced by three sources—cultural residuals from Africa, identification with American cultures, and adaptations and responses to racism and oppression. All of these factors have played a critical role in shaping African-American culture, and they still influence it today.

Because of that history, family systems may be quite open or flexible, and are often broadly defined. Individuals may have strong intimate networks encompassing kin and non-kin, such as friends and members of church or mosque. Beyond that intimate network, there may be considerable distrust of outsiders and outside attempts of assistance. The role of churches and mosques is also critical. This strong sense of spirituality and themes of sacrifice can both sustain and enable caregiving. At the same time, these strong beliefs can compel individuals to continue caregiving duties beyond a point where it may be viable. In one example, a 71-year-old African-American woman caring for both her 96-year-old mother and five-year-old great-grandson found it difficult and heartbreaking to relinquish any of her caregiving duties. Formal caregivers would do well to assess the situation with other important members of the intimate network, such as clergy.

Native Americans

Native Americans come from a wide range of tribal backgrounds, each of which has its own distinct culture. When assisting Native American caregivers, as with other ethnic groups, there is a danger in assumption and generalizations. Yet there are some common themes dominant in Native American culture as a whole. They tend to be holistic in orientation; mind, body, and spirit are intimately intertwined. There is a strong collateral sense of solidarity; decisions are generally made by group and family consensus rather than individual fiat. There is a strong value placed on noninterference; thus, individuals may be reluctant, even within a family system, to offer help when asked.

Families tend to be extended and multigenerational. Traditional healers may be consulted, as might tribal elders. Professional caregivers need to be sensitive to the interplay of all these systems in arranging and sustaining care, which may be even more complicated since Native Americans value silence and may not be outspoken about their needs, especially with outsiders. Many tribes have variations of the Alaskan proverb, "The silent hunter is the best." In working with Native Alaskans, one of us was cautioned that, "when you feel uncomfortable with the silence, they may be just getting comfortable." In short, do not attempt to rush the process. Allow considerable time to establish rapport and permit a true interactive context.

Professional caregivers should be sensitive to a number of dimensions of Native American culture. Their holism may complicate discussion of future contingencies and alternatives. Some Native Americans believe there is a power in naming or voicing; thus, to talk of a future deterioration in health, or to discuss possible contingencies, may be perceived as making them more likely. In one case, Native Americans refused an operation for a parent when the surgeon listed the possible risks. Native Americans may avoid direct confrontation; they may greet suggestions or directions for care with a silence that can be misunderstood as agreement.

A few other sensitivities are helpful. Native Americans have had a comparatively short history with alcohol, when compared with immigrants from the Old World, resulting in higher rates of alcoholism. This may, of course, complicate family relationships, creating additional challenges for caregiving. Second, among many tribal groups, there is a strong ethos of sharing. Admiring an item may lead the family to make a gift of it. Similarly, professional caregivers may wish to ask tribal elders about the etiquette of gift giving prior to bringing items, even care-related items.

Asian/Pacific Islanders

Asian/Pacific Islanders in the United States include a number of distinct cultural groups such as: Asians, Cambodians, Chinese, Filipinos, Hawaiians, Japanese, Koreans, Samoans, and Vietnamese, as well as other population groups. While relatively little data exists on the use of health services by Asian/Pacific elderly, a few significant factors have emerged. For example, certain types of cancers, hypertension, and tuberculosis are major health concerns of the Asian/Pacific elderly. And among some Pacific Islanders and Asians, the elderly are less likely to use formal health care services, such as those paid for by Medicare and Medicaid.

Professional health care workers serving these population groups should remember that cultural and language differences include a reliance on folk medicine and a distrust of Western medicine. Traditional Chinese medicine, used in China for more than 2,500 years, includes herbal medicine, herbal remedies, acupuncture, and Qi Gong.

More than 10,000 herbs and 650 patents or regular remedies have been documented and used as official medicines in hospitals and clinics. Acupuncture is a treatment in which thin needles are placed in certain body points according to the 14 Chinese meridians and 361 points, which are connected with various systems in our bodies. These needles, which are now FDA-approved medical devices, are manipulated so that they can balance and enhance vital energy flow in the body systems to normalize body functions. In November 1997, a National Institutes of Health panel reviewed the research on acupuncture and supported its use as an effective and safe treatment for various disorders, including chronic pain and the nausea and vomiting induced by chemotherapy. Qi Gong is a form of meditation with special movements that are used to balance or enhance the patients' energy. Professional caregivers must honor, respect, and assist Asians in receiving these services upon their request. This is necessary and required in addressing cultural differences.

This is by no means a comprehensive guide to ethnic differences in caregiving. It simply offers general illustrations of the ways that culture can influence the caregiving experience. Caregivers should read other sources, such as Sue & Sue (1999), McGoldrick, Pearce, & Giordano (1982), and Doka & Davidson (1998) for more specific guidance on different cultural groups.

How Can Professional Caregivers Increase Their Cultural Sensitivity?

In developing cultural sensitivity, three general and broad principles are useful: Know yourself, learn about the culture of others, and practice cultural sensitivity from what you learn and know.

It is critical to first know yourself. As we examine our own cultural roots, we become aware of how culture has influenced our sense of family, our beliefs about caregiving, and our choices of treatment. This inner reflection can even help us understand how our sense of cultural identification has changed throughout our life.

> In my family, there are many cultural differences:
> My parents and one sister were colored, other sisters
> were Negroes, two brothers were Black, and I am
> African-American (Bernice Catherine Harper).

As we examine our own roots, we also see how the interplay of ethnicity, culture, class, gender, and religion, as well as other factors, defines who we are and what we believe. It also sensitizes us to the nuances of how this is interpreted within the dynamics of our own family system.

> I remember when my sister Ruth was dying in a hospital
> in Virginia, and grieving for self, and not getting sufficient
> pain medication because she never asked for any medica-
> tion. The doctor said to me, "Your sister is not in any
> pain." I replied, "Yes, she is." The doctor questioned,
> "How do you know that? You just got here." I answered,
> "By her moans, groans, and 'oh me's.'" I explained to the
> doctor that we grew up in a family of 12 and that in order
> to be heard, you had to make a lot of noise to get atten-
> tion, whether you were sick or well. Those moans, groans
> and 'oh me's' meant 'get and give me what I need.'
> It was not required that you ask for anything. It was
> understood that you would get what you needed for your
> ailment or your pain. So when Ruth saw me, she knew
> that help was on the way. This is an interesting and mean-
> ingful familial cultural dynamic. The noise was a matter
> of getting relief from pain. I recall that the doctor was
> very empathetic and responsive, which was a great
> relief to everyone—my sister, our family and the staff
> (Bernice Catherine Harper).

Culturally sensitive practices begin with understanding personal culture. But it is furthered by a willingness to learn and respect the culture of clients. There must be a sense of openness and desire to learn not only *about* them but *from* them.

I learned about death in a Chinese family from Dr. Ho, about Japanese family life from Dr. Yanamota, about the Cherokee tribe from Dr. Garrett, Mr. Williams and Ms. Showalter, and about the Navajo tribe from Ms. Yellow-tail. I learned about the Arab family from Ms. Beckwith and her mother. I learned about the culture of the Gypsies from Mr. and Mrs. Fadad, their son Joey, and 14 family members. Ms. Lopez, Dr. Olson, and Little Teresa taught me about the Mexican, Latino, and Puerto Rican cultures, respectively. Rabbi Stechel was an excellent teacher of Jewish culture (Bernice Catherine Harper).

It may be helpful for caregivers to assume the pose of enlightened ignorance. This means not assuming knowledge but asking questions: "I don't know much about your culture; what can you tell me that will help me understand what I need to know?" Of course this is an overwhelming question that may not fit in your specific conversation, but it conveys the sense of how the professional caregiver should proceed. In addition to clients, professional caregivers can seek information from other cultural informants, as well as from popular and professional literature.

Finally, culturally sensitive practice is self-rewarding. As we practice, and reflect on, culturally sensitive practices they become part of our repertoire.

I remember once working with a Haitian woman prior to surgery. She thought herself cursed. We asked how the curse could be removed. She indicated the need for a native healer. The healer came into the hospital and performed a ritual. The surgery was then uneventful (Kenneth J. Doka).

In short, each time we practice cultural sensitivity we not only make our interventions more effective and our clients more comfortable, we learn and grow ourselves.

Conclusion

Professional caregivers have a mandate to assist family caregivers with their physical, emotional, and spiritual caregiving needs. The most effective assistance will be attuned to the general but also cultural sensitivities of how a family defines its roles, its sources of support, and its values and beliefs toward caregiving. Only then can professional caregivers do their job—helping the family offer quality care for their loved one.

Bernice Catherine Harper, MSW, MScPH, LLD, is the Medical Care Advisor of The Health Care Financing Administration, Department of Health and Human Services, Washington, DC. She is a social worker, educator, lecturer, consultant, and a health care administrator. Dr. Harper served as a Medical Social Worker for ten years with Children's Hospital, Los Angeles, CA. She was Coordinator of The Home Care Program at The City of Hope National Medical Center, Duarte, CA where she also served as Director of Social Work for 16 years. She works actively for the provision of appropriate care for all patients and their families which includes trained, culturally sensitive and competent caregivers; her work has also focused on caring for caregivers.

Michon Lartigue is the Publications Director for the Hospice Foundation of America. She oversees all HFA publications, including Journeys, *HFA's bereavement newsletter, and served as Managing Editor for this book. She also serves as Managing Editor of* Omega, Journal of Death and Dying. *In addition to her work with HFA, Ms. Lartigue has written for numerous publications and Internet sites as a freelance author.*

Kenneth J. Doka, PhD, Mdiv, is Senior Consultant to HFA and a professor of gerontology at The College of New Rochelle in New York. He is an ordained Lutheran Minister and a former president of The Association for Death Education and Counseling (ADEC) and recipient of ADEC's 1998 Death Educator Award. He is former Chairperson of The International Work Group on Death, Dying, and Bereavement. Dr. Doka has been a panelist on HFA's National Bereavement Teleconference since 1995. Dr. Doka serves as editor of Omega *as well as* Journeys, *a newsletter for the bereaved published by Hospice Foundation of America. He is the author of numerous books as well as over 60 published articles and chapters.*

Grotta Synagogue HOPE

◆

Why It Works – *From the Editor*
Faith-based organizations or faith communities play a critical role in supporting caregivers through their ministry and by becoming a practical resource for members of their congregation and community. Grotta Synagogue HOPE illustrates the concept that programs can initiate discussion of difficult issues, provide vital support, and include ritual and tradition to meet both the general and specific needs of caregivers.

For the past four years, the Grotta Foundation, a private philanthropy which enhances the quality of life for its communities' elders and their families, has made family elder caregiving and congregational-based services for older adults its two major funding priorities.

A special initiative created in 1997 by the Grotta Foundation is Grotta Synagogue HOPE (Help, Opportunities, and Programs for Elders), a collaborative effort between local New Jersey based funders, Jewish congregations, and the aging service network. Its mission is to make Jewish elders a priority in the life and programming of Jewish congregations. Grotta

Synagogue HOPE creates unique and complementary roles for congregations in the continuum of care for the elderly. Sixteen congregations, which receive seed grants and in-depth technical assistance from the program, currently participate in the HOPE Consortium. Based upon a congregational needs assessment, participating HOPE synagogues are charged with and assisted in developing special programs and services for the older adults of their congregations. Programs range from traditional "Lunch and Learn" workshops on topics of Jewish interest, to volunteer-driven transportation services for the frailer elderly (which enables them to attend religious services), to events that support spiritual and physical wellness. Synagogue HOPE is funded by four local grantmakers, and supported by an Advisory Committee of 15 community- based agencies.

In 1999, the Grotta Foundation introduced a congregational elder-care-education program, "As Families Grow Older" (AFGO), as part of Synagogue HOPE, and piloted this initiative in four HOPE congregations. The driving force behind this project was the belief that 'faith-based' caregiver orientation and training can most effectively support caregiving families by addressing their spiritual and emotional needs, while meeting their practical concerns. Through AFGO, the Foundation combines its priorities into one program that offers Jewish caregivers support drawn from the heart of their religious traditions, the life of their synagogue, and the network of their communities' service providers.

Still in pilot phase, AFGO is a 6-part volunteer and clergy facilitated workshop series. It has been adapted for a Jewish audience from a groundbreaking interfaith curriculum developed by the Winter Park Health Foundation. AFGO's package offers congregations a "hands-on" planning and program guide; technical assistance materials on volunteer recruitment, training, program publicity, and outreach; and a series of "user friendly" participant workbooks to help families make informed choices when dealing with the challenges of eldercare. The Grotta Foundation is in the process of adding to the model a special training component for participating rabbis and volunteers on ways to infuse Jewish traditions and content into the workshops. In addition, through a grant to the Jewish Family Service of MetroWest, AFGO/HOPE congregations receive technical assistance and social service back- up for participants' care management problems.

The six sessions of the adapted curriculum address critical issues in the aging/caregiver process, including:

- The Jewish Family Life Cycle and Family Dynamics
- The Health Challenges of Later Life
- Making Choices about Living Arrangements
- Financial, Legal, and Jewish Ethical Issues of Aging
- Accessing Care in Your Community: How Your Local Agencies and Congregation Can Be Your Partners in Care
- End of Life and Palliative Care: What Jewish Tradition Offers to the Dying and the Bereaved.

Sixty-six caregivers and 20 volunteers participated in the pilot phase of the project. Participant evaluations stressed the value not only of the information received, but also of the venue in which it was provided. One caregiver who was in the throes of an exhausting relationship with her elderly mother, an early stage Alzheimer's patient, was deeply saddened that they no longer seemed to have any positive experiences to share. Discussion focused on helping this caregiver reintroduce into her mother's routine some simple Jewish rituals around the preparation for the Sabbath from which they could still derive pleasure together. Another pre-caregiver noted that the information offered helped her speak about difficult end-of-life issues with her ailing 83-year-old father, who had neither completed a health care proxy nor communicated his wishes to his children. All participants felt that the synagogue provided a family-like supportive atmosphere which made them feel more comfortable in discussing delicate and sometimes painful issues relating to caregiving.

The Grotta Foundation believes that this pilot program has amply demonstrated the potential for congregations to offer solace, support, and usable information to caregivers and is considering expanding this initiative in the coming year.

For more information:

Grotta Foundation, *Help, Opportunities and Programs for Jewish Elders: An Action Guide for Synagogues,* please contact Susan Friedman, The Grotta Foundation, 76 South Orange Avenue, Suite 305, South Orange, New Jersey 07079, (973) 761-4900.

Winter Park Health Foundation, *As Families Grow Older,* please contact Cathy Michaelson Lieblich at the Miller Center for Older Adult Services, 2010 Mizell Avenue, Winter Park, Florida, (407) 629-5771.

Contributed by Susan Friedman, Grotta Foundation

Practical Suggestions

What Caregivers Need From Doctors

William Lamers

◆

Those who provide care for ill family members or friends are vital members of the health care team. Most of them have no formal training and rely to a great degree on what they learn from the attending physician and other health care professionals. Since so much care is provided in the home and few physicians make home visits, the following principles should serve as a guide to some of the things caregivers need from doctors.

Communication

Lay persons do not understand technical, scientific language and may be reluctant to admit when they do not understand what the doctor is saying. The doctor must be sure the caregiver understands what is being said. Caregivers should make notes during conversations with the doctor and the doctor must ask the caregiver to repeat what they have been told to confirm that what they heard is what the doctor indeed meant.

Contact

Caregivers need to know how and when to communicate with the doctor. The doctor must provide the numbers where he or she can be reached: office, answering service, perhaps pager, fax and email address. The doctor should also tell the caregiver what to do when the doctor or on-call doctor cannot be reached.

Questions

The doctor should assure the caregiver that there is no such thing as an inappropriate question. The doctor should encourage the caregiver to write down any questions that arise and present them at the next opportunity. The doctor should tell the caregiver that it is better to ask a question than to assume anything.

Emergencies

The doctor should let the caregiver know what constitutes an emergency and provide instructions about what to do and whom to notify.

Current Condition

The doctor should provide the caregiver with an understanding of the patient's current physical and emotional condition in terms that a lay person can understand.

Anticipated Change

The doctor should tell the caregiver about any changes that can be anticipated in the foreseeable future. This reduces the likelihood of needless caregiver concern when predicted changes do occur.

Medications

The doctor should provide the caregiver with a list of prescribed medications, indicating what they are for and what side effects to look for. The doctor should indicate when the medications should be given. Also, the doctor should tell the caregiver to request prescription refills before the weekend.

Records

The doctor should tell the caregiver what records should be kept, including notes on bowel and bladder function, sleep, the presence of pain (on a scale of 1-10) and any other evidence of discomfort. The caregiver should use these records when reporting to the doctor.

Resources

The doctor should inform the patient and caregiver of any local resources that may be of assistance to them, including information about medical supplies, durable medical equipment, home-health agencies, and sources of caregiver support.

Documents

The doctor should encourage the patient to prepare documents regarding end-of-life care, including a will, durable power of attorney for health care, and orders regarding resuscitation. If the patient no longer has the capacity to make these decisions, the doctor should encourage the surrogate to prepare the documents.

Hospice

At the same time end-of-life documents are discussed, the doctor should raise the question of hospice, especially if the patient has a life-threatening or incurable illness. Many of the services and supports listed here are available at no cost to patients with a life expectancy of six months or less who opt for palliative rather than curative therapies.

Follow-up

The doctor must assure the caregiver of continuing contact. The doctor, or someone who works with the doctor, must speak with the caregiver on a regular basis.

Recognition

Most people question their adequacy in providing care to a sick or disabled family member or friend. The doctor must let the caregiver know that his or her contribution is valuable and much appreciated. A word of thanks from the doctor helps sustain the morale of the caregiver. The doctor should also check to see that the caregiver is getting enough rest and adequate relief from other family or professional caregivers.

William Lamers, MD, is one of the first physicians to develop a hospice program in the United States (Hospice of Marin, in northern California in the mid-1970s). He helped establish the first program to train people to develop hospices. He also served as the chair of the Standards and Accreditation Committee of the National Hospice Organization (NHO). He has taught about hospice and related subjects and is currently Hospice Foundation of America's Medical Consultant.

6

Selfless Soldier

Barry Jacobs

No matter what questions we posed her, the unflappable Carla remained stubbornly upbeat, telling us that caring for her husband was her ultimate concern, regardless of her sacrifices. One of the female medical students in the room gazed at her dubiously. The other bore in with another question: "But what about a life of your own?" she asked.

"This is my life now," Carla replied spiritedly. "When I'm able to keep him calm and keep everything under control, I feel good." In the pause that followed, I saw the two medical students exchange silent glances that seemed to communicate the same thought: Her selflessness seemed too pat.

We were sitting in a close circle on the worn couches in my office during a small-group medical education session. As a psychologist-educator in a family medicine residency program, I regularly introduced residents and medical students to people with a wide variety of life problems in the hopes that it would enable these budding doctors to better help patients in similar straits. I invited Carla because selfless caregivers are among the most difficult patients for any health care professional to know how to help. These caregivers rarely seek assistance for themselves and, when they do, they frequently shrug off experts' advice as impossible or irrelevant. In my clinical career, I'd seen several caregivers eventually crash and burn because they'd steadfastly neglected to take care of themselves.

At 42, the black-haired Carla was much younger than the typical, toiling, gray-haired wife, yet she was already far more experienced at selflessness than most. In the 14 years since her husband's lower back was crushed in a work-related accident, she'd been his impassioned advocate in the hospital and at home, as much a balm to his pain as his round-the-clock meds. She was a constant presence on the hospital floors through his dozens of orthopedic surgeries and osteomyelitis treatments. She'd crack jokes with the unit secretaries and nurses or pressure them to immediately attend to his needs. When between hospitalizations he'd spend his worst days lying stiffly in their bed trying to still his pain, she'd be his Florence Nightingale, massaging his twisted muscles, doling out ice water and mounds of pills, emptying his bed pan. Carla also had to be mother and father for their four teenagers, maid and handyman for their rambling, three-story home, money manager and medical insurance expert to keep them solvent. The work showed on her. Her puffy face, deeply lined around her eyes and across her brow, suggested a decade of little sleep. Her voice, though always rapid, sounded ragged with strain.

Looking around and noting the skepticism in our faces, Carla pressed on with her explanation. "I get upset when my husband tries to do things on his own," she said. "I know he's just going to have more pain later and there'll be more work for me to do. Plus it makes me feel that he's trying to show me that he doesn't need me. I can't stand that. I feel it's my job to take care of him."

The two medical students gaped at her incredulously.

"I bet you think that's crazy," she said.

"Not at all," I reassured her. "It's all a matter of what he needs from you and what you can provide. It's important that, for his sake, you aren't doing more than is necessary; otherwise, you'll make him more disabled than he needs to be. I also worry about whether you can keep yourself going if you're forever trying to do everything for him." I paused and then added, "But we've talked about all this before."

She and I both smiled slightly and she said, turning to the medical students, "He's always so nice about lecturing me. But he doesn't know what has to get done every day."

After she'd responded candidly to all of our questions and concerns, we thanked Carla effusively for coming and sharing her story. We might question the extent to which she gave of herself to her husband but were genuinely appreciative for what she had given to us. Once she'd left the office, I told the medical students that I'd like them to view a few minutes of a videotape of Carla recorded four years earlier. "Before I ever knew her as a caregiver," I told them, "she coincidentally gave us permission to tape her medical session with a family practice resident as part of that resident's training in conducting a medical interview."

When I played the tape on the VCR, there was Carla on the TV sitting on the edge of an exam room chair while a white-coated young physician pored over her chart at a desk. She had the same dark hair and puffy face but her manner was unrecognizable— giggly and anxious as she spouted an impossible litany of her own troubles for the doctor to solve.

"I've gained 40 pounds in the last six months," she said with a flippancy that belied her obvious concern for herself. "My arm goes numb whenever I pick up a coffee cup. I have these strange pains in my chest. When I walk up the stairs, I can hear my heart beating. My psoriasis is getting worse. I have a bad taste in my mouth all the time." We watched her pause, laugh for no reason, and say off-handedly, "There's nothing wrong with me, really. I'm the one who takes care of everyone else."

I turned off the tape and asked them how they understood it in light of the conversation we had had with her a short time before. Did it capture the real Carla, full of pain and worry, hidden behind the confident caregiver's veneer? Or had she changed in the four years since then? They pondered the question with darkened looks.

"It was her last gasp," the woman who had peppered Carla with questions said sadly. "Maybe it was the last time she sought help for herself before caregiving completely enveloped her." The other student nodded knowingly.

The idea of envelopment—the slow accrual of duties and doctor appointments that grow year after year like a barnacled crust to ultimately rigidly encase the selfless caregiver—is a common clinical bias. So are the notions that within this tough exterior the caregiver's true self is suffering; that the self's liberation lies in finding a way to stand outside the confining strictures of providing care; that physicians and therapists work best with caregivers when they encourage them to give vent to their interior souls. That's why health care professionals resort to counseling the most ardent self-sacrificing caregivers about how they can break free, urging them to "make time" for themselves while pressing them with phone numbers for support groups and home health agencies and lists of nursing homes for respite care.

But if this were all selfless caregivers needed to cope better, then they would be transformed by the first such lecture from a well-meaning health expert. Instead, the imploring of dozens of professionals seems to only make them more impervious to change. With a caregiver like Carla, while she may at first have appeared to be enveloped, it became evident later that she had wrapped herself inside caregiving like a stiff muslin. Wearing the mantle allowed her to be as true, masterly, and contented as she had ever hoped in her life. She wouldn't be easily persuaded to be someone different.

However, when I first met her five years ago, her drive to perfectly take care of her husband caused her much suffering. I'd received a consultation request from nursing about a couple who were having frequent shouting matches on one of the hospital units. I learned from the head nurse that the husband had just undergone an extensive surgical revision following a fall and was in excruciating pain. She told me that his wife had been hovering over him day and night for a week despite the nurses' pleas for her to return home to take a break.

The husband refused to see me. He'd had bad experiences with mental health professionals in the past and was in no mood now. His wife was only too eager to complain to someone about him. What struck me most powerfully about Carla at first, as we sat in the unit lounge while she spoke at breakneck speed for over an hour, was how desperately she wanted her husband's approval. She seemed to experience his recent fall and exacerbated pain as some kind of critical indicator of wifely failure. That led to a pattern in which the two of them were locked. The greater efforts she made to maternally soothe him by fussing over how his blankets were arranged or whether his food tray contained the right order, the more power he had to childishly ventilate his frustrations over his condition by scapegoating her when any niggling detail was out of place. When he'd shout at her about the room temperature or lighting or lack of information from the doctor, she'd wince, then retreat to the hallway in tears. With the nurses' sympathies, her feeling of being aggrieved by what she saw as his rejection of her love would coalesce into anger. She then would tromp back into the room to pick a fight with him in order for the chance to shout back.

Describing this to me, it was clear she was hungry to be acknowledged for her indispensability, not trashed because she was close at hand. But she made the mistake of trying to wrest gratitude from a man beset with feelings of degradation and helplessness, and that made her an inviting target. I listened for a long time, empathized with the hurt she felt, and praised her awesome devotion to helping him. She beamed with apparent relief. At the talk's end, she asked if we could meet again.

Over the next five weeks, while her husband remained in the hospital for intravenous antibiotics, Carla and I met for hour-long talks each week. Even in so brief a treatment, the sessions followed the progression of stages that I attempt with most of the selfless caregivers I see in psychotherapy:

1. Listen empathically; resist premature advising: It is common for health care professionals to respond to caregivers' displays of self-sacrifice with too-ready advice that the caregivers should better care for themselves. It is nearly as common for those same caregivers to complain that the advice-givers "just don't understand." What professionals too rarely take the time to comprehend is why a person would choose to devote her life to the preservation of another. If the caregiver doesn't feel understood by a professional on that basic level, then she puts little stock in the professional's advice. Worse, a clinician's suggestions for changing her behavior may make her feel chided and miffed.

When Carla, during our first talk, muttered in irritation about the nurses' pleas for her to go home, I took it as a sign that she didn't want me to make the same mistake of asking her to back off, before understanding why she was digging in. So I was careful not to ask her to alter anything she was doing. Instead I just listened at first and empathized with the sense of mission fatigue she was feeling. It enabled her to feel that I was a supportive ally, more interested in crediting than changing her. Without that trust, all other work we'd attempt would be thwarted.

2. Encourage observation and awareness: "Living day-to-day" is a typical coping mechanism for people, such as caregivers, who are facing ongoing and arduous circumstances. While this approach has its merits, it can result in a numbing, nose-to-the-grindstone stance in which the besieged party muddles along by not allowing herself to think too much about what she's experiencing. I try to help caregivers step out of the day-to-day trance and reflect more upon what they do, in the belief that this greater awareness of self and others will provide them greater self-determination, not increased demoralization. But asking them to observe themselves mustn't be confrontational. I like to play TV's Lt. Columbo in these instances—the innocent simpleton crafting meandering questions that bring the overlooked aspects of a situation into focus.

For example, I hoped to help Carla toward a greater awareness of the dynamics leading to her conflicts with her husband. I listened supportively to her marital complaints but avoided agreeing with her characterization of him as a "bastard." Instead, I wondered aloud about the interactions that led to times when he lashed out in bastardly fashion. She resisted the idea at first that there were any factors—pain, fatigue or narcotic-induced temper—that influenced him. But when I encouraged her to take more of an observer's view of the hospital room action, she reported in ensuing weeks that there seemed greater predictability to her husband's outbursts than she had imagined. She grasped without my pointing it out that his shouting at her was only rarely a direct result of something she'd said or done. This enabled her to refrain from reacting so personally or to seek vindication. The angry shouting matches therefore were swiftly reduced to one-sided displays of frustration on his part. Soon after, without her reciprocation, these too began to subside.

3. Identify meaning; use personal and family history: Increasing a caregiver's self-awareness entails not only encouraging her to reflect upon her interactions but also helping her to identify the greater meanings she derives from caring for a loved one. Does she do what she does out of loyalty? Guilt? Are religious convictions involved? Or, does she hope she'll set an example for her children who may one day care for her when she's in need?

The answers to many of these questions are frequently found in the caregiver's personal and family histories. My conversations with Carla flowed naturally in those directions as I inquired further about why she chose to immerse herself in her husband's care. They had been wed in their early twenties in a traditional Greek Orthodox ceremony and then fallen into traditional roles. Her husband led; she supported his right to lead and the veracity of his decisions. When, with family money as backing, he launched his own plumbing and heating business, she scheduled his jobs and kept his books. When he'd arrive home wrung out from work, she kept the kids away from him and got dinner on the table. She was primed to serve him long before the day he was walking through a plumbing supply house and a heavy crate toppled onto his back, pinning him against a metal stanchion. Afterwards, the care she provided to him and their children was greater in quantity and intensity but—save having to contend with surgeons and insurance companies—not so very different in kind.

There were other strands from the past that seemed entwined in her caregiving. She alluded to how critical her father had always been of her, though she badly wanted to please him; spoke admiringly of how her mother held fast through her own familial and medical troubles; joked that her life was ruled by feelings of guilt. I found it strange at first when she talked relatively little of the losses she and her husband had endured but instead bemoaned the unfair death of a young cousin due to a rare liver disease. It was as if she used the enormity of that tragedy to justify downplaying the wrong-time/wrong-place happenstance that had broken the back of her husband and their family. At the same time, Carla drew existential and spiritual meanings from the cousin's death. She felt compelled not to squander her gift of life because the cousin had been robbed of his. That cousin, she felt, was now a guardian angel watching over her good and honest efforts to help her family to live the best that it could.

What this history-gathering impressed upon me was that Carla's caregiving was consonant with her family's values, congruent with her most deeply held beliefs, and consistent, to a large degree, with the self she'd always striven to be. There was no discerning dichotomy between her true being and a later imposed caregiver's identity. She embraced duty as fulfillment of destiny. What piqued her was having her actions criticized by the man to whom she'd given her best energies—or, rather, the best of who she was. Nearly as intolerable was when well-intentioned health care professionals condescendingly viewed her as some kind of entranced automaton and then tried to rein her in for her own good. Her sense of her own good—as well as a spiritual notion of ultimate good—was behind everything she did for others' good. She might be guilty of zealousness or even pride, but not falseness or mindlessness.

4. Applaud the meanings; worry about the methods: Because their purposes are often as pure as Carla's, I find it extremely difficult to confront most caregivers about the deleteriousness of their selflessness without risking that they will disqualify me as another patronizing expert who, stuck on the notion of a truer, hidden self, doesn't comprehend who they really are. I want them to feel that I understand and admire them without that precluding all prospect of change. To that end, I try a middle path: Applaud the meaningfulness of their endeavors but express worries about their methods.

Once I sensed that Carla felt I was supportive of her reasons for devoting herself to caregiving, I thought she might be willing to listen to my "army marches on its stomach" speech in our next-to-last session. I wanted to impress upon her that in order for anyone to continue moving toward a goal, taking in nurturance is essential. But I didn't want to tell Carla to do differently; she would swiftly reel off reasons why she had to do all that she did in the way she did it. I wanted her to conclude that making small alterations might help her better sustain herself over time to achieve what she wanted. Like an army, I suggested, she needed adequate provisions and the luxury of time to imbibe them in order to be able to fight the good fight. If she tried living indefinitely on hard tack and forced marches, she would ultimately drop in her tracks. Where was the sustenance she was allowing herself, I asked her, to be the good soldier she wanted to be?

Carla responded ambivalently. She could appreciate on a theoretical level that, without caring for herself, she wouldn't be in a position to care for anyone else. But she saw no changes she could make in her everyday life. Everything she did was that crucial. I didn't argue but instead wondered aloud: Were there sources of sustenance in her life that she wasn't fully utilizing to keep soldiering on? Could she lighten her load for the long march? She shrugged and said nothing.

I was unsure what our last meeting was going to be like the week that her husband was to be discharged from the hospital. To my great shock, she made two announcements: She had decided to enroll in a career guidance program for women who had been out of the workplace for many years. She said that she had been thinking about it for a while and that our talk the week before had convinced her to go forward with it. She also said that she felt our sessions had been good for her and that she wanted to continue talking with me on an outpatient basis. I thought this soldier was fortifying herself. I quickly agreed to meet.

In the strange turns of our relationship in the four years since, I have continued to avoid confronting her about the potential harm of her caregiving style and instead have tried to bolster the sense of purpose she derives from giving care. The results have been mixed.

I shouldn't have been surprised when she cancelled our first outpatient appointment in order to take her husband to a doctor. I still held out hope of meeting when we rescheduled for the following week. But after she cancelled again in order to do something for her children, I realized it wasn't likely she would ever follow through on our appointments. Her focus would always be her family. While talking with me in the hospital as part of her husband's overall treatment was acceptable to her, coming for treatment herself could never be as high a priority as caring for others. She as much as admitted this to me when she called to cancel a third time, saying that she did not think that she could fit psychotherapy into her life right now. During the same conversation, she also explained that, though she had signed up for the career guidance program, she was also putting that on hold until her husband and kids didn't demand so much of her time.

At first I thought Carla had completely backtracked. But there were small indications during our brief exchanges over the phone that our talks in the hospital had had some impact. She revealed none of the anger or anguish displayed when I first met her. Her rapid-fire speech sounded confident and engaged while describing her whirlwind days. Without my having to ask, Carla reported that she was continuing to closely observe the interactions with her husband. So long as she was able to keep from reacting to his occasional carping, she was able to continue side-stepping fights. Family life had settled back into its usual arduous pace. She seemed content.

Our work together could have easily ended then. But because caregiving is a long, hard campaign, I worry about how it slowly saps people over time. I consequently try to maintain some degree of contact with caregivers—sometimes years after formal treatment has ended—in order to remind them of my support. I took this tack with Carla through two additional clinical strategies:

5. Offer yourself as a long-term resource: I hope to demonstrate my availability to selfless caregivers to convey that I will be there for them should they be willing to seek help for themselves. But I don't want my occasional phone calls to seem like intrusions intended to check up on them.

I would call Carla every six months to inquire about the health of her husband. She'd report the latest round of doctoring and complications. After I had sympathized with what they were going through, I then could safely ask about how she was coping. She'd minimize any distress she was feeling but politely thanked me for my concern. Occasionally, she would call me with questions about how to handle of her teenage children or how to better communicate with one of her husband's physicians. If she wasn't going to employ me as a therapist for herself, she appeared interested in having me as an information resource and advisor for the family. This gave me a role to play and means of keeping in touch with her.

6. If they won't receive, ask them to give: When doctors or therapists offer selfless caregivers social services, respite care or medical attention, they often meet with resistance. To receive help themselves would amount to a loss of identity for many of them. Rather than attempt to persuade them to accept assistance, I've found that an effective way of helping caregivers adopt a more flexible stance is by asking them to give more of themselves to others. Specifically, I ask caregivers to be master teachers about caregiving to newer caregivers and health care professionals.

This usually has several effects: It requires that they stand back from their daily grind in order to extract the most valuable lessons they've learned to pass on to others. This serves to place caregivers in the reflective posture that I believe is necessary for productively thinking through their predicaments. Teaching about their experiences also elevates their knowledge to the level of hard-won expertise. When learners savor this expertise, it gives caregivers an added dimension of meaning about the difficult lives they lead.

I asked Carla to give of herself along these lines in two ways. When I developed a series of educational sessions for medical residents and students on various psychosocial issues, she was one of the people I immediately thought to invite to speak. She was enthusiastic about the idea of telling her story and met with students regularly. She thought nothing of challenging them about the disorganization of hospital care, the poor communication among treating physicians, the inattention of most health care professionals to patients' family members. But what was most striking to the students was her fervor for caregiving. She must be making a bid for sainthood, they thought with skepticism. Because this was an educational forum, they took license to challenge her in turn. Did she care about what happened to her? Did she realize she could be wearing herself out? Carla wouldn't have tolerated these sentiments if voiced by some know-it-all professional. But because they were students' reactions, she would listen to them respectfully and then leave the office seriously pondering their questions about the way she lived.

More recently, I asked Carla to help facilitate a caregiver support group that I was organizing. For years, she had rejected suggestions to attend such a group. It was only with the prospect of helping other caregivers that she would even consider engaging in regular dialogue with them. Of course, when she began to hear their stories, she benefited as much as anyone in the meetings. But her role had to be fashioned as one of chiefly "giving" in order for her to allow herself to "receive" at all.

Over the last two years, I've seen Carla's selflessness lessen moderately. I think it is possible that it is due in part to our periodic conversations, her educational sessions with health care professionals, and her contact with other caregivers. All have caused her to briefly pull herself out of the barrage of daily events to reflect more on her life as a whole. In such musings, a whiff of her own dreams and desires has floated back into her consciousness. She even allows herself now to occasionally appreciate her resilience through a decade-and-a-half of tough caregiving.

But I'm afraid the major engine of her change has been a shift that is more dramatic and disturbing: She has begun to have her own serious medical problems. I'm alarmed that they are symptoms of the wear-and-tear she has suffered. She had always had migraines but they have become increasingly debilitating in the last two years. Then she was diagnosed with the chronic jaw pain known as TMJ. Then, worst of all, she was diagnosed with a rheumatological condition called psoriatic arthritis that turns her fingers and hands into weakened, spastic claws. Her degree of disability waxes and wanes but there are many days she can no longer help her husband as she once did. In fact, shock of shocks, there are times she needs him to help her.

If her husband's verbal abuse toward her in the hospital angered her, then his kindness during her periods of incapacity have caused her to grieve, to become nearly depressed. She felt that she had failed at caregiving, the all-consuming mission she had poured herself into for so many years. Then she began to notice that her husband (on his best days) was doing things for her, like bringing her coffee and comforting her, that she had imagined he was too sick to ever manage. And he seemed to be less depressed in being able to finally give something back to her. Discussing this with me during one of our conversations, Carla concluded that perhaps there had been so much imbalance in their marriage before that, even as it had thrust her forward, it had held him back. Now, though he still suffered greater incapacity than she did, they were both limping through life together.

Today, Carla is still carrying on like a good soldier but has lost some of her armor and feels more vulnerable. She will call me when she is feeling stressed and even, on rare occasions, to request psychotherapy sessions. She struggles, not just with what has befallen her family over these years, but with how she has stumbled of late. She is gradually coming to the sad realization that she can no longer fight the good fight without reinforcements.

Barry Jacobs, PsyD, a clinical psychologist and family therapist, is the Associate Director of Behavioral Sciences for the Crozer-Keystone Family Practice Residency Program in Springfield, PA. He specializes in working with individuals and families struggling with chronic and traumatic illnesses. He also teaches physicians, nurses and psychologists about family systems approaches to health. A lecturer and a former journalist, Jacobs writes and edits the "In Sickness & Health" column for Families, Systems & Health: The Journal of Collaborative Family Healthcare. *This chapter is based on an earlier essay that originally appeared in that journal.*

$\mathcal{V}$ o i c e s

The Rest of My Life

Jim Skofield

Since the beginning of the AIDS crisis I have lost over 200 friends. I never imagined that I would see so much death before I was 44. And not just any deaths. In addition to the intense and frustrating level of participation demanded of both those afflicted by the disease and those caring for them, AIDS has been fraught with troubling societal and political overtones. It is like a tango, but one that exhaustingly lasts for years. I have danced that dance three times. My lover, Glenn, died in 1987, less than a year after his diagnosis. My roommate and friend Donald died in 1990. And my lover, Michael, died in 1995. It is his story that I will use to tell the story of the dance.

When the AIDS crisis began, the doctors didn't know much more about it than the patients, and the manifestations of the disease to this day remain varied and constantly shifting. While the health care system has made significant progress in treating those suffering from AIDS, the maze of bureaucracy and the human frailties of those providing care is often more than even a healthy person could maneuver.

And if the disease and its treatment were not complex enough, it is frequently compounded by difficult family situations.

In September 1995 Michael was diagnosed with progressive multi-focal leukoencephelopathy (PML) after having endured more mainstream infections for a couple of years—thrush, shingles, and Kaposi's sarcoma on one leg. I was in New Hampshire for two weeks with our cats while Mike had returned to the city to work. Our friend, Shelley, a nurse, phoned me from St. Vincent's Hospital to let me know that Mike had been admitted with headaches and slurred speech and that I should come home. A neurologist performed preliminary CT and MRI scans, and by the next morning he told us he thought it was PML, which we knew nothing about. While Mike was out having another MRI, the neurologist clearly and succinctly explained the condition. He was kind, but realistic: if it was PML, he said, Mike's decline would be swift. And it was.

The next day, after a conclusive diagnosis, we went to Mike's office at the VA Hospital in Brooklyn where he was a counselor and collected his things. He went on disability. For two weeks life was peaceful. His symptoms were present, but he was still Mike. Each day we took long walks on the Brooklyn Heights promenade in the early fall weather. Each night I lay awake thinking, "Maybe it can stay like this forever; maybe it won't get any worse." But, of course, it did get worse.

It was small things at first—an underhanded grip of his fork, food falling onto his lap; angrily tripping over furniture he thought I'd moved, though it was where it had always been—until he finally lost contact with the right side of his body. Mike was a big guy, a weightlifter who weighed over two hundred pounds before the PML set in. He resented needing help to walk or climb stairs. And mealtimes became agonizing. Friends organized feeding and dinner brigades, even though Mike would have preferred that we have dinner alone. It was only at night as we lay in bed watching TV that Mike was contented, but even then not himself— his favorite episodes of "The Simpsons" elicited an unblinking, uncomprehending concentration.

By mid-October Mike became incontinent, and caring for him became a minute-by-minute challenge. I feared leaving him alone. Once when I left him for just a few minutes to run out for some orange juice, he disappeared. It was almost an hour before we found him wandering the aisles of a nearby supermarket. He needed care 24 hours a day, and I needed help. But when we visited Mike's general practitioner to get his authorization for home health care, he refused to authorize it and the visit ended in acrimony. Mercifully, one phone call to Mike's neurologist accomplished what the difficult trip to the GP could not—the neurologist readily authorized home health care and arranged for a nurse from hospice to come the very next day. We never spoke to the GP again.

Hospice was a godsend. We had two wonderful home health care attendants—one from the Caribbean and the other from India—strong men capable of handling a large man like Mike. More than that, both were sympathetic, gentle, and caring—but most of all, they were ever present. The hospice nurse taught me how to position the bed against the wall so Mike wouldn't fall out and how to give a bed bath and change sheets without disturbing him. I can't imagine what it would have been like without them. But even with the help from hospice, fatigue began to dog my days.

As his deterioration accelerated, Mike's brother and I took him on his last trip out of the apartment. While the neurologist examined Mike, the nurse taught me to grind up his medications and mix them with water so that they could be administered sublingually in an eyedropper. More importantly, we left with a prescription for morphine. Mike's discomfort had been increasing rapidly. He started on morphine that night, and I kept the chart that allowed us to keep him as comfortable as possible.

Mike's parents came from Florida. They stayed overnight with his brother in New Jersey, but they came every morning to spend the day with Mike. They are wonderful people and their love for Mike and the rest of their family is genuine and deep. But, like many parents, they never really accepted that Mike was gay, and I doubt that they were ever comfortable with me. And beyond that, they could not accept that Mike was dying. We could not talk about his death or about funeral arrangements. They were convinced that Mike could make a full recovery if they could only get him into the hospital, in spite of the fact that Mike and I held each other's medical powers-of-attorney and he had made it clear that he did not want to die in a hospital.

He could no longer speak. Even drinking water was a problem. He was blind. He was wearing diapers. One day, when I told Mike, "When it's time to go, just go; don't hang around when you're called," it made his parents furious, and they lashed out at me. I left the apartment to take a walk to the Brooklyn Heights promenade, where a nearly full moon shone across the waters of New York harbor. I put my head on the railing. "Just follow the moon path, Mike," I whispered. "Let go. Let go. Let go . . . ." The next day, before Mike's parents arrived, I said to him, hoping that he could hear me, "Mike, I think if your parents could understand that you wanted to go, they would bless you and let you go."

Mike died the next night about an hour after his parents left. It was just past 9:00 on November 18, 1995. Our neighbor, Jacquie, helped me wash his body and dress him in a suit. I called the neurologist, who said he would sign the death certificate so that Mike's body could be turned over to the funeral home. I let his family know. Our friend Ross came by and the three of us waited for the car from the funeral home to arrive. I remember being tired. I remember it was very quiet. When they arrived I helped lift Michael's body into the body bag. I watched as the bag was zipped up. I helped lift the bag onto the gurney and helped guide it to the curbside. We all watched the hearse drive away.

I stripped the bed and we moved it from the wall. I made it up with fresh sheets. Jacquie went home and Ross and I went to the 24-hour bodega to buy milk, cereal and cat food. I walked Ross to the subway. I went home, fed the cats, and lit a couple of candles on the dresser that Mike and I had shared. The cats curled up with me on the bed and we all went to sleep.

The next morning, I got up and started the rest of my life.

In Memory of:
Michael N. Sitzer
1953–1995

7

Nursing's Role in Family Caregiver Support

Susan Reinhard

Background

Family caregiving is a significant practice and policy issue that concerns the nation's nurses. They are daily witnesses to the struggles of "informal" caregivers, the people who provide unpaid assistance to relatives or close friends. Nurse researchers have documented the consequences of caregiving (Fink, 1995; Given & Given, 1991), which involves several types of activities related to assistance with personal care and support of basic daily routines. Our experience and research tell us that family caregivers are the backbone of the long-term care system, they are not doing well, and current public policy does little to support them. Our federal and state governments usually step in only after family resources have been depleted. At best, some states offer a minimal amount of support to families to reinforce their family-based care (Family Caregiver Alliance, 1999; McConnell, 1999).

There are two main problems with this social policy. First, this is not a humane policy. It ignores the current needs of the estimated 25 million family caregivers who provide $194 billion in care (Arno, Levine, & Memmott, 1999). Second, it is not a sustainable policy. The aging of the population, and an altered dependency ratio of fewer younger adults to support an increasing number of older adults, are powerful demographic shifts. These trends will challenge government's assumption that families can continue their historic efforts to provide long-term care for dependent family members. There likely is a limit to how much families can assist without external support. And if the family system breaks down with the burden of these responsibilities, more institutionalization of older adults and people with disabilities will follow.

We need to develop and promote a new policy framework that supports unpaid caregivers who are now providing more than 80% of the long-term care for their family members (Burggraf, 1993; Families USA Foundation, 1993). We know that one in four American households currently provide some kind of care for an adult who has a chronic health condition (National Alliance for Caregiving, 1997). One out of five family caregivers are caring for a relative with dementia (Kelly, Buckwalter, & Mass, 1999). We also know that family caregivers are juggling their caring responsibilities with work demands. For example, it is estimated that as many as 15% of the United States workforce is actively involved in caring for an older adult (Wagner, Hunt, & Reinhard, 2000). Many of these employed caregivers are forced to take time off from work, forego promotions, or leave the work force for some period of time.

This is a significant issue for employers who are attempting to attract and retain a qualified workforce in a time of unprecedented low unemployment levels. The U.S. economy depends on a productive workforce. Recent research indicates that the cost of caregiving to employers due to lost productivity totals $11.4 billion a year (Met-Life Mature Market Group and National Alliance for Caregiving, 1997). This cost can only rise given the predicted demographic patterns of our society. The number of workers with significant elder care responsibilities will rise as the number of older adults doubles in the next 20 years. By 2040, there will be about 13 million Americans 85 years of age or older, the population most in need of long-term care support (National Center for Health Statistics, 1994).

Given these trends, it is in the best interest of both the public and private sectors to develop policies that support family caregivers. Their human condition calls for it. Their economic value demands it.

Challenges that Family Caregivers Face

Nurses in daily practice know that family caregivers are often asked to assume significant responsibilities without training in the knowledge and skills required to fulfill these responsibilities. As the primary social group charged with the care of society's members, families are expected to be caregivers. Social norms direct families to provide physical maintenance and care, psychological support, affection and companionship, maintenance of self-esteem, and help seeking expert advice (Duvall, 1977; Leventhal, Leventhal, & Van Nguyen, 1985). Indeed, providing care to parents has been called a "normative experience" (Brody, 1985). However, changes in health care technology, financing, and delivery have created challenges far beyond the limits of the normal expectations for family caregiving. While recuperating or dying at home may have been considered routine family care in the past, there are far more complicated caring tasks involved today. There are more complex medical procedures and pharmaceutical supports, even for palliative care. People are discharged from hospitals to family care with oxygen, feeding tubes, intravenous therapy, injections for pain relief, dressings, and catheters (Mezey, 1999). Nursing students would tremble at the idea of assuming this kind of care. Yet, we expect families to manage it all with little or no preparation. Understandably, they are frightened and overwhelmed.

The physical and mental consequences of taking on these responsibilities are significant. Decades of research document the burden and depression that families experience as a result of their extraordinary efforts to provide ongoing care to family members (Dellasega, 1989; Reinhard & Horwitz, 1995; Robinson, 1989; Whitlatch, Feinberg, & Sebesta, 1997). Almost half (44%) of family caregivers report that their responsibilities cause physical strain, and one in four caregivers reports that providing care is emotionally stressful (National Academy on an Aging Society, 2000). Without external and professional support, the toll on their health and financial resources can be severe.

Practice Considerations

Nurses are taught to consider families in all aspects of care. They are taught to consider family dynamics and resources, and to teach family members how to provide the care that is needed. Unfortunately, most settings in which nurses practice impede these efforts. In hospice-like care settings, nurses include the family as co-equals in care and are extremely sensitive to family members' concerns. However, nurses in other care settings face the pressures of early discharge from hospitals, short office visits, and the relenting forces of the medical model to treat and cure acute illness rather than to help people and their families manage the *experience* of illness.

Nurse educators, administrators, and practitioners need to constantly remember that their duty is to the person, and that care of the person includes care of the family. Discharge planning must incorporate early and consistent teaching of family members in assuming caring responsibilities, especially the technical aspects of those duties (Naylor, Campbell, Jacobsen, Mezey, Pauley, & Schwartz, 1999; Rosswurm & Lanham, 1998). They deserve home care follow-up and encouragement to seek help not just for the technical aspects of the care they give, but for the emotional demands of their caregiving. Yet, home care is increasingly difficult to arrange due to federal and state changes in payment. Hospital nurses are feeling frustrated that family members have difficulty understanding all of the information they are trying to communicate (Levine, 1998). In the press to discharge patients, nurses need to remember that the patient who is "discharged to family" is indeed fortunate. The family must be considered part of the health plan and decisions.

It is important to note that most caregivers do not think of themselves as "caregivers" but as "family." Nurses need to think of this family as an extension of the person that they are caring for. Theoretical models of nursing practice include families as part of the client. Taken together, these models of practice lead the practicing nurse to act as consultants to the client and family. Most important, the nurse should remember the following principles:

- Do not let the family member(s) leave the care setting without some connection to potential ongoing help. Nurses need to do some community resource homework to have the telephone numbers of potential supports available. There are many possibilities: hospital-based caregiving support groups; the local Alzheimer's Association chapter; the local area agency on aging; the local Visiting Nurse Association; a care management directory. Families will need ongoing concrete and emotional support. Nurses should expect this need and offer anticipatory guidance.

- Respect all family caregivers. Assume that they are doing the best that they can under difficult circumstances. Without their involvement, the client would have fewer options available for ongoing care.

- Give positive reinforcement in all settings. Help identify the strengths that family caregivers have and point them out very concretely. Help them see where they need some assistance— and help them find it.

- Help family caregivers recognize their own needs. Assess family members' needs and capacities. Melillo and Futrell (1995) urge nurses to actively assess these family members as "hidden patients" in need of nursing's help. They offer a useful guide for assessing family caregivers' needs because these people are at risk for serious health problems themselves.

Public Policy Considerations

Nurses cannot support family caregivers alone. They need a policy framework that supports these efforts. The Expert Panel on Aging of the American Academy of Nursing (AAN) has detailed several public policy recommendations for family caregiver support (Reinhard, Rosswurm, & Robinson, 2000). In addition, private industry can adopt policies that support families. Nurses need to advance policy-making in both sectors.

Given the economic value of family caregiving efforts, it is in the best interest of federal and state governments to help families continue their efforts to care for their loved ones. The primary goal of these family-sensitive policy efforts should be better balance of formal (professional) and informal (family) support so that family members can continue to confidently provide the emotional and concrete help, without becoming so burdened that they cannot sustain their caregiving efforts. Government should not substitute, but support family caregiving.

Society needs to recognize and respect the central role that family caregivers play in the health care system and provide some relief to families so they can manage their ongoing responsibilities. We need publicly-funded programs that provide choices to families so that they can balance their family, personal, and work demands. Caregivers need a range of programs that offer training, counseling, professional support as needed, and respite. Public policies should strive to facilitate the development and transfer of vital information to family caregivers about how to care for their ill family member. State and local governments can also encourage new partnerships among family caregivers, business and industry, government, and formal care providers.

Based on these policy goals, the AAN has adopted the following public policy recommendations (Reinhard, Rosswurm, & Robinson, 2000):

1. Fund and administer comprehensive, affordable, and accessible programs for family caregivers. These programs should be offered on a sliding-scale basis. It is not helpful to offer services only for those who are "entitled" by low income to receive them and turn others away to fend for themselves. We need to develop programs and delivery systems that will turn no one away. Some people can afford to pay for help. They should not be rejected because they are "not entitled" to get assistance. Programs should offer:

   • Outreach and screening to locate isolated caregivers most in need of information and referral systems

   • Education and training in how to provide care; this education should be offered in appropriate and convenient settings like homes and workplaces

   • Counseling and support services for family caregivers

   • Accessible, available, and affordable respite care provided by adequately trained individuals in homes and community settings—including weekends, evenings, and emergency situations.

2. Encourage collaboration among healthcare providers, family caregivers, governmental agencies, and business and industry:

   • Encourage private sector initiatives to support family caregivers

   • Give recognition to "best practices" of businesses that support caregivers through innovative policies and practices

   • Establish ongoing communications networks for formal and informal caregivers, and public and private stakeholders at national, state, and local levels.

3. Develop consumer-directed home care programs that are publicly supported and allow older adults to select and pay a family caregiver.

4. Encourage insurers to include benefits for family caregiver education and respite care options.

5. Support research on interventions to facilitate family caregiving.

Private Sector Policy Considerations

In addition to these public policy recommendations, nurses can promote private sector programs and policies that can help family caregivers. This is particularly true in the workplace. The General Accounting Office report (1994) of private sector activity in elder care found that elder-care benefits are only available to a small percentage of the U.S. workforce. While employers cite cost as a barrier to offering assistance to employed caregivers, there is a range of no-cost, low-cost, and more extensive options for companies of all sizes. What is needed is advocacy to advance these options. Policies and programs that help caregivers include (National Health Council, 1999; Wagner, Hunt, & Reinhard, 2000):

• Provision of information about publicly supported information and resource centers that are offered through the local area agencies on aging at no cost; at the least, posting the national Eldercare Locator toll-free number on bulletin boards [(800) 677-1116 or TDD/TTY (202) 855-1000]

• Provision of information regarding aging and caregiving in general

- Lunch-time or evening seminars given by local professionals and agencies who will often offer these seminars for free or a very low cost. Caregivers seek information about aging, caregiving, financial paperwork, paying for services needed by the family member, legal advice, how to care for themselves, and an almost endless list of other topics

- Caregiver fairs featuring booths from agencies that provide needed services like home health, respite care or counseling (see following article)

- Support groups for employed caregivers

- Wellness programs that include stress management

- Flexible work arrangements—like flex-time, compressed work weeks, job-sharing, voluntary reduced time, earned time for personal leave, and telecommuting—so that employed caregivers can balance work and caring responsibilities on an individualized basis

- Flexible benefit plans, such as flexible spending accounts and dependent care assistance plans

- Employee Assistance Programs, including stress management, bereavement counseling, and personal and family counseling

- Limited care management services

- On-site day care (including adult day care)

- Subsidies, vouchers, or discounts for elder care and respite.

This is not an exhaustive list, but examples of the range of policies and programs that employers can adopt to help their employed caregivers. Nurses can help advocate for these supports in their own workplace and in the businesses in their communities.

Summary

Nurses know the physical, emotional, social, and financial stresses that family caregivers face. They can become effective advocates for these colleagues in caring for ill, frail, and disabled family members. In addition to including the family perspective and needs in the care of the people they serve, nurses need to stand with these valiant families in seeking public and private sector policies that will better support them. The future of long-term care depends on it.

Susan Reinhard, RN, PhD, is the Executive Director of The Center for Medicare Education, Institute for The Future of Aging Services in Washington, DC, which assists professionals who are helping seniors understand and act upon their Medicare and health care choices. Dr. Reinhard also co-directs a new aging institute promoting innovative practices in long-term care, consumer education, workforce development and other areas that will affect the future of aging services. She is a Visiting Professor of Health Policy at Rutgers University's Center for State Health Policy. Dr. Reinhard served as The Deputy Commissioner of The New Jersey Department of Health and Senior Services. She holds a master's degree in nursing from The University of Cincinnati, and a PhD in Sociology from Rutgers University.

Caregiver Fairs:
Support in Action

◆

Why It Works – *From the Editor*
The day-to-day challenges of caregiving affect every aspect of a individual's or family's life, including their professional life. Caregiver Fairs offer caregiving professionals and employers an opportunity to gather and promote their communities' caregiving resources and efforts.

People who care for family members, neighbors, or friends rarely think of themselves as caregivers. Most are employed and balance careers, families, and caregiving duties. They may take time off from work or forgo promotions. They may struggle with feelings of stress or feel guilty for taking time away from their families or not doing more to help. Yet they may not seek outside help for years—in part because they do not know where to turn for support.

One way employers can help is to organize "caregiver fairs" and encourage their employees to participate. These fairs, which can also be offered by community groups and organizations, are designed to introduce people to providers and services that can help them deal with caregiving responsibilities.

The general idea is to set aside a time and place for local professionals, volunteers, and community organizations to set up tables or booths with flyers, pamphlets, and other information about the kinds of supports that caregivers need. The organizer of a caregiver fair could invite local visiting nurse organizations, hospices, assisted-living providers, nursing-home providers, day-care providers, respite organizations, the Alzheimer's Association, AARP, churches and synagogues, Medicaid staff, caregiver support groups, or any other resource available and willing to participate. Those staffing the booths should be knowledgeable about the needs of care-givers, resources, costs, and concrete details of how to get help. They should also be able to interact comfortably with people who are at various stages of caregiving—from those who do not self-identify as caregivers to those actively searching for assistance. A non-threatening atmosphere, with food, music, and colorful décor (like a fair) is ideal, and there should be plenty of space to congregate informally with peers and potential helpers.

In addition to these information booths, it can also be helpful to invite guest speakers for special topics offered in an adjacent seminar room, or at specific times. For example, an expert on caregiver stress offering insights and concrete advice can help participants understand that they are not alone. Participants can also feel valued as the speakers acknowledge the enormous contributions of caregivers and give them "permission" to congratulate themselves as they learn to take care of their own needs. A health specialist could speak about health promotion and methods to reduce stress. What is important is to invite people who know what they are talking about and who can relate to participants.

Finally, people will not come unless they know about the event and are given time off to attend. A half-day, lunchtime, evening, or all-day event may be held. The organizer should advertise the event, speakers, and locations in advance and offer staggered hours for different organizational units. When the CEO talks it up, people tend to go. Sometimes out of curiosity. Sometimes out of need. Sometimes out of desperation for help.

Contributed by Susan Reinhard

8

Self-Care:
The Path to Wholeness

Beth Witrogen McLeod

Introduction

I cannot count the times family caregivers have whispered to me, "I want my life back." They utter this confession with as much guilt as love, wondering where the familiar patterns went and feeling fearful about the future. These are common sentiments, but they are as useful as dust in the wind. They lead nowhere. The truth is, no one takes our lives away. We give them over by leaving ourselves out of our own caring circle.

The litany of long-term caregiver health complaints seems unending. Among them are fatigue, guilt, anxiety, stress, frustration, isolation, depression, anger, and resentment. Service work means that we open ourselves to the pain and suffering, as well as to the joys and victories, of helping others through difficult times. For those to whom this work is a calling, this is not just a job but a spiritual mandate. Still, it is alarming how few providers of care, whether lay or professional, have learned to balance their own needs with the attention they give others. In training for this work, even in taking it on voluntarily, most of us have failed to understand the importance of personal wellness. We do not dedicate energy to our own health with the same passion we invest in work outside ourselves.

Even though we are admonished on airlines to place the oxygen mask over our own faces in an emergency before helping others, we don't apply that rule to care on the ground. At the extreme this habit leads to burnout and disenchantment, even to clinical depression. But the reality of self-neglect goes deeper than eating poorly or failing to exercise. Burnout, also known as compassion fatigue, occurs especially when we ignore our own needs because we believe the myth that serving others means we cannot equally serve ourselves.

Placing ourselves last is an unconscious act, a common act— but a very risky act. Whereas it is true that if we do not care for ourselves we cannot care well for others, the root of self-care goes much deeper than this maxim. It is not only about physical care, but also the spiritual need to be whole and authentic. This, we find while giving to others, we have neglected to do for much of our lives. Because we have not embraced the totality of our human nature—body, mind, and soul—we bring this fragmentation into all our relationships, whether personal or work-related. This can only lead to a cycle of exhaustion and other health problems because we are not being renewed from a place of abundant energy. When we live our life for others, we give our life away.

There are additional reasons why less-than-vigorous health is common among providers of long-term care. In large part it has to do with several cultural contexts in which care is given. The most critical is that we live in an age- and death-denying society that glorifies youth and "youthful thinking." For example, even as adults we operate under belief systems that have remained unchallenged, if not also largely unexamined, since childhood. We continue to perform the socially acceptable behaviors that got us through high school and into careers, yet we work in a field that focuses on the second half of life, not on its beginnings. The tasks in middle and later years require a different set of values, which are about generativity and wisdom, about the interior life and its gifts. These tasks are about giving from our inner wholeness rather than accumulating more to enhance the image we present to the world. Yet because the social mind deems aging as something to be avoided, there are few, if any, rites or rituals in place to help us make the transition into the spiritual maturity that grows as we reclaim our deeper needs and capacities.

Moreover, we live in a society that does not validate intuition, especially the body's own capacity for self-healing. We place authority in medical science and give over our wellness to doctors, pills, and academic expertise. Because the rational mind is valued over inner wisdom, we are discouraged from paying attention to and developing our innermost guidance, which by its nature leads toward optimum wellness. Believing that others have all of our answers, we cease to look within for information.

Caregivers are further hampered in their ability to self-care because Western culture values independence so much that asking for help is seen as a sign of weakness. The fear of admitting that we are not supermen and superwomen carries such power over us that we neglect ourselves in order to measure up to an outside, disempowering ideal.

What's more, because we are mesmerized by advertising and news media that tell us we are not rich enough, thin enough, or good enough, we readily accept that we are not sufficient just as we are. With rapt attention on the rage and violence in the world, the mass media too rarely acknowledge our kindness and compassion. News reports constantly impart the message that life is not safe, and that we are inadequate to make it so. We have been scolded into believing that focusing on oneself is selfish, so we conclude that "me too" must be wrong. In molding ourselves into what is socially acceptable, we have become untrue to our whole selves, and thus invite dis-ease.

All of this sets the stage for self-neglect when we become providers of care—subtly, unconsciously, but powerfully. We willingly take on the needs of others but after the exhilaration fades, we find we don't have sufficient inner resources to feel renewed each day. What we have taken on begins to take over, and we lose more of ourselves each day, even to the best intentions. Living from the outside in, we have given our lives away.

What piece is missing in this equation? It is this: The work of caregiving is not solely about being a good provider of care to others, but also about being mindful of how we perceive, and take care of, ourselves. In aiming to do our best for others, we forget about giving 100% to ourselves. Caring so intensely for others reveals our strengths and weaknesses, where we fear moving forward and where we are stuck in the past. What a mirror caregivers have, this opportunity to go into families and see by reflection where we have stifled the flow of our own life force. Caregiving illuminates the fact that it isn't enough to witness and help resolve the pain in others; we need to trust our hearts as well.

We have been taught how to go out and give in the world. But we've forgotten how to resonate with our own lives. In growing up we grew outwardly, without also balancing our inner growth. We thus believe that service means we give our lives away, rather than connecting in a relationship where we also receive value and fulfillment. To restore our whole selves, we must go on a journey to see what people and events, beliefs and habits, fears and desires still have a hold on us in a way that no longer nurtures who we are today—or who we are still becoming. It requires courage and especially faith in goodness to discover what patterns are interfering with our innate capacity to live optimally, and then to let go of them with the gusto of an alchemist transforming lead to gold.

The Shadows

The depression, crisis, anxiety, and stress of caregiving have their foundations in our belief systems and in the emotions they engender. They are based in the degree to which we believe in our inner strength and trust life, no matter what is presented to us. This is not a linear process; it is a journey of heart and meaning. At its core is a process of coming into awareness of and integrating our shadow side, our "negative" emotions. For the best self-care, we must illuminate this side of ourselves so as to strip down the wall we have built to shield us from the effects of our fearful thinking.

Shadows are the hidden, unenlightened places where we've experienced feelings of abandonment, rejection, betrayal, conceit, greed, and self-deprecation, whether real or imagined. Shadows also consist of our perceptions, opinions, and family histories. They exist where we still hold grudges or feel wounded, where we don't feel we are good enough, where we have felt cynical or critical or judgmental, where we've built ivory towers to our own agendas and where we have constructed monuments to pain. Here are still others: Not getting what we want, getting what we don't want, the fear of losing what we have, wanting life to be other than how it is, not speaking up about abuse or violation, the fear of being rejected, and being silenced, ridiculed and criticized by others. We all experience these situations, but, unwittingly, most of us also hold on to them. Then they become the dead weight of our lives that we carry along, like the chains of Marley's Ghost, clinging to a past that sucks away the abundant life force we could have available today for vital health.

In Western culture we are socialized to fear or deny these normal feelings and to judge them as bad or harmful. We submerge them in the hope that they will go away. But they rarely do, and not until we bring them into the light of present day truth. This process, like the myth of Persephone rising from the darkness each spring, is especially visible in caregiving, when family histories and sibling rivalries surface unexpectedly, and we wonder why there is so much dysfunction where love should reign instead.

By ignoring these feelings in order to feel comfortable, we lose contact with our wholeness. Being able to control emotions is not a sign of strength or personal power, however; it is only a sign of controlling emotions. That habit will not make us whole or safe— or healthy. Disconnecting from our feelings, especially grief and anger, denies us the opportunity for inner healing by tying up our energy in remaining fragmented and frightened. The bridge to wholeness is our willingness to change our lives by choosing health.

As Dr. Christiane Northrup (1994) writes in *Women's Bodies, Women's Wisdom*, "Sadness or pain are natural parts of life. They are also great teachers. Yet our culture teaches us that there is something wrong with pain, that it must be drugged, denied, or otherwise avoided at all costs—and the costs are very high. We are not taught that we have an innate ability to deal with pain, that our bodies know how to do this."

Healing Ourselves

In a culture that encourages us to disassociate from our body's inner wisdom, it is no wonder we have difficulty balancing work and health. We think that one necessarily precludes the other. So how can we live better to do this work? How can we be renewed and remain open without giving ourselves away?

The journey of self-care means paying attention to our relationship to ourselves. It is a daily practice that starts by paying attention to our bodies. Healing thus begins with the awareness that we have given ourselves away to places and behaviors, perspectives and opinions that we thought would make us feel in control, a habit that usually translates into resistance to change. In truth, these patterns have kept us from being able to handle loss, illness, and death, and from accepting that the physical world is impermanent. Especially in the field of long-term care, we come up against issues of loss every day. If we are not in touch with our own relationship to change, we unwittingly deny ourselves a crucial regenerating element in service. We also miss an opportunity to foster healing in those we care for. For example, the quality of service we render as caregivers is affected by our own long-held negative patterns and our own propensity to empathize with old wounds. In relationships we either foster healing by coming into present time or we promote further fragmentation. If we are not mindful, these patterns spill over into the care we provide others. Then no one can be renewed.

We cannot let go of what we do not accept; we cannot move on if we are operating out of fear. Healing takes root when we connect to our own feelings and explore how to restore wholeness, breaking down the walls that restrict our life force from flowing into and through us. We cannot become whole from without; healing starts from within.

To renew ourselves each day, we need to find out what drains us. Each morning before getting out of bed, and each night before sleep, it is useful to review the thoughts, emotions, events, and people that come to mind when considering where our energy has gone.

Here are some questions to ask: What am I obsessing about? What situations or people make me feel resentful or judgmental? What emotions am I feeling? Are my beliefs and values really mine, or do they belong to my family, my religion, my workplace, my group associations? This practice helps us understand that what drains energy—and health—are feelings and actions like wanting, expecting, hoping, fearing, worrying, gossiping, generating negativity, criticizing, insisting on personal agendas or expectations of results, craving attention and validation, and needing to control or to be right.

Answers may be recorded in a daily journal or through "therapeutic writing," which can consist of exercises in a formal class (including online courses) or informally with free-form stream of consciousness written down in a notebook. If writing feels foreign or uncomfortable, caregivers can join a support group or consult a psychotherapist so that progress can be tracked. Even ten minutes a day spent excavating our negative behaviors can be cumulative and insightful. Caregivers should be encouraged to explore these normal feelings, but also to move through them and not dwell on them. This process of self-examination is the foundation of self-care and needs to become a priority. Excuses like "I'm too tired" or "I don't have time" should be addressed as the dodges they are; everyone can find ten minutes a day for themselves. If time management education is necessary, then so be it; the most important tool to give family caregivers is the knowledge that it is okay to take care of themselves, that they are not alone, and that they can do this, one step at a time.

The process of integrating mind, body, and spirit means exploring where we have invested thought, speech, and action. When we don't pay attention to the quality and integrity of every thought and action, we're not honoring and strengthening our whole selves.

All of these experiences are a normal part of human nature; however, they rule us when we are not fully present and focused on what is here and now. They disempower us when we believe that what is going on out there has more validity than our heart's desire. Optimum wellness requires putting ourselves back into the care equation by respecting our health with good nutrition, exercise, and rest, but especially by listening to our bodies even when the world is screaming at us to do it another way. As Andrew Harvey (2000) writes in *The Direct Path*, renewal necessitates a journey home to our original selves. We have identified "our essential nature with what surrounds us and with what our culture and society and parents and ordinary senses tell us about ourselves; a massive journey is then needed for us to 'dis-identify' with everything we have falsely learned about ourselves so that we can experience, with the 'hundred thousand veils' burned away, the glory of our true identity."

Every choice regarding our health is based on how much we value ourselves. As we value ourselves and remain present, we are open to receiving the flow of life force. Then we are revitalized. Self-care thus means that we are taking care of body and soul. Health is enhanced in people who are doing work that is self-fulfilling. Good health happens automatically when our talents are in full expression. But we need energy to do this. We cannot serve, we cannot bring forth our gifts, if we do not first give to ourselves. Abundant vitality comes from within; it is not something that can be bestowed from the outside. It is about putting our faith not in material goods but in the power of our inner life.

Thus the keyword in self-care is integrity: becoming whole. Integrity is based on the quality of our presence. What this requires is the practice of bringing back our focus into present time. When we live from the outside in—by rote, by what we have been told we should do or be or think or feel—we are not in present time. And if we are not here now, we are not going to have enough energy to provide good care to anyone. We must be present to be healthy, but most of us have our energy, our thoughts and feelings, tied up in the past or future. To be fully alive, we need to practice coming back to ourselves.

As medical intuitive Caroline Myss (1996) says of remaining invested in negativity, "We finance the life of our life with the dead of our life." We keep our attention on what has already passed, or on what we wish would happen. Our biography becomes our biology, she says. We carry our past in our cells; our emotions exist in body memory. For caregivers, especially empathetic ones, we also carry the stories and pain of those we care for. All of this happens because we are energetic beings as well as physical ones. But we can still care without taking on the troubles of the world. Detachment means the ability to care deeply from an objective place.

Finding Wholeness

We are by no means in total control of human nature. We are responsible for our part—and only for our part. And when we become caregivers, we find ourselves at a great crossroad where we are asked to pay attention to what matters in life. This is a rite of passage unrecognized by Western society but a very real one nonetheless. It requires that we see how we have accepted group belief and value systems in order to fit into society. We are asked to look within for our own good nature and to hear the inner voice that wants only the best for all of us.

The Greek myth of Procrustes beautifully describes this phenomenon of distrusting oneself and of giving oneself over to outside interests. Procrustes' all-powerful job was to ensure that everyone fit into society. If you were going to Athens—the cultural summit of those days—you had to pass by Procrustes and be placed on his bed, which stretched across the only road into the city. If you were too long, your limbs got lopped off. If you were too short, you were stretched to fit. Few passed by and remained whole.

This tale is a metaphor for how we betray our hearts, reconfiguring ourselves to be accepted by others (and still only rarely believing that we are). In so doing, we give our power to an ideal that cannot and will not ever care for us the way we alone can. This story suggests that when we fragment ourselves in order to bow to something outside our true nature, we cease to be connected to our true nature. Yet, if we do not value ourselves, then our work in the world becomes less valuable in turn. Then our caring does not have as much healing power as it could because the force of compassion has become choked off.

The ability to self-renew comes from restoring the totality of our being. This can come only from reclaiming our lives and from purging ourselves of the patterns that do not sustain us. Renewal comes by reintegrating the pieces of ourselves that we have given away and by bringing everything into present time and appreciating life exactly as it is. Of course, this takes dedication and practice on a daily basis.

Caregiving is clearly work of high service. But service, like healing, is mutual. It depends on a circle of connection that renders both giver and receiver more whole. One of the treasures caregivers bestow is the ability to be present with someone who is suffering, to simply validate that person's worth as a human being. This is also healing work—to witness another's emotional wounds without judgment. As we acknowledge another's pain, so we enlighten and let go of our own. Therefore it is important to be open to the reflection in ourselves that caregiving presents. It is important to love ourselves unconditionally and accept the mysterious process of spiritual evolution.

The Buddha said that you can search the tenfold universe and not find a single being more worthy of loving kindness than your-self. If we accept this message, then we can see that caregiving truly is a spiritual practice, a path with heart. Those who embark on it are called to ease suffering. That means we must become conscious of how we also create suffering in our own lives. We must listen to where we close our hearts in fear and where we need to open more in joy. We must begin to pay attention to the wisdom of our bodies, a language we can all learn to speak.

Sixteen Tips for Self-Care

1. Believe that optimum wellness is possible, and that your body has the inner guidance system to make it so. You can build a library of books and audiocassettes on energy medicine, wellness, inner healing, and self-care.

2. Listen to your body's symptoms and pay attention to its messages about health and healing. You may need to see a medical professional or holistic practitioner. Or if your primary care physician isn't helpful, there are many alternative methods to enhancing the body's natural healing abilities. These include chiropractic, acupuncture, massage, and exercises as simple as walking.

3. Work with what you have today and let tomorrow take care of itself. Say to yourself, "The energy of life is enough to dispel my fears and to give me strength to handle today."

4. Understand that if you don't value yourself you cannot receive energy to be renewed. If you have nothing to give, you will burn out. Keep reminding yourself that you have a right to self-nurture.

5. Realize that you don't have to be all things to all people. You can say no and set limits without putting others out of your heart.

6. Remember that you have a right to your own life. Giving your all doesn't mean giving up your own health and well-being. Caregiving is about caring, not martyrdom.

7. If you find yourself tired, angry, or resentful at the end of the day, ask yourself what thoughts, actions, or interactions drained you. Develop a practice to let them go.

8. Don't worry about what society, other family members, friends and colleagues think of you or how you are doing. Consider that your best is good enough; no one else has the right to judge you or make you feel guilty.

9. Keep a positive attitude and accept each day's offerings.

10. Stop trying to control people and events or expecting certain outcomes. Life happens on its own.

11. Pay attention to the people and activities that nourish you. Commit to having more of these interactions. For example, if you like to garden or look at beautiful art, make dates with yourself to do these. If you need socialization, extend yourself to friends and community. If you need quiet time, spend a day at a spa or retreat, or shut off the phone and other distractions so that you can be at peace.

12. Acknowledge negative feelings without judgment. Resolve to let them go as quickly as possible.

13. Make a list of tasks and prioritize them according to what is important for you to be involved versus things you can delegate.

14. Learn to accept and ask for help, especially from family, friends and community. Offer specific things they can do,

whether it's household chores or watching your loved one so you can have some time to yourself

15. Learn to say no to things in order to protect your time and energy. Set reasonable expectations. Don't try to be all things to all people; it is not your responsibility to make others happy or to live their lives. Remember that service means enhancing the other person's life, not giving your life away.

16. Watch out for destructive ways of coping, such as drinking too much, misusing medication, or overeating. Seek medical advice if you are experiencing changes in your health, such as blurred vision, stomach ailments, or high blood pressure.

Self-care, then, begins with self-awareness. Wellness comes from honoring our needs as whole people—mind, body, and spirit. Whatever can command us from the outside, we need to pay attention to. We need to reclaim our power from our shadows, the places where we're not accepting of life, and of ourselves. Then we have health and the capacity to celebrate each day we are alive. This acceptance of life, this flow with life, is the alpha and omega of self-care. We create health when we choose to love and bless all life, especially our own.

Beth Witrogen McLeod is a journalist, author, speaker, advocate and consultant for caregiving and aging issues. She is a double Pulitzer Prize nominee. The first was for her groundbreaking newspaper series in 1995, "The Caregivers," for the San Francisco Examiner. Her book, Caregiving: The Spiritual Journey of Love, Loss, and Renewal *(Wiley, paperback 2000), was nominated in general nonfiction. She has won many national and regional awards and has published in multiple national magazines, newspapers, and journals. She is a featured expert on television and radio programs and teaches a course on self-care and renewal through the University of California Extension system.*

Volunteer Hospices: Talbot Hospice Foundation

◆

Why It Works – *From the Editor*

Volunteer hospices are an example of how quality and dignity in end-of-life care can be achieved with a variety of models. The Talbot Hospice Foundation, a volunter hospice, is a community-based organization that widens the net of services for caregivers. This program is a reminder that funding does not always have to drive policy and that resources can be pooled to successfully achieve goals.

Passionate in its mission and evangelical in its cause, the American hospice movement is rooted in and shaped by volunteerism. Volunteer hospices (hospices who choose to forgo Medicare certification) operate with the belief that each community should define its own needs, adhere to its own set of values, and provide the workforce to care for its dying. With more than 150 agencies nationwide, over 10,000 dedicated volunteers make it possible for these agencies to carry out their missions. Furthermore, community coalitions are essential, augmenting care by working hand-in-hand with hospitals, home-care agencies, Medicare-certified hospices, and other community organizations. These partnerships create a continuum of services available to patients and families across all levels and sites of care.

The Talbot Hospice Foundation (THF) exemplifies the volunteer hospice movement and reflects the values and mission of all-volunteer hospices nationwide. Located in Easton, Maryland, THF began serving Talbot County in 1981 with one part-time staff member working out of a basement office and four volunteers providing services in one home. THF is dedicated to the concept that trained community lay people can play a significant role in providing prac- tical, emotional, and psychological support to the dying. THF currently has 216 active volunteers, and its services are available to anyone in the Talbot County community, regardless of their ability to pay.

Each THF volunteer completes a 16-hour training seminar, and those interested in providing hands-on care complete an additional six-hour course. These volunteers offer direct patient care for persons with a life-limiting illness. They main- tain an equipment loan closet and provide a wide array of community bereavement services, including a program in the schools, community education on dying and grief, a caregiv- er support group, and a referral service for the frail elderly living at home. In general, volunteer hospices like THF direct their efforts to three major areas of service:

1. **The Patient/Family Program.** Volunteers provide services to meet the myriad needs of patients, which may include comfort care, respite care, practical tasks, transportation, etc. Volunteer hospices help pull together community resources that can ease the stress of caring for a terminally ill loved one.

2. **The Community Bereavement Program.** Bereavement care is offered to the community at large as well as to hospice families. Services may include a phone program, bereavement support groups, grief workshops, one-on-one visitations, children's grief camps, or grief education.

3. **The Community Education Program.** The community is made aware of the hospice concept and how it can be broadly applied to deal with difficulties such as loss, grief, chronic illness, aging, and loneliness, as well as terminal illness. Presentations are made to groups from businesses, schools, churches, service clubs, etc. Pamphlets, books, and resources are usually available in the volunteer hospice library.

On July 1, 1998, THF opened its doors to a six-bedroom Hospice House, a 7,000-square-foot building that houses both the THF office and the Guest Wing. The Guest Wing is a residence program for terminally ill patients who, for one reason or another, cannot be cared for in their own homes. Accessible to anyone in Talbot County, inpatient services are provided through the intensive round-the-clock efforts of volunteers. Hospice House is also staffed with volunteers who do gardening, yard work, chores, and cleaning. In addition, volunteers prepare shopping lists, do grocery shopping, and prepare all meals served in the Guest Wing of Hospice House.

Several hospices have initiated a residence program like Guest Wing. Most often a community project, a house may be donated to the hospice, and people from the community contribute their skills and gifts to renovate and furnish the dwelling. Volunteers are scheduled around the clock to act as the patient's "family." Direct medical care is provided by home-health agencies or Medicare-certified hospices. There are no fees charged in most residence programs provided by volunteer hospices.

Program Note:

In 1995, the Hospice Association of America (HAA) created the Volunteer Hospice Network (VHN) to provide support, technical assistance and networking opportunities to volunteer hospices across the country. VHN members include volunteer hospices, grief support programs, and many other volunteer groups that care for the dying. Although a few volunteer hospices also provide medical care, most focus exclusively on practical, respite, emotional, and bereavement support. VHN values include respect for diversity, love of community, and championing local solutions.

For more information about volunteer hospices and VHN, visit www.growthhouse.org/hospice/vhn.html.

---

*Contributed by Rhoda Eagan, Volunteer Hospice Network &
Diane H. Jones, Ethos Consulting*

Part III

Grief, Loss, and the End of Life

There is another 'dirty secret' to caregiving: It inevitably involves loss. These losses include not only the eventual death of the person who receives care but all the losses that are experienced along the way. This can include the loss of the person as she declines, as well as the losses of time, autonomy, friends, and control as one becomes absorbed in the caregiving role. Doka's chapter focuses on all the losses of the caregiving experience, offering suggestions for adapting to grief at each phase of loss. Grief is manifested in many ways, but it often involves guilt. The demands of caregiving can be so unremitting that each day of respite, planned or not, or each burst of frustration may haunt survivors later. Zycherman's voice poignantly expresses that guilt. Both sections remind professionals of the need to allow time to truly validate and explore all the feelings, and other reactions, that emerge from the caregiving experience.

However, not every caregiver faces the death of the person for whom they care. In some cases, such as with a disabled child, the person receiving care may survive the caregiver. Here, professionals have a special role, gently assisting caregivers in planning for transitions, assessing issues of alternate and contingent guardians, and making suitable arrangements as part of their estate reference. This involves the consideration of other losses and must be carefully approached. Nevertheless, it can offer caregivers a sense of assurance and control, as well as an easing of the sense of isolation.

Spirituality, too, is a significant aspect of support, likewise providing a sense of assurance and control, helping survivors find meaning in their experiences. Blackwell and Stern, each in his own faith tradition, explore the role of spiritual support at the end of life. Each offer examples of the ways in which people can be empowered to utilize their beliefs, practices (such as prayer), rituals, and faith communities as they encounter loss. While Blackwell and Stern offer illustrations of Christian and Jewish spiritualities, their comments can be applied to other spiritual traditions. Both authors make a critical distinction between formal religion and the intensely individual spirituality by which persons seek to find meaning in the deepest sense. And both affirm that such spirituality, however defined and eclectic, is universal. The challenge for professionals, then, is to help family caregivers and dying individuals express and interpret how their own spirituality speaks to the experience.

Sherman's chapter addresses the reciprocal suffering of caregivers and patients at the end of life, which is then reflected in Groarke's personal voice. Sherman, a pioneer in palliative care, reminds us that palliation must include the suffering of both the dying and the caregiver. Part of that suffering includes struggling with the awful ethical dilemmas inevitably posed at the end of life. Price's chapter adds invaluable information for those facing such decisions. Finally, two examples of *Programs That Work*, the Whitman-Walker Clinic and Family Caregiver Alliance, offer reassurance that even during difficult experiences we need not be alone.

9

Grief, Loss, and Caregiving

Kenneth J. Doka

Introduction

- Joan has been caring for her 17-year-old son Adam, who was born with severe developmental disabilities. She is ashamed of the resentment she feels when she sees her friends with their children, knowing Adam will never experience normal milestones such as graduation.

- Manuel's wife has had Alzheimer's for nearly six years. Working, caring for her, even arranging care has been a burden for both him and his adult children. Manuel feels lonely, guilty, and depressed.

- Cynthia's husband has died after a long disabling stroke. For years she patiently cared for him, giving up activities and friendship to nurse and nurture. Now that he has died she struggles to find a new sense of identity and purpose.

- Robert has cared for his lover Lou for the nine years that Lou has struggled with HIV infection. Uninfected, Robert has supported Lou through Lou's cycle of relapses and remissions. Even though he loves Lou, Robert now just wishes he would die so he can get on with his own life.

There are two common denominators in these vignettes. All of the individuals have been intensely involved in a caregiving experience. And all of them are encountering loss and grief, which is not surprising. Grief is a constant companion in the caregiving journey.

This chapter explores the nature of grief and loss inherent in the caregiving experience and begins by reviewing the process of anticipatory grief and mourning that encompasses all the loss experienced when an individual is chronically ill or disabled. A strong emphasis is placed on strategies of intervention for patients, families and intimate networks, as well as for professional caregivers. This is critical, as grief is so stressful that a failure to provide effective care can increase the distress of the patient and lead to fatigue and burnout in caregivers.

This is especially true when an individual approaches death. Here, support will play a critical role, one that may dramatically affect the experience of subsequent grief. The chapter then considers the grief that follows a loss, addressing factors in the caregiving experience that both facilitate and complicate loss. Again, a strong emphasis is placed on intervention strategies that can assist caregivers as they cope with loss. For even though the caregiving journey has ended, the journey through grief continues.

Loss, Illness, Disability, and Grief

One of the common misunderstandings of grief is that it is only a reaction to a death. It is this misunderstanding that clouds the concept of 'anticipatory grief.' Originally, anticipatory grief referred to grief reactions that resulted from an expected or anticipated death (Lindemann, 1944). For example, if someone is diagnosed with a terminal disease, that person, as well as his family and friends, may already begin to grieve the expected and eventual death.

But grief is a far broader concept. Grief results from a reaction to a loss—any loss, not just one related to death. Rando (2000) has defined anticipatory grief as a reaction not only to an expected loss, but to all the losses—past, present and future—that are encountered in an experience of illness or disability. Anticipatory mourning, then, becomes the process whereby one continually adapts to these losses.

Loss is inherent in the caregiving experience. These losses are many. Depending on the underlying cause, clients or patients may experience losses of abilities, activities, or independence. They may have to relinquish significant roles, such as work and family roles. As one man with ALS shared: "My wife tells me I will always be a husband and father even though I no longer work. Yet it's really not true. I no longer take my wife out. I really do not function as a husband any longer. And I do not even have the strength to pick up my child."

There may be other losses as well. Some may be intangible, such as the loss of hopes, dreams or plans or the loss of body image or security. These losses may shatter the client's assumptive world, causing them to question their beliefs about the nature of the world, as well as challenging spiritual and philosophical beliefs. There may be tangible losses, too. As income declines and health-related expenses rise, lifestyles may change. And each condition carries unique losses. For example, early-stage Alzheimer's patients may grieve their loss of memory, a critical link to past, present, and others.

This grief is shared by family and others in the intimate network with whom one shares intense interaction and emotional investment. Members of that network also experience losses that are grieved. Again, some of these losses are intangible—the loss of hopes, dreams, or plans. One father, many years after his daughter was born with developmental disabilities, described his sense of loss: "Most parents over time learn that their children will not fulfill the hopes they have for them. But most parents have twenty some odd years to figure that out. My wife and I learned it in minutes." These intangible losses may create spiritual pain and confusion, challenging one's assumptions about the world.

Conditions such as Alzheimer's may generate a sense of psychosocial loss (Doka & Aber, 1989; Doka, 2001). Psychosocial loss refers to situations where the *persona* is so changed, in this case by illness or disability, that intimate others experience the loss of that person as she once was. In extreme cases, such as advanced Alzheimer's, spouses may even face *cryptowidowhood*, or hidden widowhood. Here the loss of the marriage relationship is total, though the person remains alive (Doka & Aber, 1989).

Other losses are tangible. Caregivers within the intimate network give up time, independence, roles, and activities as they tend to the person. They may experience secondary losses such as friends or income. These losses and subsequent grief may not be acknowledged by others. In fact, they may face public admiration for their selflessness, perhaps making their own feelings of resentment even harder to bear.

These losses are experienced by professional or paid caregivers as well. Over time they may become emotionally invested in the patient as well as the intimate network. Their losses may be associated with the patient or family as they watch the continued deterioration of the patient or developing dysfunction in the family due to the increased stress. They may experience a loss of their beliefs and assumptions or hopes and goals (Papadatou, 2000).

Since loss is inherent in the caregiving experience, so is grief. This grief may manifest itself in a number of ways. Physically, individuals may experience a range of reactions, including fatigue, insomnia, aches and pains, more than likely exacerbated by the fact that grief is but one source of stress. Other reactions may be emotional. Persons may experience many emotions—sadness, anxiety, guilt, anger, jealousy, to name but a few. Many of these emotions, even paradoxical ones, may be experienced simultaneously. Grief may have cognitive effects. Individuals may constantly think about the condition of the person. They may become obsessive or forgetful. Their minds may race from one thought to the next. They may be troubled by dreams or other sleep disturbances.

Spiritually, individuals may find it difficult to find meaning in the experience. They may question their beliefs or become angry with God. Others may turn even more intently to their faith for support or solace.

All of these reactions are likely to be expressed in a range of behaviors, including manic activity or lethargic behavior. Some individuals may plunge into caregiving while others become more distant and remote. Some may lash out in anger, while others act out in other ways, including substance abuse. Some may channel grief in almost transcendent ways, perhaps becoming advocates or moving into other realms of caregiving.

In summary, issues of grief and loss are inherent in the caregiving process. This grief is experienced by everyone involved—patients, caregivers within the intimate network, and paid caregivers. All will need support as they mourn their many losses.

Providing Support: Interventions and Self-Care

Strategies for intervention and support will be different at distinct periods in the caregiving experience. And, of course, they will be different for professional caregivers and family caregivers. In early phases of the disease, or in other circumstances depending on awareness, grief may be shared by the patient or client. Thus, such individuals will need support for grief as well. Patients and caregivers, then, may need to do the following.

- *Validate Expressions of Grief*
  Validation is an essential aspect of grief support. Validation means that the individual's experience of grief is listened to, understood, accepted, and explained as a valid response to the loss. Too often caregivers and patients are made to believe that natural expressions of grief are either inappropriate or ungrateful. "You shouldn't feel guilty" or "How can you be upset after all your years? Count your blessings." Such expressions, however common and well-intentioned, deny or invali-

date grief. Patients and caregivers need to have these experiences of loss and expressions of grief acknowledged, allowing space for individuals to explore their many reactions to the experience. This is critical. Professional caregivers may believe that expressions of grief are inappropriate since they do not share a kin or prior relational tie. Yet here, too, grief is an appropriate response that needs validation.

- *Inform Clients and Families*
  Patients and caregivers both may need information about the underlying condition. For example, in certain diseases, fatigue or mood swings may be a common symptom or side effect of medication. As patients and their intimate networks know more about the underlying condition, their ability to cope and sense of control is likely to be greater. In educating patients and intimate networks, it is important to recognize the phenomenon of "middle knowledge" (Weisman, 1972). This means that dying persons and members of their network drift in and out of the awareness of dying or other serious conditions. This means that patients and families will sometimes accept, and sometimes fail to accept and acknowledge, the information they have been given. The implication of middle knowledge is that one should always follow the patient and family member's lead. They will let us know what information they are ready to hear. It is critical to understand that patients and families may choose, at times, not to acknowledge information they once seemed to accept.

- *Help Patients and Families Deal with the Affective Issues Aroused by the Loss*
  Patients and their networks often lack opportunities to ventilate the emotions aroused by the situation. Because the patient is alive, family and friends may feel disloyal, unfeeling, or inhibited in expressing emotion. The patient, too, may feel it is inappropriate to express his emotional reactions. All parties

may struggle with a wide range of emotions, among them anger, guilt, anxiety, and shame. Education about the condition may alleviate some of the affective issues, but clients may need additional opportunities to explore and ventilate their emotions. Counselors should encourage emotional expression, identify and validate the emotional responses that clients experience, and explore strategies for coping with these emotions. Questions such as, "Many times clients in your situation have expressed to me feelings of _____. Have you experienced this?" can provide the freedom to explore previously unacknowledged affect.

In addition to the illness, the caregiving experience may arouse feelings as well. Caregivers may feel resentful of the burdens placed on them, perhaps angry that others are not more helpful. These feelings are likely to be exacerbated when the relationship before illness was ambivalent. Caregivers may feel resentful of their new responsibilities, guilty about lapses of patience, or even regretful that they cannot do more. Patients may resent their increasing dependence, or be ambivalent about the help they are given. Exploring these reactions can allow them to acknowledge their own limits or to develop alternative strategies for future contingencies that can reinforce a sense of control. It is critical that counselors recognize the broad range of ways in which clients may achieve emotional release. For some, ventilating by crying can be helpful; for others emotions can be expressed in activity or cognition (Martin & Doka, 1999).

- *Help Clients Recognize and Respond to the Changes in Their Own Lives*
An individual who experiences loss is likely to experience a series of secondary losses that spring from the initial loss. In psycho-social loss, these secondary losses can be profound. As mentioned earlier, clients may lose prior companionship, shared activities, and contact with others. They may have less

personal time and thus be forced to relinquish other significant roles or pleasurable activities. And the changes may occur so rapidly (or so gradually) that they may not realize how significantly their lives have been altered and how the changes have added to their stress.

Many times helping clients to acknowledge these changes can be beneficial. Simply asking, "In what ways has your own life changed since _____?" allows clients to enumerate these losses. Sometimes clients themselves will be surprised at the extent to which their lives have changed. Having identified the losses, they can then develop strategies for coping with them, perhaps regaining some of what was lost (possibly in modified form) and mourning the loss of what cannot be salvaged.

- *Explore Methods of Coping*
  Coping can be defined as the "constantly changing cognitive and behavioral efforts to manage specific external and/or internal demands that are appraised as passing or exceeding the resources of the person" (Lazarus & Folkman, 1984, p. 141). Coping strategies can be diverse. Some may be helpful, such as reframing thoughts or sharing emotions with others. Because the conditions surrounding loss can create periods of sustained stress, counselors will find it useful to explore individual clients' coping strategies. In this exploration, coping strengths can be identified and encouraged. Unhelpful coping strategies, such as substance abuse, can also be identified, and clients can then assess alternative strategies.

  Among the issues that might arise in a discussion of coping strategies are concerns about support and respite. One key coping skill is utilizing one's support system effectively. Asking clients to identify and assess their informal support systems can be useful in many ways. It can reinforce the idea that there are others to whom they may turn. It can lead to discussions about who has or has not been forthcoming, allowing the assessment of "surprises"—that is, individuals who did not come through as expected or those who provided unexpected support. This discussion can also identify barriers to support, such as a reluctance to use or seek support.

These considerations can in turn lead to a discussion of respite. For the aware patient, respite in the form of visitors or other activity can provide needed diversion. For family caregivers, respite is essential to effective adaptation. Counselors may find these caregivers reluctant to consider their respite needs for a number of reasons, such as the inability to find or trust alternative caregivers, concerns of the patient, feelings of guilt, or perhaps even the gratification experienced when one feels essential and needed. Nonetheless, family caregivers should be encouraged to explore both their respite needs and their respite strategies. The very question of how they meet their own needs for respite validates the legitimacy of deriving strategies to meet their own needs.

- *Help Clients Plan Realistically for the Future*
Aware patients, as well as their family members and friends, need to plan for the future. Clients may be resistant to planning for three reasons: First, in many situations, future possibilities may seem dismal. Second, many may have learned to adapt by simply taking each day as it comes. Third, given the reality of middle knowledge, clients, whether patients or families, may simply choose not to discuss an uncertain future. For all of these reasons, counselors should respect their decisions.

This concern has many dimensions. One issue involves the question of advance directives. It is important to allow discussions of advance directives should the subject arise, even to invite clients to address these issues. First, in addition to the process of anticipatory mourning, there is a concurrent process of anticipatory bereavement (Gerber, 1974). This means that patients may need to take objective actions prior to further decline. Second, addressing future possibilities allows patients to consider available options. Even if certain options are not viable, the discussion of alternatives still reinforces a sense of control.

- *Explore Spiritual Issues Raised by the Patient's Condition*
  Much of the time, clients experience a shattering of assumptions—most of their beliefs about the nature of the world or the future—which can give rise to a profound spiritual struggle. This struggle can be complicated, particularly as the demands of caregiving can limit opportunities for spiritual support— for example, limiting time for participation in religious services or spiritual practices. Counselors can validate this struggle, provide space to explore the spiritual issues raised by the illness, and allow clients to assess the ways in which they can effectively utilize their beliefs, rituals, and faith communities.

  Counselors may employ many resources as they assist patients and caregivers in dealing with losses. Support groups can offer respite and validation, as well as ways for individuals to explore their response to the underlying condition. Support groups exist for cognitively functioning persons with a variety of conditions, as well as for caregivers. Some of these groups may be specific to a given condition such as ALS, Alzheimer's or developmental disabilities. Others focus on the caregiving experience and are open to any caregiver. The list of resources in the appendix offers information about national organizations that can refer to local support groups.

  In many of the same ways, bibliotherapy, the use of books or self-help literature, can be helpful. Like groups, bibliotherapy offers validation, help, and suggestion for coping. And it has the advantage of being available whenever an individual needs support and comfort.

  Other techniques may also be helpful. Caregivers and patients may find complementary therapies such as meditation, imaging, or other approaches to be useful. These strategies can reduce stress and reinforce a sense of control.

Rituals, too, may be offered. Rituals are acts that evoke meaning. Through the experience of caregiving, rituals may offer individuals a sense of both meaning and control, allowing one to act out reactions. One man dying of cancer turned over his checkbook to his adult daughter, conveying his trust in her ability to now handle things. This ritual allowed him a dignified way to relinquish a significant role.

It is critical to remember that the needs addressed here are shared by all—patients, caregivers with the family or intimate network, and professional caregivers. It is especially critical to offer support for these professionals. Not only can they become close to their patients, but to the families as well. The very nature of their work means that they may experience cumulative losses leading to compassion fatigue and burnout. Their own sense of grief can easily be disenfranchised (Doka, 1989, 2001).

As the Patient Approaches Death: Needs and Interventions

In many cases the role of a caregiver can go on for many years, perhaps even across the life span. But in other cases the underlying condition of the patient moves from a chronic to a terminal phase. When families and intimate networks approach the imminent death of a patient, they may need the following help as they deal with their ongoing needs.

- *Dealing with Affect*
  Families may struggle with a series of ambivalent emotions as death approaches. They may feel relief and subsequent guilt as they anticipate the end of caregiving. They may struggle with all the emotions of grief. They may be fearful and confused as to what they will do as caregiving responsibilities, once a large part of their lives, cease. As noted earlier, they will need opportunities for validation and information.

- *Balancing Demands*
  For many caregivers, responsibilities and demands may
  increase. Caregivers may need assistance at this time in
  prioritizing and balancing the varied responsibilities they face,
  as well as finding and accepting support from formal and
  informal networks.

- *Preparing for Death*
  Families may need to focus on what must be done as death
  approaches. Have they made plans for a funeral? Are legal
  documents such as advance directives in order? What personal
  acts might they need to do prior to a patient's death? Is there
  a particular way in which they need to say goodbye?

  Individuals can assist family caregivers in a number of ways
  here. First, family members will need information on what to
  expect as death occurs. They may need to review advance directives and other decisions. For example, family members may
  need to be reminded that feeding tubes or hydration may cause
  additional discomfort at the end of life. Such information at
  this time may eliminate potential conflicts and mitigate later
  distress over decisions. Second, family caregivers may need to
  review and rehearse final actions. As death approaches, for
  example, they should know whom to call and what they need
  to do.

- *When Death Occurs*
  At the time of death, a number of interventions will assist
  caregivers:

  —Allow time alone. Do not rush removal of the body.
    Remember that the family may need time alone to say
    goodbye.

  —Allow the expression of grief. It is appropriate at this
    moment for families to express their grief. Do not inhibit
    that expression, and, as much as is in one's power, do not
    let others inhibit that expression.

—Empower ritual. The moment of death is a sacred time. Offer loved ones the option for a ritual. Perhaps they wish to light a candle, say a prayer, or find another meaningful way to address the moment.

—Help with the details. Families may be confused and disoriented at this time. They may value assistance in calling the funeral home and informing others.

And finally, at the moment of death, it is critical not to neglect professional caregivers. They, too, may need to mark the moment and grieve.

After the Death: Grief and Caregiving

It is often said that sudden loss is difficult for survivors, while prolonged loss is easier for survivors (though more difficult for the dying person). In fact, some of the early thought was that anticipatory grief often mitigated the grief survivors experienced at the time of death—that is, that much grief work had been completed. The reality is different. In any loss, survivors will experience the many manifestations of grief we have mentioned. When illness is prolonged, there are factors that will facilitate the grieving process, but there also are factors that complicate grief.

Prolonged illness, especially when it involves caregiving responsibilities, does allow survivors to become aware of the severity of the problem as it continues to unfold. As one caregiver shared: "Each time I came to take care of my father, I realized how much he had declined—even from the past week. Bathing him, I could see the progress of the deterioration. When he died I was ready. I felt he was, too." Moreover, prolonged illness gives individuals the opportunity to finish business—to say goodbyes, talk over past issues, and possibly resolve conflict. And the very experience of caregiving can be a demonstration of love that may be perceived as atoning for prior conflicts and difficulties.

Other aspects of prolonged illness may complicate the grieving process. Prolonged illness and caregiving are both stressful, affecting grief in at least three ways. First, the cumulative effects of prolonged stress from the illness and caregiving are draining, sapping one's ability to respond to yet another series of stressful events. Second, these effects may be experienced throughout the network, limiting opportunities for support. Third, the stressful context of caregiving can fray relationships, creating or exacerbating conflicts between caregivers or with the dying person that may need to be addressed later.

Other factors may complicate grief as well. Survivors may be troubled by the extent that the deceased suffered. Such experiences may challenge spiritual assumptions and beliefs. Survivors may also be concerned about care decisions, such as the timeliness or appropriateness of particular medical decisions.

There are a number of interventive strategies that can assist. It is critical, of course, to validate loss. There is often an assumption by others that now that the illness has ended and caregiving has ceased, the ordeal is over. In fact, grief now continues, and survivors are likely to experience a roller coaster of reactions that will, in an individual way, ebb and flow over the next years.

In the grief process, the individual will deal with many emotions. He or she will struggle with spiritual issues and concerns such as the meaning of the experience, will readjust to a life without the person, will continue to adjust to the reality of the death, and will relocate the deceased. The latter refers to the ways in which one continues a relationship with the deceased, who, while not physically alive, still lives in memory (Worden, 1991).

In caregiving after prolonged loss, a number of issues may emerge that may complicate a survivor's attempt to deal with the grieving process.

- Survivors may need to review the caregiving experiences, addressing the times they felt positive about, the times that concerned them, and the lessons they learned from the process. For some, journaling may be an effective way to gain perspective on the experience.

- Survivors may need to review the illness, focusing once again on treatment decisions. Opportunities to review those decisions with medical personnel may help reassure them that choices made, given an appreciation of context and information they knew at that time, were appropriate.

- Survivors will often struggle with memory. The later experiences of caregiving and illness can overwhelm other more pleasant memories. It may be helpful for survivors, when they are ready, to review photographs or videos of the deceased as a way to regain earlier images and recollect other experiences.

- In some situations, especially those where the caregiving role was all-absorbing, survivors may need to re-establish and develop identity. Redefining oneself as something other than a caregiver and finding new meaning in life may take time and considerable reflection.

Professional Caregivers and Grief

As noted throughout this chapter, as well as in other chapters in this book, professional caregivers will need to confront their own grief. Both Vachon (1987) and Papadatou (2000) found that both environmental and individual factors influence adjustment to the effects of cumulative losses, mitigating compassion fatigue. Individuals benefited from effective lifestyle management. Their grief, too, was facilitated by their ability to validate their own grief and to find their own spiritual center. But environmental factors also were critical. Professional caregivers benefited when organizations acknowledged and supported their grief in such ways as offering grief education, support groups, effective and caring supervision, and rituals in which they could acknowledge their loss.

Conclusion

Grief is a constant companion to the caregiving experience, one that affects everyone involved. That grief cannot be minimized. Effective interventions, however, have a critical role in making the experience of grief understandable and shared. That illumination and support is the gift that can be offered to caregivers. Perhaps it will be enough.

Kenneth J. Doka, PhD, Mdiv, is Senior Consultant to Hospice Foundation of America and a professor of gerontology at the College of New Rochelle in New York. He is an ordained Lutheran minister and a former president of the Association for Death Education and Counseling (ADEC) and recipient of ADEC's 1998 Death Educator Award. He is former Chairperson of the International Work Group on Death, Dying, and Bereavement. Dr. Doka has been a panelist on Hospice Foundation of America's National Bereavement Teleconference since 1995. Dr. Doka serves as editor of Omega *as well as* Journeys, *a newsletter for the bereaved published by Hospice Foundation of America. He is the author of numerous books as well as over 60 published articles and chapters.*

Voices

The Wife:
Seven Months Later

Lynda Zycherman

*T*hey said then and they say now: "You were a good wife to him, during the marriage and during the final crisis—such strength, such fortitude. He was in the SICU for three weeks and you were with him, all of the day and part of the night. At the dinner hour, you carefully told the kids just enough. Not all of it, because they are so scared, but enough of the reality; after all, they're 16 and 18, practically adults, almost ready to leave the nest anyway." Yes, a brave and competent woman.

But later, after he's gone and the fleeting relief of the finality of his death has also come and gone, guilt joins up with grief and begins to lap at my confidence. Could they all be wrong? Did I fool them all and myself as well? Does no one recognize my massive, irreversible failure? I got sick. Three days at home with fever, antibiotics, and bed rest. The family said to me and I agreed, "You couldn't/shouldn't go in—you might infect the patient with more than he's already got. You need to conserve your strength."

Here is the worst part and the best. When I recovered and finally went in, there was the broadest, most joyous grin on his face, such as I had never seen. His head and eyes followed me as I moved around the room. I asked him, "Why are you grinning like that?" He mouthed, "I am so glad you've come back." I was deeply happy to be so loved and, at the same time, furious with myself for losing even one second of togetherness.

And, in my two- or three-day absence (who remembers details now?) the downward spiral had begun.

My brain says, "It's not your fault, anyone can get sick, there are all these pathogens flying around the SICU and you were run down." The heart says, translating from the universal language of guilt, "You let him down. You should have been there for him. When you didn't come, his fear and loneliness allowed another, more dreadful visitor to enter." Irrationally, I think that by my will alone I could have pulled him through, or forced him to get better.

I tell myself that it was just a few days out of 23 years and after all, anyone can get sick. But I don't believe it yet.

In Memory of:
Joseph Zycherman
May 21, 1947–January 12, 2000

10

Providing Spiritual Support to Family Caregivers

Reverend George Blackwell & Rabbi Harold Stern

Reverend George Blackwell:

Whether or not a person is religious, all people have some sense of their own spirituality, and no life-affirming event brings this to light more than the end-of-life experience. We see this frequently in a hospital setting where patients may designate that they have no religious affiliation, yet when we get to know them we find that they are nevertheless people of faith. Death brings us face to face with our limitations as mortals and with the part of our existence over which we have no control. No matter which of the many ways we express our spirituality or religious beliefs, we are all searching for meaning; therefore, it is almost always possible to connect with patients and caregivers on a spiritual plane, whether or not it is discernible at first glance.

In providing spiritual support to families as they journey through a time of illness, death, and bereavement, it is helpful to have an appreciation for the basic properties of spirituality. While faith is usually understood as trust or belief in something or some-one, it does not require a formal system of practice or even a super-natural personage. Everyone has faith, but not everyone has faith in the same things or for the same reasons. It is our role and our challenge to meet people where they are. My grandfather taught me that powerful lesson when I was a young man. He was a deacon in his church, and I had a pretty lofty impression of what it meant to be a deacon, because my grandfather was a man who worked hard, loved the church, and lived and prayed faithfully. So you can imagine my self-righteous indignation when, during a hospital visit to my grandmother, one of the other deacons showed up with alcohol on his breath. After he left, I asked my grandfather, "How could a deacon drink liquor?" and I will never forget his response: "Sometimes a man feels he must put his faith in a medicine that someone else doesn't have to. If that's the man's medicine, leave him to it." The point here is that faith in a doctor, a drug, or even in oneself may not be spiritual faith, but there is value in learning to respect whatever it is a person chooses to put faith in. It is all too often our nature, as humans, to be judgmental of others people's choices and paths.

As caregivers we must always be vigilant in ensuring that our religious framework is helpful and not harmful to those we are supporting. To really 'be with' someone exactly where they are, even when we don't agree with it, is one of the greatest gifts we can give. While we each have to do this in a way that's authentic for us, I have found six courses of action to be useful in this area.

The first is validating your *own* expression of spirituality, realizing it may well be different from those you care for. By doing so you will come to recognize that your own spiritual voice will lend itself to the experience of illness and dying by helping you to connect on a meaningful level with other spiritual voices. Own your spirituality first and then lovingly raise the spiritual question with those you are caring for by asking (not necessarily in these exact words), "Where are you?" Remember, you can't help them if you can't find them, and you won't find them if you are not certain of your own spirituality, and, then, willing to touch theirs. Often, your own spirituality is the vehicle that transports you onto that common plane. This is true for both the givers and receivers of care. Seeing that a connection is made between you and the family caregivers validates your experience of this process because through that you are saying, "I am strong enough to walk with you through the valley of the shadow of death."

Second, meeting them where they are means accepting that they feel what they feel, no matter how irrational others perceive it to be. Once we can accept that, they can stop trying to convince us and can go about the business of understanding what is behind their feelings. We will gain their trust, and they will gain a worthy companion for their journey.

In the third course of action, we must commit ourselves to engaging in validation. How does one validate the experience of dying and death? By committing to it fully. If you're gonna go, then go boldly! For example, when you shake hands with someone who gives you only their fingertips in a weak fishtail sort of shake, it can give the impression that they don't want to shake hands. It makes you wish they hadn't put their hand out to you at all! Still, there are people who grasp your hand fully, with strength and enthusiasm. You can feel them transmitting genuine regard and concern. Well, people can feel when you are really 'with' them in the experience of illness and dying and when you are not. If you're not going to commit to the process, you're not going to connect with the very ones you propose to care for, and that makes it uncomfortable for you *and* for them.

I remember being with a particular family as their loved one was dying and looking for a way into their time of suffering. They gingerly and with reservation expressed feeling disappointed with God, but were obviously exercising restraint. I felt strongly that they needed permission to be angry with God, so, softly but clearly, I said to those gathered in the room, "You know, there's nothing more disconcerting than the thought that God has abandoned you or someone you love. Not everyone will be angry with God, but everyone ought to know that God cares enough to expect that we may be angry with Him, and that's all right." In saying that, I committed myself to their experience. By affirming their anger, they were empowered to speak openly about the hurt, pain, sorrow, loss, and, yes, anger.

A fourth course of action is to "show up and shut up." One of the pitfalls of caring for others is our need to resolve problems or fix the hurt. In doing so, we may not only contribute to others' fear and weakness, we may also allow them to be a drain on our own spiritual strength. It is not always necessary to give advice or tell stories. And every question does not require an answer. Don't be afraid of silence. A serene and caring presence is more healing than words. Think of yourself as a conduit through which God has chosen to be present. It is a humbling experience, when we can be still and know that God is present.

One of the benefits of modeling this approach to caregiving is that family caregivers often begin to see the enormous value of their own 'mere' presence. Recognizing this can liberate them from feeling they must 'do more, fix things, make it better.' They can truly be with their loved one in a spiritual sense, reclaiming the precious gifts of love and peace.

Fifth, pay attention to personal boundaries. As the Serenity Prayer admonishes, we must seek the wisdom to know the difference between those things we can change and those we can't. Many professional caregivers damage their spiritual health by crossing over and extending themselves beyond what is productive and healthy for their own spiritual well-being. Surely there will be people who are in such a deep, dark place that they are actually beyond your reach. To pursue them is to ask for trouble. I have seen far too many professional caregivers give up because they venture too far out in deep water and have trouble getting back to dry land. They begin to feel overwhelmed and ineffective, and, of course, one of our primary needs as caregivers is to feel helpful and effective. So we must protect our own spiritual and mental well-being. It's not healthy to give everything we have. Unlike the

Apostle Paul, we need not be "made all things to all people, so that by all means we might save some" (I Corinthians 9:22). It is a caregiver's nature to think of others first, but if we don't restore and replenish ourselves, we are susceptible to feelings of hurt, anger, guilt, fear, pain, and powerlessness. We may begin to feel responsible for the well-being of those in our care, and blame ourselves for their decline. That is when we know our own spiritual strength is being depleted, and by depleting our reservoir we not only become ineffective, we harm ourselves.

Which brings us to the sixth course of action—to recognize the importance of maintaining our own spiritual optimism, even in the face of chronic sorrow. While God is present with us in a time of suffering, God is not the author of suffering. Our spiritual practices, whatever they may be, are the mechanism for our continued strength, serenity, and resilience. Each of us knows that place where we meet God. We must go there regularly and often if we are to be of service to those in their darkest hour. For they will benefit most from the 'peace that passes understanding,' the peace that comes *through* us but not *from* us.

Rabbi Harold Stern:

The current rebirth of spirituality, which addresses core values of meaning, purpose, and personhood, has application to end-of-life care issues. Our extended longevity has resulted in longer periods of illness and therefore presents us with both the blessing of time and the challenge of viewing the experience with a spiritual lens, even as the practical demands of care may be overwhelming. We as spiritual caregivers are challenged to journey with these individuals. Our 'mere' presence sends the important and unmistakable message that they are not abandoned by society or by God.

The Role of Faith

The construction of meaning and the community of others who share that meaning can be enormously helpful. It is well-documented that the celebration of faith—through adherence to religious dogma or by non-traditional expressions of spirituality in the cosmos, in Nature or in one's support system of family and caregivers—has a positive effect on individuals struggling with their own or a loved one's life-threatening illness. In his book *Timeless Healing* (1996), Herbert Benson, professor of medicine at Harvard Medical School, cites research showing that faith in an eternal or life-transcending force is supremely soothing to the body and the mind. He quotes Anne Frank's diary (1952), in which she wrote, "He who has courage and faith will never perish in misery."

People leading good and decent lives who are afflicted, or whose loved one is afflicted, with catastrophic illness often ask, 'Why is this happening to me now?" They struggle to find meaning in the experience. And in spite of the fact that death comes to all of us, many individuals in Western culture tend to view this experience, and themselves, as abnormal.

While individual and cultural differences influence pain management and treatment decisions, we can all learn to advocate for what feels appropriate to patients and their families within their cultural and religious context (Congress, 1999). Health care professionals should not only be receptive to making referrals to pastoral care, they should also be open to talking with clients about their spiritual beliefs. And we should avoid interpreting all behavior as stemming from the patient's terminal illness.

Perhaps the most important message of this chapter is that one does not have to be a clergy person to offer spiritual solace to another who is suffering. Anyone who has worked in end-of-life care for any length of time has heard countless patients and family caregivers express that they found profound solace from the caring presence of health care professionals of various disciplines. Patient and family testimonials to care-team members reinforce the fact that often the most profound impact of these professionals was not medical intervention but their presence and humanity in the face of suffering. This understanding of the ministry of presence can be a liberating and empowering concept for professional caregivers of all disciplines and for anyone who wishes to offer comfort to people experiencing life's darkest moments.

Sometimes the best spiritual care comes from people with no pastoral training at all. I have seen nurses, nursing assistants, and housekeeping staff provide meaningful spiritual care to dying people and their loved ones. Eileen Chichin (1999) relates the story of a CNA in a nursing home who cared for a dying resident: "I knew she was dying. I'm from a different religion—I'm Hindu and she was Catholic. But I just took her hand and sat with her and I said, 'I know you are very tired now. It's okay for you to go. I will stay and hold your hand.' And then she died."

Suffering

Can we moderns envision a merciful God who allows suffering to occur? Can we be comfortable in the presence of terminal patients and their loved ones who may interpret pain and suffering as expiation for misdeeds and transgressions? During my Clinical Pastoral Education at a hospital I encountered a Catholic bishop who, though he was in great pain, refused pain medication. When the nurses prevailed upon him to take his medications, he responded that the redemptive value of suffering was a desirable theological commodity. He likened his situation to Jesus' offering up his suffering for the benefit of his flock. Frustrated with her failure to persuade him, the nurse manager, an observant Catholic herself, implored the archbishop to prevail upon the bishop to take his pain medication. The archbishop admonished the bishop, telling him that he was "not up for beatification any time soon." The bishop dutifully complied with the prescribed pain regimen.

The Judeo-Christian tradition has language that supports the redemptive qualities of pain and suffering, while simultaneously validating the sacredness of life. Judaism affirms the utilization of pain management, even when the effort to manage intractable pain may result in the patient's death. Eastern religious systems speak of the transmigration of the soul to other life forms, which may have implications supporting this redemptive, or supernal, nature of physical pain and the psychic torment known as suffering.

The Talmud cites Rabbi Eleazar, who was afflicted with a degenerative and painful ailment. He was visited by Rabbi Johanan, who asked him, "Are your sufferings welcome to you?" (i.e., Do you derive spiritual reward by virtue of the redemptive value of suffering?). Rabbi Eleazar replied, "Neither they [the sufferings] nor their rewards [spiritual growth]." Rabbi Johanan said, "Give me your hand," and he took his hand and raised him up, because, the Torah tells us, "The prisoner cannot free himself" (Babylonian Talmud, Berakhot 5b). This is a powerful insight into the experience of the dying. The terminally ill person and her loved ones may view illness as a prison from which there is no escape. Just as Rabbi Johanan reached out his hand and lifted up Rabbi Eleazar, so may we help 'free' people from their psychic suffering through the intervention of empathic caregiving—through caring presence and a hands-on approach that includes touch and 'co-weeping.'

Making Decisions at the End of Life

Religious interpretation impacts on medical decision making along the continuum of care, including prolonging life or prolonging pain and suffering. No health care or psycho-social clinician should be expected to be an encyclopedia of knowledge regarding the position of every religion on these important issues, but we must all be willing to ask honest questions. We also need to know where to find resources for this information. There are many excellent overviews of the practical application of religious dogma to everyday medical reality.

Both Christianity and Judaism sanctify every moment of life as a precious gift from the Divine. Therefore, is it ever permissible to cease treatment and pave the way for death? Rabbinical literature (Midrash to Numbers Rabba 22:2) records a concern for psychological suffering. A very old woman came to Rabbi Yose ben

Halafta complaining that her life held no meaning. She had lost her appetite and desire to live and wanted to die. He asked her, "How did you reach such a ripe old age?" She replied, "I attend synagogue every morning and allow nothing to interfere with that sacred duty." Rabbi Yose instructed her not to attend synagogue for three days. She consented, and on the third day she became ill and died. Parallel Talmudic texts support this position of withdrawing whatever elements sustain life beyond meaning.

Other faith communities delegate decisions related to withdrawal of life-sustaining support to 'formation of individual conscience,' allowing an individual to make personal decisions based on his internal moral compass. Protestant theology would support the notion that, when faced with morally tinged questions regarding medical care, the affected individual, rather than a clergy person, is the preferred decision maker. Hinduism and Zen Buddhism also support similar notions based on their respective, albeit different, theological foundations.

The Value of Prayer

Many clinicians in Western medical practice view prayer as taboo and thus deny a powerful tool with which to help effect healing for their patients. Only clergy or clinical chaplaincy staff are granted societal permission to invoke the healing tonic of prayer with patients. Fortunately, the resurgence of spirituality into everyday life has begun to change the negative value associated with invoking ancient prayer in the contemporary health care setting. A number of physicians and health care professionals, especially those associated with hospice teams and palliative care, have begun to break the 'stained-glass ceiling' that relegates prayer and spiritual expression to the four corners of the chapel, church, or synagogue. There is great value in having caregivers in every discipline feel comfortable with various forms of prayer—both traditional and spontaneous—in the service of meeting the holistic needs of the suffering individual and loved ones. Whereas prayer cannot 'fix' the stressor, it can validate the feelings of patients and family in a comfortable and familiar manner. Steeped in ritual, prayer often offers a safe and comforting port for individuals who may have journeyed away from ritual observances.

An appropriate expression of prayer may well inform the compassionate caregiver's ability to help patients and caregivers open new vistas of healing. We must learn to utilize our rituals and faith communities to access these gifts. Rev. Ken Doka has stated that "rituals . . . empower families and can be powerful reminders of how we are connected in relationship. Nostalgic experiences, role models, and sacred stories within religious traditions often achieve far-reaching results that cannot be realized utilizing traditional medical protocols" (Doka, 1997).

Faith Community and Personhood

In his book *Asylums* (1972), Erving Goffman describes the devastating depersonalizing effect of institutionalization and illness on the individual. He describes how a patient, whom he defines by the Latin root *patiens*, 'one who suffers,' is stripped of his identity and denuded of personal effects and dignity. Goffman tells of a female patient who used a pillowcase in lieu of a handbag to store personal items that helped define her personhood.

A friend tells the story of visiting her mother, who was in the throes of advanced Alzheimer's, in a nursing home. The mother had long since failed to recognize her daughter and could no longer express coherent thoughts, but as they sat together, she looked around in bewilderment and said, "I've lost. . . I've lost . . . ." The daughter asked, "What have you lost, Mother?" And her mother looked her directly in the eye and said, with heart-rending clarity, "Well, just about everything."

In the throes of a life-threatening disease process, both patient and caregiver often feel isolated from, perhaps even rejected by, their community, increasing their experience of suffering. The advent of spiritually-based communal groups that seek the company of the patient *qua congregant* or 'fellow sojourner' reconnects the individual to her personhood, often lost and denuded in the process of becoming a patient. The Bikur Cholim group in Jewish practice, as well as the congregation of Friends in Quaker practice, provide countervailing influence to this diminishment of personhood. Their intervention begins the process of reinstating the 'non-contributing patient' to the status of 'contributing member of society.' In Jewish tradition, the imperative to engage in Bikur Cholim activity is an example of *Imatio Dei* (imitating God's) behavior, a practice found in many religious traditions. The Talmud, for example, exhorts that, as God is merciful, people should model the Divine paradigm.

Upon hearing of a parishioner's terminal diagnosis, a priest rushed to be with her and her husband. The husband's first words to the priest were, "Father, why has God forsaken us?" and the priest replied, "He hasn't forsaken you. He sent me here to be with you."

The Final Days

The actively dying person may consciously withdraw from life-affirming behaviors physiologically, cognitively, and spiritually. At this point an important aspect of providing spiritual support to family caregivers is to offer comforting interpretations of this phenomenon, offering them the language with which to relate it to life's continuum. We can help families understand that this is a normal experience. Some have identified the intuitive experience of the actively dying individual as 'travelling.' We can facilitate open discussions regarding funeral planning and unfinished business, such as "I love you, I'm sorry about . . . I will always treasure . . . ." We must not, however, always expect these eleventh-hour reconciliations to bring resolution to what I sometimes refer to as "the Samsonite collection" of family dysfunction and dynamics.

As companions along the way, we can encourage family members to continue their established relationships. In response to the question, "What should we do in the final hours and moments?" Ken Doka responds, "Too often we think of the dying person as a different person. Do what you have always done" (1997).

Here again, rituals can play a powerful role. Recitation of the Sacrament of the Sick in Catholicism, of the Proclamation of One God in Islam, and of the Viduy confessional prayer in Jewish practice can serve as an expression of forgiveness and affirmation of faith as signifying much as acceptance of the finality of death and the preparedness of the patient to move on to a different form of existence.

Rabbi Maurice Lamm (1984) tells the story of two Chinese sisters whose father was dying. A nurse urged them to put their father into a hospital. "We'll give him his pills and his injections. We'll keep him comfortable and clean. We'll turn him and prevent bedsores." The Chinese sisters discussed the proposition and concluded, "No, he'll not go to the hospital." The nurse said, "But we'll give him everything!" The sisters replied, "Who will give him love?" At a time of terminal illness, the family must demonstrably give love, and the giving may exalt love to a level hitherto unimagined. Death ends a life, not a relationship. Let us strive to value our relationships at all levels of presence.

Editor:

Both authors have addressed the importance of creating a safe environment for the patient and caregiver to tell their stories in order to address the meaning of their life and the dying experience. One of the characters in Barry Lopez's tale *Crow and Weasel* (1990) explains the power of story this way: "The stories people tell have a way of taking care of them. If stories come to you, care for them. And learn to give them away where they are needed. Sometimes a person needs a story more than food to stay alive. That is why we put these stories in each other's memory. This is how people care for themselves."

So how do we use patients' and caregivers' stories in order to assess their spiritual needs and provide the best possible spiritual support? There are a number of tools for assessing spirituality at the end of life. Maugans (1996) suggests the acronym SPIRIT as one tool to help professional caregivers:

Spiritual belief system (formal dimensions, often overtly religious)

Personal spirituality (informal dimensions, often very personal and individualized)

Integration and involvement in a spiritual community (supportive environment)

Ritualized practices and restrictions (personally meaningful activities, including dietary/treatment restrictions)

Implications for medical care

Terminal events planning (advance directives, funeral arrangements, etc.).

Listening to the patient's and caregiver's stories in terms of these six areas will help us meet them where they are. Both Rev. Blackwell and Rabbi Stern have stressed the importance of listening carefully to the language people use in describing their spirituality and then responding with compatible language in order to create a comfortable atmosphere. If, on occasion, we feel we cannot do that, we should attempt to find another spiritual care provider who is more comfortable with the patient's and caregiver's language of faith. According to Lewis and Butler (1974), most people have the capacity to reconcile their lives, to confront real guilt, and to find meaning, especially in the presence of acceptance and support from others. It is the role of all caregivers to create a safe place for them to do so.

Reverend George Blackwell, DMin, is a certified chaplain who provides spiritual and bereavement support at University Hospital in Newark, NJ. He is also the pastor of the Good Neighbor Baptist Church in Newark.

Rabbi Harold Stern, a certified chaplain and pastoral counselor, has provided spiritual care in nursing homes and hospices in New York City for over fifteen years. He is currently the Spiritual Care Coordinator at Hospice of New York.

11

The Reciprocal Suffering of Caregivers

Deborah Sherman

Family caregivers are often the continuous companions of individuals with life-threatening, progressive illness from the first symptoms until the time of death. The individual's illness alters the family member's world, as they become involved and committed to the care of the patient, both at home and in institutions (Andershed & Ternestedt, 1998). Like patients with a terminal illness, family members are in transition from living with the disease to anticipating the death of their loved one from the disease (Davies, Reimer, & Marten, 1994). In witnessing the patient's pain and suffering, family caregivers may experience a sense of powerlessness, and are often frightened and confused by the dramatic physical and emotional changes they perceive in their loved one as the disease progresses (Loscalzo & Zabora, 1998). Despite the acuity of the patient's condition, current changes in the health care system frequently mandate the early discharge of patients from hospital to home, with the expectation that family members will accept the physical and emotional responsibility of being the patient's direct care provider. However, most family members are unprepared to deal with the physical and emotional needs of their loved ones and the intense demands inherent to the caregiver role.

For both patients and family caregivers, suffering becomes an innate component of incurable, progressive illness, as they experience or witness the struggle with discomfort and disability, and contemplate the impending loss of all they have been and all they imagined they could be (Byock, 1997). Chapman and Gavrin (1993) characterize suffering as the perceived physical and psychological threat to the integrity of self, negative affective quality, sense of perceived helplessness, and perceived loss. Suffering, in the form of physical, emotional, social, and spiritual distress, becomes a reciprocal experience of family caregivers as they attempt to meet the dying patient's needs and anticipate their own loss and sorrow. During this life experience, the family alternates between two roles, that of caregiver/worker and that of patient, being both givers and takers of care (Andershed & Ternestedt, 1999).

Health care professionals are now realizing that family caregivers are indeed "second order patients" who are in need of care and support (Lederberg, 1998). Furthermore, as the patient's illness progresses, the family's needs intensify and change. There is the potential that both the patient and family caregiver will experience a significant compromise in the quality of their lives. Given that the 'unit of care' is the patient and family, hospice and palliative care offer a support system not only to help patients live as actively as possible until death, but also to help the family cope during the patient's illness and in their own bereavement (Bone, 1995). This chapter will focus on the reciprocal suffering of caregivers and the opportunities for health care professionals to improve family caregivers' quality of life through hospice and palliative care.

The Suffering of Caregivers

When individuals are seriously ill and dying, their primary source of physical and emotional support is often their family. However, there has been recent recognition of the intimate reciprocity of suffering by patients and families experiencing terminal illness, as the suffering of one amplifies the distress of the other (Foley, 1995). Although family members express the rewards of caring for terminally ill relatives, there may be major psycho-social and physical effects experienced by caregivers, including heightened symptoms of depression, anxiety, psychosomatic symptoms, restriction of roles and activities, strain in relationships, and poor physical health (Higginson, 1998).

As a result of the illness, both patients and their family caregivers experience multiple aspects of loss and face major changes in their lives that necessitate both internal and external adjustments in coping. Family caregivers may refuse to leave the patient's side for even a moment, for fear that their loved one may die in their absence. As a result, caregivers often have a strong compulsion to attend to the patient's every need with disregard for their own needs (Klein, 1998). Yet if they do tend to their own needs, they are often wrought with a sense of guilt regarding their own health and their desire to live life (Loscalzo & Zabora, 1998).

Family caregivers may also experience stress from having strangers in their home, as well as from the physical changes to the home to accommodate the patient's needs. When forced to modify their work schedule or to leave their jobs, the time away from work and friends exacerbates their sense of isolation and burden of caregiving. The quality of the caregiver's life is therefore negatively affected by the overall disruptions in his social life, the loss of social mobility, as well as by potential social isolation, and even abandonment by friends (Lederberg, 1998). It is not unusual that these stressors result in feelings of anger and resentment, as well as an increase in the caregiver's own needs because of heightened psychological distress.

When anticipating the death of a family member, caregivers often spend considerable time reviewing painful aspects of the past, with feelings of regret for disagreements, conflicts, or failures and a wish that relationships with the patient and with other family members were somehow different. With each family member's unique experience of stress, families may find it difficult to pull together to effectively cope with the imposed life changes. In families where communication is indirect, little agreement about the nature of the problem may exist. Roles may be rigidly entrenched, resulting in conflict with regard to the delegation of the role responsibilities formerly assumed by the ill family member. The dynamics of families in times of crisis may exacerbate a lack of tolerance for differences in opinion. Additional conflict may also occur when family members differ in their preferences for the location of care. Certain family members may prefer to care for their relative at home, while others may be reluctant or refuse to provide such care, given their perceived limitations in coping with the physical and emotional stress, and the fears related to such a responsibility. And these conflicts may bring up other, earlier family conflicts.

In a study of spouses of patients with cancer, Beeney, Butow, and Dunn (1997) reported heightened psychological distress due to many conflicting emotions, including conflict among feelings of loss, sadness and guilt, difficulty in knowing how to talk with the person who has cancer, worry about the possibility of death, as well as the task of adjusting to the bodily changes of their partner. The study participants also expressed that health care professionals often placed additional pressure on them to be strong and supportive to the patient, with the expectation that they assume the caregiving role.

Such expectations can be extremely unrealistic given evidence that the level of distress for spouses becomes at least as severe as that of the cancer patient as the disease progresses (Hoskins et al., 1996; Kaye & Gracely, 1993; Omne-Poten, Holmberg, Bergstrom, Sjoden, & Burns, 1993). Based on a sample of 77 adults with terminal cancer and their relatives, Hinton (1994) found that relatives suffered their own grief, strain, and ill health, with serious depression and anxiety in the later stages of illness.

Through a descriptive study of 50 patients and caregivers in a hospice program, Hays (1986) also reported an increase in family caregiver's anxiety and fatigue in response to uncontrolled patient symptoms in the last 10 days before the patient's death.

Based on a longitudinal study, reciprocity of suffering was also noted by Ell, Nishimot, Mantell, and Hamovitch (1998), who reported that caregivers of terminally ill family members experienced distress one year after diagnosis with 30% reporting a decline in their mental health. Hodgson, Higginson, McDonnell, and Butters (1997) further found that 32% of caregivers experienced severe anxiety at the time of referral to home care for their terminally ill family member and that 26% remained severely anxious during the last week of life. Indeed, such results indicate that caregiver distress is heightened along the illness/dying trajectory and that caregiver support is essential to their adjustment and their future health.

Furthermore, while attempting to meet the increased emotional needs of other family members and performing standard family functions, family caregivers must also adapt to changes in family roles and responsibilities by filling in for or delegating the role and responsibilities of the ill family member (Doyle, 1994). Blanchard, Albrecht, and Ruckdeschel (1997) noted that cancer causes changes in the family's identity, roles, and daily functioning, with 20 to 30% of partners suffering from psychological impairment and mood disturbance as a result of a spouse's cancer.

As key providers of patient care, family members also have informational needs as they address the ongoing, intimate daily needs of the patient and participate in decision making. Twenty-five percent of caregivers lose their job due to caregiver responsibilities, and nearly one third of families lose their major source of income or their savings (Lederberg, 1998). A national population-based investigation of people who die from cancer found that 81% of the sample were cared for by relatives and that more than half of the relatives were unable to obtain the information they wanted from physicians regarding diagnosis, prognosis, and plan of care. Furthermore, over 25% of relatives reported the need for greater financial support, as well as help with domestic chores (Addington-Hall & McCarthy, 1995).

In a recent study of terminally ill patients and family caregivers, Emanuel et al. (1999) reported that 87% of patients required help, specifically with transportation (62%), homemaking services (55%), nursing care (28%), and personal care (26%). The majority of patients (52%) were women over the age of 65, and the majority of caregivers (71%) were women. Most patients relied completely on family members and friends for assistance, with only 15% relying on paid help and fewer than 3% receiving help from volunteers. Concern was expressed that women are called upon to provide care for the dying, but when they themselves are dying they must rely to a greater extent on paid help. The implications of this study centered on the need to recognize the stress imposed on family caregivers and the importance of increasing family caregiver support.

Through qualitative inquiry, Andershed and Ternestedt (1999) have provided insight into the involvement of relatives in the care of the dying. The themes that revealed the nature of family caregiver involvement included: *to know, to be,* and *to do. To know* captured the relatives' endeavors to increase their understanding of the patient's situation, seeking knowledge of the patient's diagnosis, how ill the patient was, how the patient viewed his/her illness, and what assistance would be needed by the staff and family caregivers. The theme *to be* reflected the importance of relatives' being physically present with the patient, as well as showing an interest in and openness to the deeper level of the patient's world. For example, finding out what was important to the patient, and supporting the patient's wishes and preferences. The theme *to do* involved caregiving actions, such as offering physical care and providing support by being the patient's spokesperson. It was concluded that health care professionals must guide the relatives on the patient's final journey, by knowing what the family and the patient want and can do.

The experience of transitions in families and ways of coping

By documenting the experience of transition in families with terminal illness, as well as their ways of coping, Davies, Reimer, Brown, and Marten (1995) have provided insight into what patients and families want and can do. Within the context of advanced illness, the transition begins when family members make significant attempts to redefine their life situation in terms of how they view themselves, the patient, and each other. Although both family caregivers and patients may acknowledge the extra responsibilities and burdens of care, there is often a mutual offering of support and reassurance to alleviate the sadness and depression that may accompany role changes.

Contending with change also includes attaining or maintaining meaningful relationships, as both patients and family members recognize the limited time they have together and grieve the loss of their social connections with others. Like the patient, family members struggle with the paradox of living with and dying from the illness, with the conflicting desire to fight and keep going versus the desire to give up. In their search for meaning, patients and families affirm spiritual values, change life priorities, and examine how the experience of illness has contributed to their personal growth. Importantly, like their dying loved one, they live day to day to make the most of the present as they prepare for death on practical, cognitive, and emotional levels.

In their work with family caregivers of patients with end-stage dementia, Szabo and Strang (1999) also recognized the caregivers' need to maintain a sense of control. Through qualitative interviews, caregivers revealed the importance of being able to articulate confidently their ability to anticipate and solve problems. Control was maintained by reflecting on their positive internal resources with open acknowledgement of their caregiving abilities.

Caregivers emphasized the importance of knowing when they needed help, asking for it, and taking corrective action when they began to lose control within caregiving situations. Amid such life transitions as the dying and death of a family member, an understanding of how caregivers maintain control, lose control, and regain control can be valuable in the provision of supportive care, thereby promoting their quality of life.

The effect of suffering on caregivers' quality of life

Although the quality of life of patients and families is important across all stages of the illness trajectory, it becomes extremely important during the final phases of an illness (Cella, 1992; Finlay & Dunlop, 1994). From the patient's perspective, quality of life is described based on the impact of sickness and health care on a person's daily activities and sense of well-being (Ragsdale, Kotarba, & Morrow, 1992). Most often it is the individual's subjective evaluation of his life experiences and ability to control all aspects of his life and illness that relates to the perception of the quality of life (Hanestad, 1990). Researchers are now focusing not only on the global perception of an individual's quality of life, but also on the measurement of the dimensions of quality of life that include physical well-being, emotional well-being, social well-being, health and functioning, spirituality, and treatment satisfaction (Aarson, 1990; Cella & Tulsky, 1990; Ferrans & Powers, 1995). Finlay and Dunlop (1994) also believe that, in addition to these dimensions of quality of life, both the financial burden on family caregivers and grief and bereavement issues should also be examined.

Research indicates that physical, emotional, social, and spiritual concerns are experienced by patients and their family caregivers, particularly as illness progresses, and that, furthermore, these concerns may adversely effect the quality of their lives. Based on a study of 50 patient-caregiver dyads in the terminal phase of illness, Kruse (1995) found that patients' and caregivers' coping with the end stage of life was significantly related. Other researchers report that the quality of life of family members revolves around meeting the patient's needs (Kristjanson, 1989), and that terminal illness often has extremely deleterious effects not only on the patients' but also on the family caregivers' quality of life (Smeenk et al., 1998).

In a study of family members of patients during the terminal phase of illness, Kristjanson, Sloan, Dudgeon, & Adaskin (1996) concluded that patients' quality of life was moderately correlated with family members' health during the palliative-care phase ($r = -0.38$, $p < 0.05$). Furthermore, family members' scores on the health index (symptoms of stress scale) were significantly lower than normative scores based on a healthy population.

Miaskowski, Zimmer, Barrett, Dibble, & Wallhagen (1997) also found that differences in the perception of pain between patients and their family caregivers were associated with harmful outcomes for both. Based on a sample of 78 patient-caregiver dyads, it was reported that in non-congruent dyads with regard to pain perception, caregivers had significantly higher caregiver strain and patients reported significantly more mood disturbance and lower quality of life than in dyads reporting congruence in pain perception.

Weitnzer, McMillan, and Jacobsen (1999) found that the quality of life of family caregivers of patients receiving palliative care (n = 134) was significantly lower than for those receiving curative care (n = 267). This finding supported the prediction that as the patients enter the final stages of life, represented by receiving palliative rather than curative care, the patient's physical and emotional burden lowers the caregiver's quality of life.

A study of the quality of life and coping of patients with gynecologic cancer (n = 40) and their spouses also confirmed that patients and spouses recorded similar responses with regard to overall quality of life and its domains, and that the family domain was the most important domain in both groups (Zacharias, Gilg, & Foxall, 1994).

The quality of life and level of subjective burden on family caregivers of patients with end-stage renal disease was examined by Wicks, Milstead, Hathaway, and Cetingok (1997). Based on a sample of 96 caregivers and their relatives, it was reported that caregiver quality of life was related to caregiver burden ($r = -0.40$, $p < .0001$), and caregiver self-rated health ($r = 0.67$, $p < .0001$). From the above research findings, health care professionals have come to understand the vulnerability and risks to the health and quality of life of patients and family caregivers experiencing life-threatening illness, as well as the need for caregiver assessment across the illness/dying continuum and into the bereavement period.

Family Caregiver Assessment

In improving the quality of life for patients and their families, it is suggested that palliative-care clinicians begin with an assessment of who constitutes the family and the dynamics of the family caregiving system (Medalie, 1997). By assessing the family's strengths, weaknesses, opportunities, and threats in dealing with the life-threatening or terminal illness of one of its members, optimal support and care can be offered by the interdisciplinary team to address caregivers' concerns and needs and to promote their caregiving ability.

An important aspect of assessment is the organization and functioning of the family, particularly as it relates to family membership, structure and roles, family cohesion, and decision making processes. When caregiving responsibility is delegated to one member of the family, particular attention must be given to the assessment of the caregiver's state of physical and emotional health by asking the simple question, "How are you feeling and coping?"

Of great importance is the assessment of the family's communication patterns, particularly regarding the openness or closure of communication, directness or indirectness, verbal and non-verbal messages, acceptance or inhibition of the expression of emotion, and validation or dismissal of feelings (Rando, 1984). Clinicians must also learn about the boundaries in communication with regard to ethnic or cultural rules of who interacts or communicates with whom, in what setting, and in what way. The communication in families becomes even more difficult when family members vary in their knowledge and degree of acceptance of the patient's illness (Rando, 1984). As the illness progresses, it is important to gain an understanding of the caregiver's knowledge about the patient's illness, their expectations regarding care, the degree to which they are comfortable in participating in the care, and their level of caregiving knowledge and skill.

Another important assessment parameter is the family life-cycle stage and the developmental tasks of the main family caregiver and each family member. A serious or terminal illness may result in the postponement or cancellation of educational plans, life events such as marriage, or career goals, thereby heightening the caregiver's distress. The level of distress experienced by family members may also be related to the patient's emotional adjustment, gender, age, socioeconomic status, personality, social support, and coping skills, as well as the marital adjustment of the patient and caregiver (Blanchard, Albrecht, & Ruchkdeschel, 1997). These factors are therefore important to consider in the assessment process.

Ethnic, cultural, and spiritual values associated with illness and caregiving are equally important to assess, as is the family's previous experience with illness. Medalie (1997) further suggests assessing family caregivers' willingness to care for the patient and provide emotional support, their own personal needs, their knowledge of community resources, and their willingness to accept external support. The assessment of the physical, emotional, social, and spiritual well-being of family caregivers should continue during the bereavement period to identify those who are at risk for complicated grieving and who need ongoing support.

Improving Caregivers' Quality of Life through Palliative Care

As a philosophy of care, hospice and palliative care provide both active and compassionate therapies intended to comfort and support patients and families who are living with life-threatening illness with the goal of promoting quality of life (Canadian Palliative Care Association, 1995). Both provide support by respecting patients' and caregivers' right to be informed, including timely access to information and services in a language that can be understood; assurance of confidentiality; emphasis on the availability of services 24 hours a day, seven days a week, with the assurance of continuity of care; and a holistic approach to care, which is offered by an interdisciplinary team of health professionals who work collaboratively with the patient and family to meet their physical, emotional, social, and spiritual needs (Ferris et al., 1995). As a dynamic process, palliative care is responsive to the changing needs of patients and their families across the illness continuum until death and, like hospice care, into the bereavement period for caregivers.

Palliative-care interventions that support the patient and family will change as the patient's disease progresses. Helping family caregivers and patients deal with imminent death must involve discussing advance directives and preferences regarding where to die; preparing for death both emotionally and practically (making funeral arrangements); helping families deal with unfinished business and resolving family-patient conflicts; and relieving emotional or spiritual suffering through active listening, meaningful presence, and the teaching of healing strategies such as relaxation, imagery, or meditation.

In palliative care, it is important to respect the family caregiver's knowledge of the patient, including the patient's desires and preferences; and to encourage family caregivers to participate in all aspects of the patient's care. However, it is also important to recognize the stress of being both caregiver (that is, 'pillar of strength') and griever in need of support and to frequently assess the caregiver's well-being, coping abilities, needs, and expectations. The clinician needs to acknowledge the caregiver's efforts and assess her relationship with the patient and other family members, while encouraging the expression of fears, concerns, loss and grief. It is important to put the caregiver in touch with respite services before stress, emotional and physical exhaustion, and depression take their toll.

Within the context of the family as a system, keeping other family members informed of the progression of the patient's illness and providing an opportunity to share information and expectations through periodic family meetings is often appreciated. Family differences regarding values, priorities, and attitudes, which may place the main caregiver in a difficult or confrontational position, may be more objectively discussed in this forum. Family meetings also provide the family and interdisciplinary care team members an opportunity to discuss treatment goals and options, to solve problems, and to identify available resources and support networks. The meetings allow family members a chance to vent, to voice their opinions, discuss feelings and needs, describe related painful past experiences, and discuss changes in role responsibilities and potential role conflicts.

Health care providers may also use this occasion to reinforce the importance of their continued support of the patient and primary family caregiver (Medalie, 1997). Through such open discussions with patients and family members, it is possible that each may come to a new appreciation of their relationship with an expression of care and concern for the other's needs. The intent is that the supportive efforts of the palliative care team or hospice care team may protect both the patient's and family's quality of life as death approaches.

The Importance of What the Family Experiences and Remembers

Dying is "not only what the patient experiences but what the family remembers" (Lynn, Teno, & Phillips, 1997). Berns and Colvin (1998) remind health professionals of the importance of listening to the family caregivers' final story as they recall the death of their loved one. Based on the interviews of 416 family members who were involved with the care of the deceased or involved with decisions about end-of-life treatments, the following themes were identified through their stories:

- Being present or absent at the death of their loved one was a significant memory for survivors;

- Survivors need and expect honest and open communication from a consistent health care provider during the dying process;

- Families want information about the dying process and want to know what to expect;

- Keeping promises and wishes made to the dying person helps families cope with death;

- Giving the patient the permission to die is a powerful directive that families feel should be in their control rather than stated by the health care provider; and

- Families remember the details of events surrounding the death as either peaceful and comfortable or painful and struggling.

The authors conclude that when family members tell the story of the death of their loved one it becomes part of their relationship with that person and helps the caregiver to understand and cope with the loss. The stories told by family caregivers may also change over time, reflecting the development of a new relationship with the deceased, or may indicate the need for bereavement intervention.

McSkimming et al. (1999) studied the needs of family caregivers in caring for their loved one with a life-threatening illness and following the patient's death. Through focus groups involving 67 family caregivers, several major themes were expressed that describe the caregivers' experience and perceptions, and the memories they hold onto. One theme expressed by caregivers was that, "It is my illness, too." This reinforced the reciprocal suffering of caregivers and their belief that the illness was also their own, since the caregiving demands had dramatically affected their lives and relationships. A second theme captured the belief that, "I know my loved one best." Indeed, family caregivers wanted health professionals to recognize their expertise about their loved one's condition and wanted information they provided to be taken seriously in developing the patient's plan of care. The third theme expressed by caregivers was, "I am exhausted," revealing the burden of care, sense of isolation, balancing of multiple roles and responsibilities with insufficient rest, all with a lack of resources to provide temporary relief from caregiving duties. The caregiver's last theme was, "I am afraid of missing the doctor," which captured the family's frustration in wishing to speak with the physician in order to ask important questions and receive current information regarding their family member.

During the bereavement period, family caregivers reflected on the significance of sharing the last few days of life with the patient, viewing it as a special time of intimacy. The caregivers did not appreciate the physicians' emphasis on prognosis, but preferred to receive reassurance of the comfort of the patient and the promotion of his dignity. Caregivers also felt that patient's wishes were often ignored and that this increased and protracted the patient's suffering. As they reflected upon the death of their family member, caregivers wished that they had understood their loved one's last messages. They emphasized how important these last communications were in finding meaning in their loss. Caregivers also explained the importance of health professionals acknowledging their loss and of the importance of hearing "I am sorry," which conveys health professionals' concern and caring. Lastly, the caregivers of this study expressed a strong desire to hear from their family member's physician and caregivers following the death of the patient, which was perceived as a source of support. Caregivers also expressed a sense of comfort when health professionals shared a personal memory of their loved one. This study emphasizes the importance of health care professionals in addressing family caregivers' needs and underscores the potential value of palliative care in providing support in the final stage of life.

Evaluating the Hospice and Palliative Care Offered to Caregivers

As more patients and families receive hospice and palliative care, there is a need to evaluate its effectiveness in promoting both the patients' and family caregiver's quality of life. The value of hospice and palliative care to the quality of life for the terminally ill and their family caregivers has been supported by two studies by McMillan and Mahon (1994a, 1994b). Based on a sample of 31 patient-caregiver dyads, over half the patients reported an increase in their quality of life three weeks after their enrollment in hospice or palliative care, while an even higher percentage of caregivers reported a significant increase in the patient's quality of life. In the second study, based on the 68 adult primary caregivers of 68 patients with cancer, it was found that the caregiver's and patient's quality of life were positively correlated and that the caregiver's quality of life was maintained during the first month of hospice care.

To date, few studies have systematically documented the family's and patient's quality of life and their experience in dealing with a terminal illness, as well as the value of palliative care to patients and family caregivers along the illness trajectory (O'Boyle & Waldron, 1997). Documenting the quality of life experiences of terminally ill patients and their families will enable researchers to compare the relative importance of the various dimensions of quality of life along the illness trajectory; compare alternative approaches to end-of-life care, such as traditional care versus hospice and palliative care; compare outcomes across health care settings, specifically home, inpatient or outpatient hospice and palliative care settings; and compare the impact on quality of life made by different types of health care providers (Stewart, Teno, Patrick, & Lynn, 1998).

Furthermore, most studies that have been done are retrospective, using interviews with family members after the patient's death. Longitudinal, prospective quality-of-life studies are needed, to help providers determine the type and timing of appropriate health care interventions. Given that the patient is central to the family's experience, it is now recognized that both patient and family should be included in the research (Davies, Reimer, & Marten, 1994). Although studies have identified the stress of family caregivers, particularly in caring for a relative with terminal illness, there has also been little or no agreement about the characteristics of caregivers who may benefit from intervention (Meyers, 1997). The assessment of caregivers' functional and emotional status is extremely important, particularly in light of the current restrictions in health care reimbursement for hospitalization and palliative care services for patients with advanced illness, and the imposed expectations on families who may not be physically and emotionally able to handle the responsibility of end-of-life care.

Conclusion

In clinical practice and through research initiatives, health care professionals must continue to focus on ways to best support not only the dying patient, but his family, and to protect the quality of their lives. The suffering of patients and family caregivers can be alleviated through hospice and palliative care. The comfort of family caregivers is achieved when they perceive that all that could be done was done, to achieve a peaceful, dignified death for their family member. The pain experienced by witnessing the suffering and experiencing the loss of their loved one can be relieved when health care professionals acknowledge their reciprocal suffering and respond with sensitivity and compassion. The expectation that family members will give care must be balanced with the understanding that family members also need care to replenish their energy as caregivers and heal their grieving hearts.

Deborah Witt Sherman, PILD, RN, ANP, CS is an assistant professor in the Division of Nursing at New York University where she is the program coordinator of the first nurse practitioner palliative care master's program in the United States. She completed an Aaron Diamond Post-doctoral research fellowship, and is the awardee of the prestigious Project on Death in America Faculty Scholars Fellowship funded by the Soros Foundation. Dr. Sherman has various publications, national and international presentations and awards for excellence in scholarship and leadership. She is a member of the editorial boards of numerous journals and a member of many professional organizations. She serves on the advisory board and as faculty on the End of Life Nursing Education Consortium. and has also served on the New York Academy of Medicine Senior Advisory Board to integrate palliative care into medical school curriculums.

In Memory of:
Lothar Henry Witt
September 24, 1926–October 4, 2000

Family Caregiver Alliance

◆

Why It Works – *From the Editor*

*Often, sharing a personal experience helps others recognize
that they too have similar needs. With vision and commitment,
those needs can be recognized and supported through the work
of grass-roots organizations. Family Caregiver Alliance is an
example of the types of self-help networks that can arise
to meet those needs. Such networks have great value.
They can offer respite and support, share knowledge
and information, allow hope, and validate feelings
and reactions. And they can advocate, turning
individual stories into collective issues.*

––––––––––

In 1977 in San Francisco, Anne Bashkiroff made her
private sorrows public as she spoke about her isolation, loss of
control, and the lack of understanding from the medical and
social service communities as she struggled to care for her
husband with Alzheimer's disease. Many nodded their
agreement and voiced their personal understanding of
the issues of caring for their loved ones with chronic health
conditions. Later, many in the group became founders of

Family Caregiver Alliance (FCA), the first grass-roots organization in the country to recognize and advocate for the needs of family caregivers of adults with cognitive impairments. FCA has had a consistent mission for over 23 years: *to serve as the public voice and to improve the quality of life for family caregivers through services, education, advocacy and research.*

In 1980, Family Caregiver Alliance sponsored landmark legislation that recognized the heroic efforts of families as the primary providers of long-term care and created a program to assist them. From the beginning, FCA saw that families needed emotional support and practical services to enable them to make choices, provide care, and promote self-care for the caregiver. FCA recognized that families were, in fact, their own "case managers" and sought to incorporate consumer direction as an underlying philosophy. Working across multiple diagnoses, age of onset, and care needs, FCA developed a consistent approach to working with different family constellations to determine the best outcomes for all involved.

Families need an array of services accessible at various points in their caregiving career: specialized information about medical conditions, planning issues, and care provision; linkage to qualified services that fit their situation; continuing assessment of psycho-social and health needs of caregivers; ongoing consultation on care planning; emotional support via support groups and professional counseling; and legal and financial information. Caregivers also need respite services and a range of options to choose from: in-home, day care, short-term stays in facilities, and weekend camps or retreats. Building on the success of this service prototype, California enacted legislation in 1984 to create the Caregiver Resource Centers so all families would have access to the service package.

Family Caregiver Alliance knew that research and outcome data would be needed to move a policy agenda forward and provide the rationale and direction for improved service development and practice. The 1984 legislation also created the Statewide Resources Consultant (SRC), housed at FCA, to operate a statewide information clearinghouse on caregiving and brain disorders; conduct education, training and applied research; carry out program and policy development; maintain a statewide database on CRC clients served; and provide technical assistance to the CRC sites. The SRC provides technical information to state administrative departments, policy makers, advocates, academics, and the media—in California and nationally—on the issues of family caregiving and long-term care.

For over a decade, the statewide information collected from thousands of families caring for a cognitively-impaired adult across economic, ethnic, and geographic boundaries has been clear and consistent. Those who provide the care, especially older spouses, are at risk for serious health and mental health problems. Data from the California Caregiver Resource Center System Annual Report for Fiscal Year 1998-99 shows that six in ten (60%) families exhibit symptoms of depression (scores of 16 or higher on the Center for Epidemiological Studies Depression Scale). Caregivers report being highly stressed by their situation and 44% report high burden levels. About 29% report their physical health to be fair to good. Typically caregivers provide over 11 hours per day in care and more than one-third (36%) report receiving far less help from their own family and friends than they need. Thirteen percent say they get no help at all.

While the experiences may seem bleak, families using the array of options offered by the Caregiver Resource Centers report an increasing sense of control and mastery of caregiving tasks, especially with problem behaviors. With intensive counseling and medical help, depression can be lowered. And with assistance and support, families will use community services and ask for help from family and friends.

For families who have identified themselves as caregivers and have sought help, the burdens sit a little lighter on their shoulders. However, many caregivers do not seek help. It is imperative that health providers, social service professionals, and helping communities such as churches recognize the significant impact of caregiving on individuals and encourage those who give care to take care of themselves. Professionals, especially those in the medical fields, need to recognize that a stroke or a diagnosis of Alzheimer's disease affects a family system, not just the patient. And they need to view referrals to programs offering assistance as an essential health maintenance function for those caregivers in need.

From one person's speaking out, many voices added their stories and a movement was born. Long-term care is ultimately both a personal family issue and a looming policy challenge. As we move into the 21st century, how we care for both persons needing care and for their family caregivers will grow increasingly important. Society cannot risk the breakdown of the main providers of long-term care and needs to seek compassionate and practical supports for families.

More information on Family Caregiver Alliance can be found on the website at www.caregiver.org or by contacting Family Caregiver Alliance, 690 Market Street, Ste. 600, San Francisco, CA 94104 phone (415) 434-3388, fax (415) 434-3508.

Contributed by Kathleen Kelly, Family Caregiver Alliance

12

Hard Decisions in Hard Times: Helping Families Make Ethical Choices During Prolonged Illness

David M. Price

This chapter focuses upon the kinds of health care decisions that face patients and their loved ones at the end of life. The intention is to show how health professionals and other support persons often make these decisions more difficult than they need to be and to identify a few basic ideas for how to facilitate responsible health care decision making by those who are experiencing major loss in the context of prolonged and progressive illness.

Every medical treatment decision is an ethical decision. That is to say, every such decision is an answer to a *should* question:

- Should I undergo another round of chemotherapy?

- Should we bring Grandma home to die?

- Should we begin dialysis?

- What should we do about this low blood count?

A sound answer to each question depends on technical information or expert advice. But none can be answered by reference to technical knowledge alone. Each decision has a value component. Each turns, in significant part, upon some notion of what is worth what; that is why every medical decision is an ethical decision.

In the course of a prolonged illness, the patient and (usually) her close family members or friends will make many such ethical decisions. They will make them in conjunction with health care professionals who bring to the decision-making process relevant knowledge and experience and, one hopes, skillful, empathic support.

Patients and caregivers will need such support, not only because these decisions tend to be difficult and couched in unfamiliar terms, but because the decisions must be made in the context of grief. A prolonged illness, even if it is not perceived as necessarily ending in death, nonetheless entails prolonged grief. A long, often progressive illness typically includes loss of well-being, vigor, function, social status, and self-image. Responses to such losses are profound, whether they are losses in one's self or in a partner, parent, child, or sibling.

Sudden death or death after a brief illness compresses grief. There are relatively few health care decisions to make and they tend to seem largely apart from real life. In a brief, fatal illness, survivors are actually excused from making some decisions. Other decisions and major pursuits are postponed. Life seems to stand still. One takes time out for a brief illness and for acute grief. By contrast, in prolonged illness, life must go on and health care decisions that must be made are made in the midst of life and in the midst of grief. Moreover, these decisions tend to be more complicated in terms of their impact on ongoing family patterns and interests:

- Should we put Mother in a nursing home?
- Should Peter be taken off the ventilator?
- Is it right to let Dad make this decision about amputation?

- Should we feed her by mouth even though we know she could get pneumonia?

As these questions or ethical dilemmas illustrate, many health care decisions are choices among 'least worst' alternatives. Accordingly, the guilt that is a familiar component of grief can easily find a focus. Guilt, whether real or imagined, is no friend of sound and timely decision making. It is easy to see how the interaction of grief and ethical decision making cuts both ways: the nature of the decisions prompts grief responses, while aspects of grieving tend to complicate decision making.

Shared Decision Making

Important health care decisions tend to be shared decisions; more than one person is usually involved in the process. This appears to be true both in the sense that it is proper that it be so, and in the sense that that is what generally happens.

Decisions are shared in two dimensions: First, the clinician (the physician or other health professional) and the patient (or surrogate for the patient, if the patient is incapacitated) share decision making in a process known as 'informed consent.' The clinician lays out options, provides explanations and predictions and, perhaps, offers advice. The patient or surrogate assimilates, analyzes, and evaluates. The process is properly and, indeed, necessarily a dialogue. It ends with a decision to which both parties agree, and a plan of care that they then implement cooperatively. Though this process is often flawed and occasionally is so flawed as to support a judgment that there was no informed consent at all, this shared decision making is the ethical (and legal) ideal. Most of the time, clinicians, patients, and families manage a rough approximation of the ideal.

The second dimension of shared decision making is what happens between the patient (or surrogate) and his significant support people. Patients and principal family caregivers rarely act alone, despite the fact that they might be fully within their rights to do so. Even when one member of a family is clearly authorized to make decisions, it almost invariably happens that others are informed, involved, and consulted. Dying mothers and fathers frequently reshape their decisions to accommodate the sensibilities and preferences of their grown children. Spouses typically take each other into account and do not act on their individual preferences alone. Even deeply estranged family members commonly make room for each other in family councils. The sole signature on a consent form belies the typical array of stakeholders and the fact that, as hard as it may be to do so, they do tend to acknowledge and include each other when there are important health care decisions to make on behalf of a common loved one.

In two senses, then, health care decisions at the end of life ordinarily come out of a process of shared decision making. Not only do patients or their surrogates decide in conjunction with professional advisors, but those who are bound by familial duty or affection generally consult broadly as important end-of-life decisions are made. They do so for a variety of reasons. The one most often is articulated is, "I want this to be something they can all live with." It would not be too far off to rephrase this sentiment as, "I want to decide in such a way as to not unduly complicate their grieving."

Responsibility

People faced with difficult health care decisions are often most impressive, even inspiring, in their bravery and selfless devotion to duty. The young parents of a child with devastating congenital problems who, despite the fact that nothing in their short lives has prepared them for this responsibility, learn what they have to know, master their urge to flee, and face into an ordeal that one might expect would overwhelm them. A daughter manages to put aside her own deeply held preferences in order to honor her father's wishes. A husband who is very nervous about bringing his dying wife home does it anyway. The neighbor of a woman who has no family volunteers to become the legal guardian in order to authorize her friend's removal from life support. To work with such people as they make these decisions is a great and humbling privilege.

A few families are seriously dysfunctional and some patient surrogates are thoroughly irresponsible. Occasionally, decision makers or whole families manage to evade responsibility in ways that defy the conscientious efforts to assist and support. There are passive-aggressive personalities who make a pretense of responsibility, while the patient languishes and clinician frustration mounts. Fortunately, these are relatively rare.

All of what follows in this discussion of ethical decision making as it impacts upon grieving persons presumes that most patients and most family members are basically responsible, and that, with proper assistance, they will engage in good faith efforts to discern the right thing to do.

Sound Decision Making

It is possible to identify certain features of a good decision-making process without requiring subscription to any particular methodology or ethical theory. In general, the marks of sound decision making include:

Adequate information. Good decisions require good information. The very first step in any sound decision-making process is to assess whether the relevant information is reliable and complete. *Information* includes both fact and interpretation, both description and judgment. The perceived adequacy of the information may depend in significant measure on the reputation of those who have gathered the facts and made the interpretations.

Appropriate identification of alternatives. A frequent and serious mistake in decision making is to proceed to make a choice between two or three perceived options when, in fact, more care or imagination would have revealed additional alternatives. Sometimes the choice is framed in a way that distorts or obscures the nature of the real options. It is possible to do everything else flawlessly and still miss the best alternative because it was never identified or adequately articulated.

Identification of decision makers. It may not be obvious who should make certain decisions. This uncertainty can derail an otherwise good process. Shared decision making as discussed above entails an often delicate apportionment of decision-making power or complementary aspects of a complex decision.

Identification of stakeholders. For many decisions, persons or organizations who would not be identified as rightful decision makers nonetheless have a discernable interest in the outcome. Interests may include money, prestige, ego, ideological stance, or expected courtesies. Full understanding of the social, political, organizational, and economic context within which the decision process unfolds requires attention to interested parties as well as to those who have direct decision-making roles.

Tolerance as affirmative respect. Those who share responsibility for a joint decision may or may not come from the same place ethically. If they approach the decision in basically the same way (for example, from the perspective of 'rights' and centrality of the principles of personal liberty), then decision making is apt to go smoothly. However, it commonly happens that those who share decision making proceed from different starting points or along divergent paths. In such cases, sound and efficient decision making depends upon a common commitment to tolerance and respectful listening.

We seem to be becoming a more tolerant people, despite signs of a worldwide resurgence of religious fanaticism and ethnic jingoism. Most of us seem to be more aware of pluralism and less certain that our cultural perspective is the only one worth notice. One hopes that this modern awareness does not lead to a moral relativism in which one opinion is thought to be as good as any and morality is equated with mere preference. Tolerance is a much more robust and demanding virtue. It respects persons, especially as they attempt to make principled decisions. True tolerance succeeds not by devaluing the issues or traditions that divide us, but by affirmatively respecting those who differ in good faith.

Clarity about key terms and concepts. Good decision making is marked by precision of language, especially with respect to those words that are central to moral reasoning, emotionally loaded or heavy with obscure authority. In short, good decision making is careful to either avoid or to define exactly those kinds of evocative terms and allusions that are deliberately used by advertising writers and campaigning politicians. In the language of morals, as in political speech, there is a time and place for rhetorical flourish and emotional appeals. But when there are important decisions to make in difficult circumstances, sound decisions depend in part upon a good-faith effort to be as clear as possible about what is meant by key words and important ideas.

The above six marks of good decision making are all the more important when some of the parties are simultaneously coping with significant loss. If prolonged illness means 'living with grief,' it means deciding with grief. This realization underscores the importance of optimizing the decision-making process along the lines just suggested.

Common Decision Points in Prolonged Illness

The balance of this chapter is devoted to some of the common decisions faced by or on behalf of patients with prolonged and ultimately fatal illnesses. Against the background of earlier discussions of the shared nature of health care decision making and the characteristics of good decision-making process, we now proceed to examine some practices that militate against good decision making, entailing added stress and, perhaps, longer term complications for grieving patients and their loved ones.

We will also consider alternative strategies consistent with the foregoing marks of good decision making. These are potential interventions by which professionals and caregivers can make hard choices not easy but more satisfying and more healing. Assuring sound and confident health care decisions is a way of facilitating, rather than complicating, the adaptive process known as grief.

Foregoing Cure-Oriented Treatment. At some point in many prolonged and progressing illnesses, there comes a point (or points) when those who share responsibility for the treatment plan will ask, "Should we stop our efforts to 'beat' the disease in favor of efforts to promote quality of life?" This development begins with an acknowledgment that the likelihood of cure or remission is fading and that the patient and the therapies are being overmastered by the disease. In the terms of grief dynamics, denial and bargaining give way to acceptance. This is not a happy moment, though it is often accompanied by a sense of relief or release.

Of greatest importance to these decisions is the availability of adequate information and accurate identification of alternatives. Physician judgment and physician communications are key to good decision making, though other parties to the process, including other health professionals and loved ones, can be either helpful or hindering.

Prognosis, a judgment about what the future is likely to hold both with continued treatment and without it, is the sort of judgment that physicians are uniquely trained to make. Patients, family members, and even other health professionals are dependent upon physicians to make these judgments and to communicate them. Failure to do so is not uncommon and is the proximate cause of much disordered decision making and much unnecessary suffering.

When Elisabeth Kübler-Ross began her ground-breaking research a generation ago, the first thing she learned was that few of her physician colleagues at a large public hospital acknowledged having any dying patients. Thanks to Dr. Kübler-Ross and many others, the incidence of professional denial is surely lower today. However, it is still common to find patients whose acknowledgment that they have come to the end of their lives is achieved without any direct help from their medical advisor. In every hospital there are nurses and senior residents who can identify a handful of attending physicians who seem never to recognize impending death until it is unmistakable to even untrained observers. Here, the failure to provide adequate information is not a matter of factual inaccuracy, but flawed judgment.

It is also not uncommon for physicians and other professionals to acknowledge among themselves that a patient is irretrievably dying, but not to communicate that effectively to the patient or family. Few of us like to be bearers of bad news; but if that is part of one's job, then a failure to effectively communicate it is a failure of duty and a subtle form of the ancient 'physicianly' sin of abandonment. Other members of the health care team may be slow to compensate for the physician's failure. Nurses, consulting physicians, social workers, respiratory therapists, and other professionals are often reluctant to assume a function often thought to be, and sometimes jealously guarded as, the exclusive province of the attending physician.

Put most plainly, many patients and families cannot and do not make good and timely decisions in large part because they are not told the truth and are either given, or allowed to persist in, false hopes for recovery or survival. Whether because of ignorance, a lack of nerve or a powerful need to avoid, some physicians all of the time and many physicians some of the time seem unable to effectively communicate to their patients or their patients' families that death is near. The consequences for sound health care decisions are serious. Appropriate choices about when to switch from curative care to comfort care depend absolutely upon medical judgments about what is reasonable to expect.

More common than the failure to make or communicate the medical determination that a patient is entering the final stages of his disease process is the failure to appropriately identify alternatives. The main culprits here are attitudes and habits of thought—the modern notion of the physician as one who 'fights' disease and our liberal faith that there is a potential technological solution for every problem.

Acknowledgment that cure-oriented treatment may no longer be appropriate is often presented as though it means the end of therapy. 'There's nothing more we can do' is a familiar refrain. The alternative to more chemotherapy or other life-prolonging intervention is seen as 'giving up.' This defeatist language both reflects and creates negativity and hopelessness. It suggests abandonment and, because of relentless specialization, may indeed signal a change to a completely new set of professional caregivers.

Dr. Patricia Murphy, a nurse specializing in bereavement and clinical ethics, has proposed a more positive and accurate way to frame the ethical question about foregoing cure-oriented treatment. The core idea is to characterize the choice as between two vigorous and ongoing forms of therapy, rather than seeing one choice as doing nothing or giving up. To counter the passivity and defeatism of the common perception, Dr. Murphy has coined the acronym ACT, or Aggressive Comfort Treatment, as a way to characterize the alternative to aggressive efforts to reverse or arrest the disease process.

ACT is not merely a way to put a positive spin on an otherwise depressing decision point. It actually helps correct a false impression that palliative care is 'nothing' and the misleading notion that medicine has no concern for the alleviation of pain or enhanced quality of life.

It is true that palliative care has been overshadowed by curative medicine for the past fifty years. Most physicians and nurses do a notoriously poor job of pain control at the end of life, according to many observers and several important national studies. The negative language typically used to characterize the option of shifting treatment to comfort-oriented goals has affected the attitudes and shriveled the competencies of health care professionals. It has undoubtedly influenced patients, families, and professionals to pursue life-prolonging treatment long after they might otherwise have switched to therapies that maximize quality of life.

Language is powerful. It shapes perceptions and conditions choices. Perhaps ACT will prove to be a semantic force for the rehabilitation of palliative care as an essential medical competency. In the meantime, it suggests a way to help patients, families, and professionals to avoid guilt-driven and misbegotten pursuit of elusive goals because they did not want to 'give up.'

Do-Not-Resuscitate and Do-Not-Hospitalize Orders. In hospitals, decisions to forego cardiopulmonary resuscitation (CPR) are the most frequently made decisions with regard to withholding potentially life-sustaining treatment. Outside hospitals, the most frequent such decision is probably the decision not to send a dying patient to the hospital when that patient shows signs of impending cardiopulmonary failure. Such decisions are properly recorded in medical orders entered into the patient's record after agreement by the patient or patient surrogate that CPR and its usual intensive-care aftermath would not be of net benefit.

Do-Not-Resuscitate (DNR) orders and Do-Not-Hospitalize (DNH) orders are appropriate for patients who are dying, permanently unconscious or seriously demented, in a condition that is both very burdensome and irreversible, or unlikely to survive in other than an intensive-care environment. It should be obvious that sound decisions about DNR or DNH orders are dependent upon the sort of prognostic judgments discussed at length in the preceding section. Patients or patient surrogates depend upon physicians to make and communicate these prognostic judgments upon which they can then form an opinion about whether CPR and its aftermath is 'worth it.'

Patients and caregivers need to know about the probabilities of success for CPR relative to the patient's condition. Lay people are commonly shocked to learn that the success rate (measured in survival to discharge) of many of the hospitalized patients most likely to receive CPR is as low as one percent. Physicians who

simply ask, "Do you want us to try to restart her heart if it stops?"
are likely to get an answer that is unsound by virtue of its being
grossly uninformed or misinformed. The remedy is clear. Patients
(and, more often, families) need to be told about the probability
of success.

Physicians or other professionals who engage in these decision-
making dialogues can (and arguably should) also recommend or
advise, rather than merely dispassionately ask. There is something
ironic about a physician who has always offered recommendations
at each treatment decision point until death is in view, and then
suddenly has only questions and no more advice. This not-so-
subtle behavioral shift suggests that the physician is disengaging at
precisely the point at which a grieving patient or family most needs
the constancy of a trusted and familiar medical advisor.

The choice about DNR is often presented as though it were a
choice between life and death. It is ordinarily not really that at all.
DNR should be more accurately and realistically seen as a choice
between two kinds of death. Health professionals (or perceptive
nonprofessionals) should frame the DNR decision for grieving
family members in terms like this:

> Your dad has come close to the end of his life. While
> it is impossible to predict how long he might manage to
> live, we can say with considerable confidence that he will
> not get significantly better and that his heart will fail—
> probably sooner than later. You all understand that, do
> you not?
>
> OK, since we are agreed that your dad's death is close,
> I think the goal of care from this point forward should
> be to do everything we can to assure his comfort and
> to enhance his chances to enjoy whatever life remains.
> I think we're all committed to that goal. Right?
>
> Now, when his heart does finally give out, it would be
> technically feasible to try CPR. I don't think we should
> do that. The chances of it working are practically nil and

I'd rather see you all gathered at his bedside, speaking soothing words to him and each other and putting a cool washcloth on his forehead and telling him you love him. *That's* good care for him when his poor old heart finally gives out. CPR won't really help and doing it will mean that you can't do what we know *will* help. What do *you* think about this?

This kind of decisional guidance is notable, not only for its accurate information about the probabilities of successful CPR and for the helpful advice offered by the physician, but also for the way in which the alternatives are framed. The choice is not between doing something and doing nothing, but between two differing interventions, one aimed at life extension and one aimed at life enhancement. If the reframing were motivated by a desire to sugar-coat and obscure, it would not be a worthy suggestion. Rather, it is justified on the basis of giving this family a more realistic and accurate understanding of the nature and consequences of the decision at hand. Finally, this approach is much more apt to afford the survivors the comfort, support, and confidence of a caring, fully engaged professional who shares in the decision with them.

Tube Feeding

The provision of hydration and nutrition through plastic tubing is a technological intervention frequently considered when patients cannot take food or drink by mouth. Tube feeding can be accomplished by way of tubes inserted through the nose and into the stomach (*nasogastric* or *NG tube*), or surgically implanted through the abdominal wall into the stomach (*C tube* or *PEG*) or (less commonly) into the small intestine (*J tube*). Also, for shorter periods, nutrients can be delivered through small-bore tubes directly into the bloodstream (*hyperalimentation* or *HAL*).

There is rarely any question about the appropriateness of artificially delivered hydration and nutrition when the intervention is employed as a bridging maneuver to support the patient over a critical period until relative health is restored. However, questions may and often do arise when the incapacity to take oral feedings is a feature of a condition from which the patient is not expected to recover. Examples include:

- a 60-year-old woman who has suffered a massive stroke from which recovery is thought to be remote;

- a 75-year-old man with far-advanced Alzheimer's disease who does not eat enough to maintain good nutrition;

- an 88-year-old woman with congestive heart failure which confines her to her bed and bedside chair and who, despite 'having her full mental faculties,' has little appetite and wishes that her daughter would just stop constantly pressing her to eat.

In each of these cases someone among the professional or family caretakers will suggest—and perhaps passionately insist upon—artificial hydration and nutrition. In each case, someone else will almost surely wonder aloud whether tube feeding is appropriate or vigorously argue that it is not. The symbolism of food and drink and the emotionally loaded associations of food with caring, nurturing, comfort, and family duties will almost surely play a role in decision making about the care of these patients.

Very careful attention to the way key words and concepts are employed would be required as the family members of each of these patients think and talk about whether to institute, withhold, or withdraw tube feeding. They will almost surely be vulnerable to emotional and intellectual manipulation. Someone—perhaps, regrettably, a nurse or physician or clergy person—may say to them, "you wouldn't want your mother to starve, would you?" Sound decisions in such cases require that great care be taken to preserve important distinctions and remain clear-headed. For example, while 'starvation' may describe what would happen in the body of an unconscious patient, there would be no subjective experience of deprivation in that patient. An emotionally laden statement such as "your mother will starve" conjures up images of concentration camp victims whose experience is totally unlike that of a profoundly brain-damaged, permanently vegetative stroke victim.

Dying patients who are alert, like the 88-year-old woman with end-stage heart disease, typically lose interest in food, a kind of anorexia of the dying. There is no evidence that they suffer. In any case, if such patients become hungry or thirsty, they can simply ask for or accept food and drink.

In all these instances, allusions to starvation are misleading. Such language by well-meaning people turns out to arise from ideological agendas or careless assumptions. It is not helpful for emotionally vulnerable family members trying to discern the right thing to do in confusing circumstances.

Careful attempts to distinguish between 'feeding' and mechanically mediated nutritional support are important to clear thinking. There is a world of difference between patiently offering Grandma a few spoonfuls of applesauce or Ensure pudding and pumping a pharmaceutically-prepared preparation directly into her stomach through a length of plastic tubing. A whole lot more than calories and minerals is being conveyed through spoon-feeding. Offering that spoonful is what we have been doing for our young, our old and our sick since time began. That, not tube feeding, is what is always obligatory.

One of the often overlooked consequences of resorting to tube feeding is that we stop or reduce the symbolically and interpersonally rich 'nourishment' that accompanies assisted feeding. To speak carelessly, or rhetorically, of tube feeding as if it were the same thing as a daughter lovingly helping her dying mother sip some broth or ginger ale is inaccurate and unhelpful. It does not lead to sound decision making, especially by those who are making choices in the context of anticipatory grief.

Summary

Family members, friends and health care professionals who share responsibility for health care decisions with or on behalf of persons during a prolonged illness make those decisions in the midst of their grieving. Grief can complicate the decision making; less-than-optimal decision making can complicate the grieving.

Both as a way to assure sounder decisions and as a way to avoid unnecessary complications of grief, those who would support others through such hard times would do well to pay attention to the characteristics of sound decision making. In this chapter we have identified some marks of good ethical thinking:

- adequate information
- appropriate identification of alternatives
- identification of decision makers
- identification of stakeholders
- tolerance as affirmative respect
- clarity about key terms and concepts.

Finally, we have looked at several specific decisions or ethical dilemmas commonly faced in the course of prolonged illnesses. In the context of these situations, we have identified some unhelpful behaviors and suggested strategies that support quality decision making.

David M. Price, MDiv, PhD teaches ethics at the University of Medicine and Dentistry-New Jersey Medical School and is Clinical Ethicist at University Hospital in Newark, NJ. He has helped found ethics committees in five hospitals, multiple nursing homes and two hospices. Dr. Price is Chairman of NJ Health Decisions and Director of the Center for Healthcare Ethics, a non-profit educational agency. His articles appear in medical, nursing, ethics and legal journals.

The original version of this article appeared in *Living With Grief: When Illness is Prolonged*, Kenneth J. Doka and Joyce Davidson, Eds., Hospice Foundation of America, 1997.

programs · that · work

Whitman-Walker Clinic

◆

Why It Works – *From the Editor*
*A caregiving crisis, especially a widespread crisis,
can be a devastating and crippling ordeal, one that by
sheer scope impairs the abilities of caregivers to adequately
provide quality care. In such crises, it is critical that community
organizations play a role—coordinating services and marshalling
volunteers. Whitman-Walker Clinic is a powerful example of one
community's response to the HIV/AIDS crisis. It began as an
outreach to an isolated community whose needs were
often ignored, and has now expanded its services to
touch the lives of many people living with HIV/AIDS.*

In 1982, the Washington, D.C. area had 22 of the 1,300 cases of AIDS that were then reported in the United States. All 22 were gay men. By the end of 1996, there were 602,014 cases of AIDS in the U.S.; 371,783 had died. In the Washington area there were 16,677 AIDS cases; 9,677 had died. By that time the epidemic had spread to the African-American and Latino communities, among others.

In the early seventies, Whitman-Walker Clinic began as an all-volunteer service for the gay men's community, providing

STD screening and treatment. The Clinic then expanded its services to include other programs for both gay men and lesbians, and developed a vision for a diversified health care organization that provided medical care, alcoholism treatment, and a variety of mental-health counseling programs.

Officially chartered in 1978, the Clinic had only three years to strengthen this initial vision before 1981, when the staff recognized the projected impact of HIV/AIDS in Washington. From that point on, Whitman-Walker Clinic has focused on providing a wide array of services to those affected by HIV/AIDS, while still providing comprehensive services to gay men and lesbians.

Whitman-Walker Clinic's success is due primarily to two dynamics: a strong mission statement that supports the Clinic's work, and a diverse community-based board of directors who work as volunteers to ensure that the organization's programs and services reflect the changing needs of the communities it serves.

Mission Statement

Whitman-Walker Clinic is a non-profit, volunteer-based, lesbian and gay community health organization serving the Washington, D.C. metropolitan area. Our volunteers and staff are dedicated to providing or facilitating the delivery of high quality, comprehensive, and accessible health care services. Our services are directed to all gay men and lesbians. We are proud of the Clinic's substantial contribution in the fight against AIDS. Our historic commitment to accessible health care moves us also to share our programs with anyone in need of HIV-related services.

The changing dynamics of this epidemic dictate the changes in programs and services. Today, Whitman-Walker Clinic serves more than 5,000 people through its main medical facility in downtown Washington, and through three regional centers in Anacostia, Suburban Maryland, and Northern Virginia. A staff of more than 250 clinicians, program specialists, and support staff provide comprehensive health services to those living with or impacted by HIV/AIDS.

Whereas in the 1980s most of the Clinic's programming was focused on helping gay men die with dignity and comfort, much of its work today involves helping people from all walks of life to *live* with this disease. This has been possible because of close work with communities who are projected to be increasingly affected by HIV and AIDS, setting up the necessary programs and services well before the clients walk through the doors.

For example, the Legal Services Program once was involved primarily with helping clients write wills, advance directives and other legal documents needed once a person died from complications associated with AIDS. Today, much of the work done in that program involves immigration problems, debt consolidation, permanency planning and other services needed by people who are planning on living.

Also, much of the Clinic's programming is devoted to providing direct primary medical and mental-health care for those living with HIV/AIDS. The historic commitment to providing the gay and lesbian community with high-quality health care has not been abandoned.

The Clinic is often asked "how have you survived," when many sister agencies across the country have had to lay off staff and cut back on programs. Without the strong and consistent support of the gay and lesbian community, survival of the financial crises brought on by a burgeoning HIV/AIDS epidemic might not have been possible.

And the gay and lesbian community continues to provide Whitman-Walker with a substantial portion of funding, even though the epidemic is raging through other communities which are served by the Clinic.

The board of directors takes an active role in ensuring that the Clinic has a strategic plan that requires careful budgeting and monitoring of expenses. In every activity, the first question asked is how this directly supports the expressed mission of Whitman-Walker Clinic. If it does, the program is then examined to determine if it is an already budgeted activity. If it is not already included in the budget, there has to be a compelling reason to modify the adopted budget and work plan. This may seem like a reiteration of Organizational Management 101. However, when an agency is in the business of saving the lives of those with an incurable disease, all too often empathy and compassion at any cost win out over sound fiscal policy and planning.

As difficult as it is to put off otherwise worthwhile programs and services, it is the scrupulous attention to planning and expense monitoring that has enabled Whitman-Walker Clinic to continue to provide these services to a growing population of neighbors, family and friends living with HIV.

For more information on the Whitman-Walker Clinic see the Resource Section

Contributed by Michael Cover, Whitman-Walker Clinic

Voices

I Know Now

Desmond Groarke

*N*ow, at the beginning, I know the ending.

I didn't know then. I didn't know when. I didn't know how. I didn't know where. I thought I knew why. You smoked. You were 73. A large mass, right lobe, squamous cell, stage four. Then another, on your larynx, reaching into your trachea. The otolaryngologist shows me that one, before I have time to think. He puts the scope to my eye: An egg-shaped, vibrant bulge, transected by a network of blood vessels.

How red and moist and familiar is this inner tube of your being, Mom. But I should not be here. I am your son, but no Oedipus! It was multiple myeloma killed my father 20 years ago, not I.

So, Doctor, what are the risks of that surgery? If the removal of the tumor fails, will she be left with a hole in her throat? Yes, of course, a tracheostomy. By the way, who can say now which of the tumors has come first? Who can say what will come at the last? At this moment I would gladly give my right eye to know. But I am no Oedipus.

Another doctor speaks of "losing your airway." I picture your eyes bulging out of your head, blindly pursuing your airway. A nurse speaks of "bleeding out." The tumor in your throat might penetrate a major vessel. It will be "frightening and messy but very quick." Some form of respiratory failure is certain. Technically, that is happening now.

We want the end to come at home. Is that too much to ask? Will you die easily in your bed, spectacularly on a public bus?

I know the ending, now.

We decide against surgery. How can you shout "Bingo!" with a hole in your throat? And you don't like the doctor who would do the job. You love the one who offers radiation. She is kind, and she listens. She is a mother-to-be; a blind man could see that. And you like planning and dressing and travelling to get there, by car or bus, accompanied by one of us, three times a week. You feel as if you're doing something to defeat this thing. Privately to me, a nurse compliments you: "Your mother is the type who will die on her feet." I cannot find a context to tell you in.

We have two uneventful days, a third, then fourth. Could this be a routine? We go to Mass four, then five, then six Sundays in a row. Then just at the start of consecration you falter in your kneeling down. You fade. A noise in place of breath comes from your lungs, a knocking sound. Who's there?

Suddenly and certainly I am losing you, and I know it. People want to help. An ambulance? A cell phone? I hold you in my arms and whimper. Who's there? But we are not at home, and there has been no kind of warning. None whatsoever. Nobody is ready now. Everyone is looking. I will not let you go like this, so I tell you, "It's not time, Mom. It's not time." You settle back as if you were just practicing. But a little while later, back at your home, you ask me if you are going to die from what you have, and I tell you yes, although we do not know when or where or how.

Which comes first: the knowledge that you are dying or the cause of it?

You are feeling pain in your arm, your throat, your ear is killing you. You ask the radiation oncologist for something to help you sleep. She tells you that for medication you need a medical oncologist. We meet with one. He says you should come back in a few weeks, after your radiotherapy. He'll assess your treatment at that time. In the meantime, we try to contact your first specialist, the pulmonologist who made your diagnosis. He does not return our calls. His private secretary is seriously pissed off when you call on her direct line. How did you get this number? Discouraged now and feeling abandoned, we call the radiation oncologist, since you say she listens. Well, you have declined surgery, you are receiving maximum radiation, your symptoms are multiplying, and you are unhappy and in pain; there is no recourse but to refer you to the Palliative Care Service. What's that? They'll relieve your discomfort.

Oh, I thought you'd *all* do that.

The palliative care nurse is unembellished, unselfconscious. Yeah. Yeah. Yeah, she says as she takes notes, listing phone calls she will make to arrange for a visiting nurse, another for oxygen, a nebulizer, another for a home health aide, another to your insurer. The doctor is soft-spoken, with just a tinge of deliberateness. He writes the third, fourth, fifth prescription—two for controlled substances. He holds you enthralled. I have trouble looking at his eyes. Life has too much to do with death these days.

You, Mom, are completely at ease, palliated already. This man and this woman care about you, and you look at them as if you've known them all your life. When I am ready to speak up, the doctor asks if I am in the medical profession. I know the names and uses of so many drugs, serious drugs administered to the seriously ill. No, but I have had many friends who . . . . He knows what I mean. He is one of us.

Finally, three months after seeking care at one of the world's pre-eminent teaching hospitals, you have a doctor who will take care of you, a nurse, the promise of an entire team. It's only been three months since you were introduced to a renowned pulmonary specialist by a hospital board member, the sister of a law partner of your other son. Good thing you didn't wander in off the streets, unknown, uninsured. Who knows where you'd be? It's only been three months that we are making our way out of the medical battle zone (you win some/you lose some) and its assault technology, and into the care of human beings with knowledge and licenses to practice the ancient art of medicine: Do no harm. Palliative Care Service.

Before you leave, you have three phone numbers: the doctor's direct line, the nurse's, the palliative care service's beeper. You have a fistful of scrips and oft-repeated verbal directives. You have the promise of a phone call from the nurse as soon as she speaks with your insurer. You have a message from her on your machine by the time you return home. Everything is arranged.

You tell me you want to make a trip home, to Ireland. You want to say goodbye. I am terrified, not of my own fear but of your courage. But I am willing. The doctor says yes, go soon, as soon as possible. Everything is arranged.

In the airport lounge you talk of getting on a ship, but you haven't crossed on a ship in fifty years, not since you first made the crossing, alone and ill from a vaccination, long before a husband, even longer before a child. Now, above the jet stream, over the north Atlantic at an hour indeterminate a sunrise sheds its red glow on a couple holding hands in oversized leather seats, on their way home to say goodbye. She sleeps. He watches. She is 30 years his senior, she hasn't long to live. Against all odds, all caution to the wind, are they falling deeply in love?

You ask the hostess: When is Father giving out Holy Communion? She is one of us—yes, Irish. She replies: I'll ask.

How easy it is, selecting your outfits and laying out your clothes, bathing and dressing you. Your sisters praise me for my taste. "No husband would do it," Agnes proclaims. "Or could do it!" Maggie adds. You had a petticoat, four full hoops, when I was a boy. I liked to dance around in it, until I was caught by the other boys. We never talked about that petticoat—outgrown no doubt and out of fashion, like my boyhood fantasy—but it is not in your closet now. And it is most assuredly not in mine.

On the ground, you have moments of startling clarity. You organize a dinner for 23 guests. You stand at the bedside of your favorite uncle—92 years old—who is in agony after some heroic surgery. You tell him: I know what I have.

He, for his part, claims to know nothing. He will not leave this hospital again. He will die the same night as you, two weeks hence.

Yes, I know the ending now.

You give up your mind on this trip, too, spells at a time. You haven't a clue who that is, where you are, how to find a bathroom. But at the graveyard, when I return to the car despairing of finding your sister's grave, you get out the passenger side, climb the wall and walk directly to it. You stumble and fall returning to the car, and I remember the superstition about falling in a graveyard.

After the big dinner, we turn to wave to lingering guests and what passes between us but a hearse headed towards Galway. The drama is fading, a fairy tale instead, any uncertainty becomes a mock.

We are back in New York, but you are not returned. Minute-to-minute symptoms flare and fizzle. You cannot walk; you don't want to stay home. Pale yellow vomit flows effortlessly from your mouth; you eat a huge meal.

But this constant talk of home is maddening. When are we going home? When are we going home? Finally, I get it. You no longer mean Ireland, and you no longer mean New York. So, instead of telling you once again that you are at home, I tell you that you will go home but I do not know when or where or how.

I know the ending, now.

Walking you to bed this Saturday night I know it is your last walk. So tired, so deeply tired. You bless yourself with a heavy cross given you by a priest friend. You kiss the cross and say: I tell you if you got hit in the head with this you'd know it.

This is your last joke. Your last sentence comes Sunday afternoon: Bye, Des, I'll see you soon.

I have held up well under the lack of sleep, under the sudden calls, under the strain of traveling and carrying two. Family members hover about these last couple days. They talk trivia; they eat sandwiches; they choke on their own emotions. The doctor and nurse from palliative care pay a house call this afternoon. They assure me you are comfortable. The doctor tells me to call him as soon as anything happens—or tomorrow.

Now, at nine or ten o'clock on Monday night a few of us are around your bed, including your two other children. This is the bed in which you conceived us. You haven't spoken or opened your eyes in a few hours. The caesura between your breaths lengthens. We are losing you, and we are at home this time, and there has been plenty of warning.

I lose it first, Mom, in just that way most forbidden in this family: a spasm, a moan, a roar comes up and out of me and I burrow my head helplessly against your arm, imploring comfort but expecting a blow. My partner says: She's reaching for you. You raise your arm, clutching my head onto your breast. You, who are about to lose everything we think we've ever known, turn to me now to comfort my pain. Footsteps, or is it the beating heart the fetus hears in his sanctuary, pounding in my head, in your breast? Mom, you come one last time down that corridor we each inside know so well yet manage to forget, and give me once again to life while I, I give you to death.

I know the beginning, now.

In Memory of:
Mary Dolan Groarke
August 16, 1925–June 29, 1999

Part IV

Conclusion

Joyce D. Davidson

So Now What Do We Do?

Today my friend Helen told me about her recent hysterectomy. She said that as she went to the hospital alone that morning she was more terrified than she had ever been in her life. She thought her knees would buckle. With her heart pounding, she stepped onto the elevator, and then another woman got on. As the two rode the elevator Helen couldn't stand it any longer and blurted out, "Please, please tell me you're having a hysterectomy, too!" The woman said yes, she was. Helen told me that an immediate, overwhelming sense of relief enveloped her, and as the two women approached the reception desk in the surgical area, she called out brightly, "Two uteruses to go, please!"

Now, the other woman's presence had absolutely no bearing on Helen's surgery, but it had everything to do with her feelings about it. Somehow, no matter what we humans are going through, nothing gives us more comfort than the presence of someone with whom to share our journey.

That may be an oversimplification of what we, as professional caregivers, are called upon to do for the family caregivers we support, but that's basically it. We are called to be, as the song goes, their "brave companions of the road."

Both being brave and being a companion, however, are enhanced if we equip ourselves for the trip. The goal of this book is to do just that. It reinforces the importance of caring presence, practiced expertise, and vigorous advocacy.

There are those who are particularly suited to providing empathic presence and active listening—what Doug Manning (1999) refers to as the three H's: someone to Hang around, Hug them, and Hush. Others' talents may lie in connecting caregivers to concrete services and community resources, or in providing hands-on medical care. Still others are drawn to the arena of public policy and community networks. All are essential. That is one of the miracles of humanity—that all of our gifts are needed to enhance our own lives and the lives of others.

No matter where our gifts and our skills lie, we are best equipped when we bring to our calling a balance of head and heart. Families are helped most when we are calm, capable and compassionate. Manning emphasizes two key concepts in providing support to family caregivers: first, understanding, and second, significance. Caregivers often minimize their suffering because the patient's suffering is 'so much worse.'

"Large sorrows," says Manning, "hit us out in the open and we are well aware of their effect on our lives. Small sorrows creep in unaware and silently collect in the bottom of our soul." (p. 30) Validating the significance and meaning of the caregiver's experience is our most basic task. The opposite of understanding, says Manning, is not misunderstanding, but trivialization. It is important that we not only validate the significance of the caregiver's experience, but also encourage them to advocate for themselves with family and friends who may complicate their caregiving role. Manning offers the "Primary Caregiver's Bill of Rights" (p 71):

- The right to rest

- The right to honesty

- The right not to be second-guessed about medical decisions

- The right to family sensitivity about time and expense

- The right to receive thanks.

And finally, we must open ourselves to experiences of extraordinary grace, even in the midst of sorrow, suffering and exhaustion. In a recent magazine article, Elizabeth Halling, one of the contributors in this book, tells the poignant, powerful story of her family's journey with Gabriel, their severely disabled three-year-old son. She describes Gabriel's birth defect as the "hollow in the center of his brain . . . that invited in sadness, which sits at the kitchen table with us at every meal." She talks about a grueling caregiving schedule that goes from six in the morning to ten at night, the house full of medical equipment, the multitude of appointments with doctors and therapists, repeated hospitalizations, her husband's career sacrifices in order to care for Gabriel—and the exhaustion, the fear, the anger, the heartbreak.

But she also describes the "small but deeply fulfilling moments of unexpected happiness." They go to church, she says, not to ask God to fix Gabriel, but to "bow our heads and receive our blessings, and we are blessed to know what our blessings are." She speaks fondly of the church ladies who "smile and bring us cakes and casseroles," and others who pray for Gabriel and "reach out to touch his little cheeks and turn around in the pew to get a look at him."

These are moments of grace, which Anne Lamott (1999) describes as "unearned love—the love that goes before, that greets us on the way. . . the help you receive when you have no bright ideas left, when you are empty and desperate . . . . The light . . . that takes you from that isolated place and puts you with others who are as startled and embarrassed and eventually grateful as you are to be there."

All these experiences and emotions make up the caregiving experience. It is our charge to bear witness to the whole of it and to hold it in our hearts. To embrace ambiguity with serenity. To forgive patients and families for their imperfections and to forgive ourselves for ours. To remain open so that we may give without breaking. To acknowledge the profound significance and meaning of each family's journey.

To be their brave companions of the road.

Joyce D. Davidson is a hospice and palliative care counselor in the New York City area. She provides end-of-life and crisis/trauma counseling at University Hospital in Newark, NJ. She also provides bereavement support at Broadway House in Newark, a nursing home for AIDS patients.

Resource List

Both Hospice Foundation of America and the National Family Caregivers Association recognize that the responsibilities and requirements of caregivers can be overwhelming. Whether your caregiving efforts guide you personally, professionally, or both, support is available.

We hope that the following list can serve as a guide to meeting some of your needs. You will find national organizations and resources that offer general support, disease-specific support, respite care, and elderly information. The Internet sites can provide you with online support and resources. In addition, there are many excellent organizations that provide assistance on a local level. A select list is included, but you may contact any of the national organizations listed for local information.

While your individual experience dictates specific needs, when you contact one or more of the organizations listed, you will find that you are not alone.

Caregiving: General Support
National Organizations

American Self-Help Clearinghouse
100 E. Hanover Avenue, Suite 202, Cedar Knolls, NJ 07927-2020
(973) 625-7101 Fax: (973) 326-9467
www.selfhelpgroups.org
email: ashc@cybernex.net

Not caregiver specific, but serves as an information clearinghouse for various self-help groups. Also provides information on how to start a support group.

Family Caregiver Alliance
690 Market Street, Suite 600, San Francisco, CA 94104
(415) 434-3388 or (800) 445-8106 (CA residents only)
Fax: (415) 434-3508
www.caregiver.org
email: info@caregiver.org

FCA is a nationally recognized information center on long-term care
and the lead agency in California's system of Caregiver Resource
Centers. FCA serves as a public voice for caregivers, illuminating the
daily challenges they face, offering them assistance and championing
their cause through education, services, research, and advocacy.

Friends Health Connection
P.O. Box 114, New Brunswick, NJ 08903
(800) 483-7436 Fax: (800) 384-7436
www.48friend.org
email: FHC@pilot.NJIN.NET

Links persons with illness or disability and their family caregivers
with others experiencing the same challenges.

Interfaith Caregivers Alliance
One West Armour Street, Suite 202, Kansas City, MO 64111
(816) 931-5442 or (800) 350-7438 Fax: (816) 931-5202
www.NFIVC.org
email: NFIVC@aol.com

Provides respite support and a variety of other services through local
congregations working together. Services vary by site. There are
currently 1,300 programs throughout the country.

National Alliance for Caregiving
4720 Montgomery Lane, Suite 642, Bethesda, MD 20814
(301) 718-8444 Fax: (301) 718-0034
www.caregiving.org
email: gailhunt.nac@erols.com

The National Alliance for Caregiving (NAC) is a non-profit joint
venture created to support family caregivers of the elderly and the
professionals who serve them. Recognizing that family caregivers provide
important societal and financial contributions toward maintaining the
well-being of older Americans, the Alliance was created to conduct
research, develop national projects, and increase public awareness of
the issues of family caregiving.

National Family Caregivers Association
10400 Connecticut Avenue, Suite 500, Kensington, MD 20895
(800) 896-3650 Fax: (301) 942-2302
www.nfcacares.org
email: info@nfcacares.org

The National Family Caregivers Association (NFCA) is a grassroots organization created to educate, support, empower, and advocate for the millions of Americans who care for chronically ill, aged or disabled loved ones. NFCA is the only constituency organization that reaches across the boundaries of different diagnoses, different relationships, and different life stages to address the common needs and concerns of all family caregivers. Members receive the quarterly newsletter, *Take Care!*, inspirational greeting cards, and access to an experienced staff which provides information, referrals, and caregiver support counseling

Rosalynn Carter Institute
Georgia Southwestern State University
800 Wheatley Street, Americus, GA 31709
(912) 928-1234 Fax: (912) 931-2663
http://rci.gsw.edu
email: rci@canes.gsw.edu

The RCI provides educational programs for caregivers; conducts research on the caregiving process; disseminates information on caregiving to a wide audience; consults with agencies, organizations, and individuals about caregiving activities; provides a forum for a discussion of issues concerning informal and formal caregiving; and advocates for public awareness and policy changes which enhances the lives of caregivers.

Strength for Caring—Hotline
(888) 422-7380
www.oncolink.upenn.edu/sfc

A free comprehensive education and support program for family members caring for patients with cancer at home. The program is intended to help family caregivers feel better equipped and more confident in this role.

Well Spouse Foundation
30 East 40th Street, New York, NY 10016
(800) 838-0879 Fax: (212) 685-8815
www.wellspouse.org
email: wellspouse@aol.com

A national, non-profit membership organization that gives support to husbands, wives and partners of the chronically ill and/or disabled. They offer support group information for spouses.

Caregiving: Hospice & End-of-Life Care

Hospice Foundation of America
2001 S Street, NW, Suite 300, Washington, DC 20009
(800) 854-3402 Fax: (202) 638-5312
-or-
777 17th Street, Suite 401, Miami Beach, FL 33139
(305) 538-9272 Fax: (305) 538-0092
www.hospicefoundation.org
email: hfa@hospicefoundation.org

Hospice Foundation of America is a non-profit organization that provides leadership in the development and application of hospice and its philosophy of care. The Foundation produces an annual award-winning National Bereavement Teleconference and publishes the *Living with Grief®* book series in conjunction with the teleconference. In addition to the annual teleconference, HFA provides a variety of other resources. *A Guide to Recalling and Telling Your Life Story* is a tool to assist people in writing their autobiographies. *Clergy to Clergy: Ministering to Those Facing Illness, Death, and Grief* is an audiotape series developed to help clergy members of all faiths minister to their communities and see to their own needs as caregivers. HFA publishes *Journeys*, a monthly newsletter for the bereaved, as well as special issues for adolescents, the newly bereaved, and those facing the anniversary of a death. HFA serves as the Managing Editor for *Omega, Journal of Death and Dying*. HFA offers brochures on *Choosing Hospice, Hospice Volunteers*, and *Living with Grief: At Work, At School and At Worship*; has published a series of educational articles; and provides resources to hospices, schools, military service centers, and other organizations. HFA is a member of the Combined Federal Campaign through Health Charities of America.

Last Acts Campaign
c/o Barksdale Ballard, 1951 Kidwell Drive, Suite 205,
Vienna, VA 22182
(703) 827-8771 Fax: (703) 827-0783
www.lastacts.org

Last Acts is a national campaign to engage both health professionals and the public in efforts to improve care at the end of life. Last Acts is made up of more than 400 partner organizations that believe that every segment of society, employers, clergy, voluntary health organization leaders, medical and nursing professionals, and counselors, among others, has a role to play as a part of a larger movement that addresses end-of-life concerns at the national, state, and community levels.

National Hospice and Palliative Care Organization
1700 Diagonal Road, Alexandria, VA 22314
(703) 837-1500 Fax: (703) 525-5762
www.nhpco.org

The oldest and largest non-profit organization in the U.S. devoted exclusively to hospice and palliative care. NHPCO operates the Hospice Helpline (800-658-8898) to provide the general public and healthcare providers with information about hospice and palliative care.

Project on Death In America
Open Society Institute
400 W. 59th Street, New York, NY 10019
(212) 548-0150 Fax: (212) 548-4613
www.soros.org/death/index.html
email: pdia@sorosny.org

The mission of Project on Death in America is to understand and transform the culture and experience of dying and bereavement through initiatives in the provision of care, public education, professional education, and public policy.

Caregiving: Specific Support
Disease-Related Support

[AIDS/HIV] Whitman-Walker Clinic
1407 S Street, NW, Washington, DC 20009
(202) 797-3500
www.wwc.org

The ALS Association National Office
27001 Agoura Road, Suite 150, Calabasas Hills, CA 91301-5104
(800) 782-4747 (Information and Referral)
(818) 880-9007 (All Other Calls)
www.alsa.org

Alzheimer's Disease & Related Disorder Association
919 N. Michigan Avenue, Suite 1100, Chicago, IL 60611-1676
(800) 272-3900 Fax: (312) 335-1110
www.alz.org
email: info@alz.org

American Brain Tumor Association
2720 River Road, Suite 146, Des Plaines, IL 60018
(800) 886-2282 Fax: (847) 827-9918
www.abta.org

American Cancer Society
1599 Clifton Road, NE, Atlanta, GA 30329
(404) 320-3333 Fax: (404) 325-2548
www.cancer.org

American Heart Association—National Center
7272 Greenville Avenue, Dallas, TX 75231
(800) 553-6321 Fax: (214) 706-5231
www.americanheart.org

American Parkinson's Disease Association
1250 Hylan Boulevard, Suite 4B, Staten Island, NY 10305
(800) 223-2732 Fax: (718) 981-4399
www.apdaparkinson.com

National Alliance for the Mentally Ill
Colonial Place Three
2107 Wilson Boulevard, Suite 300, Arlington, VA 22201
(800) 950-NAMI (6264) Fax: (703)524-9094
www.nami.org

National Mental Health Self-Help Clearinghouse
1211 Chestnut Street, Suite 1207, Philadelphia, PA 19107
(800) 553-4KEY (4539) Fax: (215) 636-6312
www.mhselfhelp.org

Elderly Referral Resources

AARP
601 E Street, NW, Washington, DC 20049
(800) 424-3410
www.aarp.org
email: member@aarp.org

Supplies education and information about caregiving, long-term care, and aging, including publications and audio-visual aids for caregivers.

Children of Aging Parents
1609 Woodbourne Road, Suite 302A, Levittown, PA 19057
(800) 227-7294
www.careguide.net

CAPS assists caregivers of the elderly with information and referrals, a network of support groups, and publications and programs that promote public awareness of the value and the needs of caregivers.

Eldercare Locator
National Association of Area Agencies on Aging
927 15th Street, NW, 6th Floor, Washington, DC 20005
(800) 677-1116 Fax: (202) 296-8134
www.n4a.org

Referrals to Area Agencies on Aging via zip code locations. Offers information about many eldercare issues and services in local communities.

The National Association of Professional Geriatric Care Managers
1604 North Country Club Road, Tucson, AZ 85716
(520) 881-8008 Fax: (520)325-7925
www.caremanager.org

Geriatric care managers (GCMs) are health care professionals, most often social workers, who help families in dealing with the problems and challenges associated with caring for the elderly. This national organization will refer you to their state chapters, which in turn can give you the names of GCMs in your area.

Ethnic and Minority Caregiving Resources

Coalition of Limited English Speaking Elderly
53 West Jackson, Suite 1301, Chicago, IL 60604
(312) 461-0812

Jewish Council for the Aging
11820 Parklawn Drive, Suite 200, Rockville, MD 20852
(301) 255-4200

National Association for Hispanic Elderly
1015 18th Street, NW, Suite 401, Washington, DC 20036
(202) 293-9329

National Caucus and Center on Black Aging, Inc.
1424 K Street, NW, Suite 500, Washington, DC 20005
(202) 637-8400 Fax: (202) 347-0895
www.ncba-blackaged.org

Financial Support Programs: (Prescription Drug & Medical Care)

Federal Hill-Burton Free Care Program
(800) 638-0742 (message center)

Offers referrals to agencies that offer free medical care.

Health Care Financing Agency
Office of the Administrator, Room 314G Humphrey Bldg.
200 Independence Avenue, SW, Washington, DC 20201
Medicare Hotline: (800) 638-6833
www.hcfa.gov

HCFA provides health insurance for over 74 million Americans through Medicare, Medicaid, and the State Children's Health Insurance Program (SCHIP). In addition to providing health insurance, HCFA also performs a number of quality-focused activities, including regulation of laboratory testing (CLIA), development of coverage policies, and quality-of-care improvement.

Medicine Program
P.O. Box 520, Doniphan, MO 63935
(573) 996-7300 Fax: (573) 996-3304
www.themedicineprogram.com.
email: help@themedicineprogram.com

A means-tested program for persons who do not have coverage either through insurance or government subsidies for outpatient prescription drugs, and who cannot afford to purchase medications at retail prices.

National Patient Advocates Foundation
753 Thimble Shoals, Suite B, Newport News, VA 23606
(800) 532-5274 Fax: (757) 873-8999
www.npaf.org
email: action@npaf.org

The Patient Advocates Foundation is a national non-profit organization that serves as an active liaison between patients and their insurer, employer and/or creditors to resolve insurance, job discrimination and/or debt crisis matters relating to patient's conditions.

Pharmaceutical Research and Manufacturers of America
1100 15th Street, NW, Washington, DC 20005
(202) 835-3400 or (800) 762-4636 (message center)
www.phrma.org

Provides a patient assistance directory that includes a list of pharmaceutical company-run programs which help people without insurance or with low income to obtain medications.

Grief and Bereavement

Association for Death Education and Counseling
342 N. Main Street, West Hartford, CT 06117-2507
(860) 586-7503 Fax: (860) 586-7550
www.adec.org

A multi-disciplinary professional organization dedicated to promoting excellence in death education, bereavement counseling, and care of the dying. Based on theory and quality research, ADEC provides information, support, and resources to its membership and the public.

Hospice Foundation of America
2001 S Street, NW, Suite 300, Washington, DC 20009
(800) 854-3402 Fax: (202) 638-5312
-or-
777 17th Street, Suite 401, Miami Beach, FL 33139
(305) 538-9272 Fax: (305) 538-0092
www.hospicefoundation.org
email: hfa@hospicefoundation.org

The Compassionate Friends
P.O. Box 3696, Oak Brook, IL 60522-3696
(630) 990-0010   Fax: (630) 990-0246
www.compassionatefriends.org

The Compassionate Friends is a self-help organization whose purpose is to offer friendship and understanding to families following the death of a child. They have 580 chapters nationwide that provide monthly meetings, phone contacts, lending libraries, and grief-related literature. Also provides training programs and resources for local chapters and answers referral requests.

Widowed Persons Service
4270 Chicago Drive, SW, Grandville, MI 49418
(616) 538-0101

WPS is a self-help support group for men and women who have experienced the loss of a spouse through death. They offer daytime and evening support group meetings, seminars, social activities and public education of the widowed experience. They have a directory of the 270 programs across the country as well as videos.

Home Care, Assisted Living, & Nursing Facilities

Consumer Consortium on Assisted Living
P.O. Box 3375, Arlington, VA 22203
(703) 841-2333 Fax: (703) 243-3342
www.ccal.org
email: membership@ccal.org

CCAL is a national consumer–focused organization dedicated to representing the needs of residents in assisted living facilities and educating consumers, professionals, and the general public about assisted living issues. Also provides tools to help consumers to make informed choices including a checklist for evaluating assisted living facilities.

National Association for Home Care
228 7th Street, SE, Washington, DC 20003
(202) 547-7424 Fax: (202) 547-3540
www.nahc.org

NAHC is a trade association that represents the interests of home care agencies, hospices, and home care aide organizations.

National Citizens Coalition for Nursing Home Reform
1424 16th Street, NW, Suite 202, Washington, DC 20036
(202) 332-2275 Fax: (202) 332-2949
www.nccnhr.org
email: nccnhr@nccnhr.org

Serves as an information clearinghouse and offers nationwide referrals for help with concerns regarding long-term care facilities.

New Lifestyles
(800) 869-9549 Fax: (214) 515-9202
www.NewLifeStyles.com

Publishes free regional directories of nursing homes, assisted living and retirement communities.

Senior Alternatives
26211 Central Park Ave, Suite 512, South Field, MI 48076
(800) 350-0770
www.senioralternatives.com

Publishes regional directories of nursing homes, assisted living and retirement communities.

Visiting Nurses Association of America
11 Beacon Street, Suite 910, Boston, MA 02108
(617) 523-4042
www.vnaa.org
email: vnaa@vnaa.org
Promotes community-based home health care.

Internet Resources

There are a variety of websites that offer information and support for family caregivers. This is a general listing and many of these sites offer access to local resources. To locate other sites, type "FAMILY CARE-GIVER, CAREGIVING, CAREGIVER" on any major search engine.

www.caregiver.com
Internet home for *Today's Caregiver* Magazine. Site includes topic specific newsletters, online discussion lists, back issue articles, chat.

www.caregiverzone.com
Offers referrals for senior housing, home health care and support,
senior centers, medical professionals, emotional and financial counseling,
additional resources, and caregiving tips.

www.careguide.com
Careguide is a care management company dedicated to helping people
at every stage of the aging process lead more comfortable, secure and
independent lives.

www.carescout.com
CareScout is a company dedicated to helping Americans make
intelligent, informed eldercare decsions by connecting Americans to
eldercare information, ratings, comparative data and products.

www.carethere.com
Provides a broad national database of information and services in the
areas of health care, finance, insurance, legal products and emotional
support—all specifically designed to assist caregivers.

www.ec-online.net (eldercare online)
An online community of peer and professional support for people caring
for aged loved ones.

www.extendedcare.com
Offers Internet-based solutions and resources that connect hospitals,
consumers and extended care providers (i.e. nursing, assisted living
and other senior living facilities, home health care agencies, etc.) to
each other.

www.familycareamerica.com
Offers varied resources to meet caregivers' specific needs in their own
localities, provides caregiver support, solution sharing, and discussion
forums.

www.growthhouse.org
Growth House, Inc. improves the quality of compassionate care for
people who are dying, through public education about hospice and
home care, palliative care, pain management, death with dignity,
bereavement and related issues.

www.homecarecompanions.org
Works to ensure that people living with a life-threatening illness receive
sufficient, appropriate, and affordable care in their homes, by training
families, friends and partners in basic home care nursing skills.

www.webofcare.com
Offers advice on disease-specific care situations, caregiver chats, product information, health news, and local resource searches.

www.widownet.org
WidowNet is an information and self-help resource for, and by, widows and widowers.

Respite Services
National Organizations

Easter Seals
230 West Monroe Street, Suite 1800, Chicago, IL 60606
(800) 221-6827
www.easter-seals.org
email: info@easter-seals.org

Provides a variety of services nationwide for children and adults with disabilities. May include adult day care, in-home care, camps for special needs children and more.

Family Friends
National Council on the Aging, Inc., 409 3rd Street, SW, Washington, DC 20024
(202) 479-6675 or (202) 479-6672
www.ncoa.org/friends
email: miriam.charnow@ncoa.org

A project that provides respite for families of children with special needs by men and women volunteers over the age of 50. Programs located throughout the country, with over 2000 volunteers, families, and friends.

Shepherd's Centers of America
One West Armour Street, Suite 201, Kansas City, MO 64111
(800) 547-7073
www.shepherdcenters.org
email: staff@shepherdcenters.org

Provides respite care, telephone visitors, in-home visitors, nursing home visitors, home health aides, support groups, adult day care, and information and referrals for accessing other services available in the community.

Referral Resources

National Association of Adult Day Services
National Council on the Aging, 409 3rd Street SW, Suite 200,
Washington, DC 20024
(202) 479-6682
www.ncoa.org/nadsa

Promotes the concept of adult day services; provides information on
many aspects of of adult day services; works to improve and extend adult
day service programs; develops social and public policy positions related
to the needs of adult day service programs.

National Respite Coalition
4016 Oxford Street, Annandale, VA 22003
(703) 256-9578
http://chtop.com/NRC.htm.
email: jbkagan@nrc.com

National Respite Coalition works to preserve and promote respite
programs and policy at the national, state, and local levels, by providing
caregivers the needed resources for locating respite services.

National Respite Locator Service
800 Eastowne Drive, Suite 105, Chapel Hill, NC 27514
(800) 773-5433
www.chtop.com/locator.htm.

Helps parents, caregivers, and professionals find respite services in their
state and local area.

This list was compiled by the National Family Caregivers Association,
with additional information from Hospice Foundation of America
and the Family Caregiver Alliance.

References

Levine: *Introduction*

Arno, P.S., C. Levine, & Memmott, M.M. (1999). The economic value of informal caregiving. *Health Affairs 18*, no.2: 182-188.

Donelan, K., Hill C.A., Hoffmann, C., Scoles, K., Feldman, P.H., Levine, C., & Gould, D.A. (2000). *Challenged to Care: Perspectives of Informal Caregivers.* (In Press.)

Jacoby, M.S., Sullivan, T.A., & Warren, E. (2000). Medical Problems and Bankruptcy Filings. *Norton Bankruptcy Law Adviser*, Issue No. 5 (May):1-12.

Levine, C. (1998). Rough Crossings: Family Caregivers' Odysseys through the Health Care System. *A United Hospital Fund Special Report (1998). New York: United Hospital Fund*, 1998.

Levine, C., Kuerbis, A.N., Gould, D.A., Navaie-Waliser, M., Feldman, P.H., & Donelan, K. (2000). *A Survey of Family Caregivers in New York City: Findings and Implications for the Health Care System.* A United Hospital Fund and Visiting Nurse Service of New York Special Report.

Levine, C., ed. (2000). *Always On Call: When Illness Turns Families into Caregivers* (2000). New York: United Hospital Fund.

Lipsyte, R. (1998). *In the Country of Illness.* New York: Alfred A. Knopf.

Mazzocco, Robert (1996, June 17). *Dynasty.* The New Yorker p. 64.

National Alliance for Caregiving and American Association of Retired Persons 1997). *Family Caregiving in the U.S.: Findings from a National Survey.* Washington, DC.

Schulz, R., & Beach, S.R. (1999). Caregiving as a risk factor for mortality. *Journal of the American Medical Association 282(23)*: 2215-2219.

Stone, D. (2000). *Reframing Home Health-Care Policy*. Cambridge, MA: Radcliffe Public Policy Center.

Stone, R. I. (2000). *Long-Term Care for ther Elderly with Disabilities: Curernt Policy, Emerging Trends, and Implications for the Twenty-First Century*. New York: Milbank Memorial Fund.

Strong, M. (1997). *Mainstay: For the Well Spouse of the Chronically Ill*. Northampton,

Lattanzi-Licht: *Chapter One*

Corr, C. A. & Corr, D. M. (Eds.). (1985). *Hospice approaches to pediatric care*. New York: Springer Publishing Company.

Connor, S. and Lattanzi-Licht, M. (1995). Hospice Trauma Response Survey. NHO Newsline, Arlington VA: National Hospice Organization, Nov.1 (5)21, 4-5, Gallop Poll Survey. (1996). Commissioned by the National Hospice Organization.

Lattanzi-Licht, M. (with Mahoney, J. J. & Miller G. W.) (1998). *The hospice choice*. New York: Simon & Schuster/Fireside.

Rezendes, D. & Abbott, J. (1979). Hospice movement: Way stations for the terminally ill. *Perspective on Aging, 8*.

Saunders, C. (1978). Quoted in S. Stoddard. *The hospice movement*. New York: Vintage Books, 120.

Wolfe J, et al. (2000). *New England Journal of Medicine*, March 4.

Weinberg & Ellison: *Chapter Two*

Metropolitan Life Insurance Company, The MetLife Study of Employer Costs for Working Caregivers, Westport, CT, June 1997.

National Alliance for Caregiving and the American Association of Retired Persons. (1997). *Family Caregiving in the U.S.: Findings from a National Survey*. Bethesda, MD: National Alliance for Caregiving.

National Health Council. (1999). *Family Caregiving: Agenda for Action*. Washington, DC: Author.

U.S. Department of Labor. (1998). *Facts on Working Women* (U.S. Department of Labor No. 98-1). Washington, DC.

Workplace Task Force (now called the Workplace Committee), Last Acts, Research Findings from Studies with Companies and Caregivers, 1999.

Workplace Task Force. (1999). *Research Findings from Studies with Companies and Caregivers.* Washington, DC: Robert Wood Johnson Foundation.

Gaventa: *Chapter Three*

Fitchett, G. (1994). *Assessing spiritual needs: A guide for caregivers.* Minneapolis: Augsburg Press.

Gaventa, W. (1993). Gift and call: Recovering the spiritual foundations of friendships. In A. Amado (Ed.), *Friendships and community connections between people with and without developmental disabilities.* Baltimore: Paul Brookes.

Gaventa, W. (1996). Re-imaging the role of clinical training for hospital chaplaincy and pastoral care: Moving beyond the institutional walls to the community. *Journal of Religion in Disability and Rehabilitation, 2*(4).

Gaventa, W. (1998). Recovering the meaning of professional. *Frontline Initiative.* Newsletter of National Alliance for Direct Support Workers. Fall, 1998.

Kretzmann, J. (2000). *Building Communities from the Inside Out.* (Audiotape presentation). New Brunswick: The Boggs Center-UAP.

Kretzmann, J. and McKnight, J. (1993). *Building communities from the inside out: A path toward finding and mobilizing a community's assets.* Chicago: ACTA Publications.

McKnight, J. (1996). *Everyone has a gift.* (Video). Toronto: Inclusion Press.

McKnight, J. (1995). *The careless society: Community and its counterfeits.* New York: Basic Books.

Mount, B. (1995). *Capacity works.* Manchester, CT: Communitas.

Nemey, T., & Shuruway, D. (1996). *Beyond managed care: Self determination for people with disabilities.* Durham, NC: National Program Office on Self Determination.

O'Brien, J. (Ed.). (1998). *A Little Book About Person Centered Planning.* Toronto: Inclusion Press.

Pearpoint, J. (1990). *From behind the piano: the budding of Judith Snow's unique circle of friends.* Toronto: Inclusion Press.

Pearpoint, J., O'Brien, J., & Forest, M. (1998). *PATH: A Workbook for Planning Positive Possible Futures.* Toronto: Inclusion Press.

Palmer, P. (1992). *The active life: A spirituality of work, creativity, and caregiving.* San Francisco: Harper and Row.

Palmer, P. (1998). *The courage to teach: exploring the inner landscape of a teacher's life.* San Francisco: Josey Bass Publishers.

Preheim-Bartel, D., & Neufeld, A. (1986). *Supportive care in the congregation.* Goshen, MD: Mennonite Mutual Aid.

Schwartz, D. (1996). *Who cares? Rediscovering community.* Denver: Westview Press.

Programs that Work: *CARE-NET*

Carter, R. (1994). *Helping yourself help others: A book for caregivers.* New York, NY: Times Books.

Haigler, D.H., Mims, K.B., & Nottingham, J.A. (1998). *Caring for you, caring for me: Education and support for caregivers, Leader's guide.* Americus, GA: The Rosalyn Carter Institute, Georgia Southwestern State University.

Haigler, D.H., Mims, K. B., & Nottingham, J.A. (1998) *Caring for you, caring for me: Education and support for caregivers, Participant's manual.* Americus, GA: The Rosalynn Carter Institute, Georgia Southwestern State University.

Nottingham, J.A., Haigler, D. H., Smith, D.L., & David, P. (1993) *Characteristics, concerns, and concrete needs of formal and informal caregivers—Understanding their marathon existence.* Americus, GA: The Rosalynn Carter Institute, Georgia Southwestern State University.

Chichin, Burack, & Carter: *Chapter Four*

Aroskar, M. A., Urv-wong, E. K., & Kane, R. A. (1990). Building an effective caregiving staff: Transforming the nursing service. In R. A. Kane and A. L. Caplan (Eds.). *Everyday ethics: Resolving dilemmas in nursing home life* (pp. 271-290). New York: Springer.

Burack, O. R., & Chichin, E. R. (in press). A support group for nursing assistants caring for nursing home residents at the end of life. *Geriatric Nursing.*

Burack, O.R., Chichin, E. R., & Olson, E. (2000). *Teaching end-of-life ethics to CNAs.* New York: Springer.

Cantor, M. & Chichin, E. R. (1990). *Stress and strain among homecare workers of the frail elderly.* New York: Third Age Center, Fordham University.

Chichin, E. R. (1992). *Home care is where the heart is: The role of interpersonal relationships in paraprofessional home care.* Home Health Care Services Quarterly 13, 161-177.

Chichin, E. R. & Olson, E. (1997). Reasons for staff discomfort with dementia patients' requests to withhold or withdraw life-sustaining treatment. Final Report. New York State Department of Health Bureau of Long-term Care Services Dementia Grants Project.

Chichin, E. R., Burack, O. R. Olson, E. & Likourezos, A. (2000). *End-of-life ethics and the nursing assistant.* New York: Springer.

Collopy, B., Dubler, N., & Zuckerman, C. (1990). The ethics of home care: Autonomy and accommodation. The Hastings Center Report, March/April Suppl. 1-16

Fischer, L. R. & Eustis, N. N. (1988). Relationships between home care workers and their clients in rural Minnesota. Grand Rapids, MN for 1988 Blandin Foundation Fellowship Program.

Kaye, L. (1985). Worker views of the intensity of affective expression during thedelivery of homecare services to the elderly. *Home Health Care Services Quarterly 7*(2), 41-54. Institute of Medicine (1986). Improving the quality of care in nursing homes. Washington, DC: National Academy Press.

Karioth, S. (1997). A loving good-bye. *Nursing Assistant Monthly 4*(2), 2.

Lerea, L. E., & LiMauro, B. F. (1982). Grief among health care workers: A comparative study. *Journal of Gerontology 37*(5), 604-6-8.

Lev, E. (1989). A nurse's perspective on disenfranchised grief. In K. Doka (Ed.), *Disenfranchised grief: Recognizing hidden sorrow.* Lexington, MA: Lexington Books.

Waxman, H. M., Carner, E. A., & Berkenstock, G. (1984). Job turnover and job satisfaction among nursing home aides. *The Gerontologist 24*(4), 503-509.

Harper, Lartigue, & Doka: *Chapter Five*

Barrett, R. (198). Sociocultural considerations in working with Blacks experiencing grief and loss. In K. Doka and J. Davidson (Eds.), *Living with grief: Who we are, how we grieve* (pp. 83-96). Washington, DC: The Hospice Foundation of America.

Doka, K.J. and Davidson, J. (1998). *Living with grief: Who we are, how we grieve.* Washington, DC: The Hospice Foundation of America.

Harper, B.C. (1997). Growth in caring and professional ethics. In B. Jennings (Ed.), *Ethics in hospice care.* New York: Haworth Press.

McGoldrick, M. (1982). Irish families. In M. McGoldrick, J. Pearce, J. Giordano (Eds.), *Ethnicity and family therapy* (pp. 340-363). New York: Guifford.

McGoldrick, M., Pearce, J.K., & Giordano, J. (1982). *Ethnicity and family therapy.* New York: Guifford.

Pinderhughes, E. (1982). Afro-American families and the victim system. In M. McGoldrick, J. K. Pearce & J. Giordano, (Eds.), *Ethnicity and family therapy* (pp. 108-122). New York: Guilford.

Sue, D. W. & Sue, D. (1999). Counseling the culturally different: theory and practice. New York: Wiley.

Yeo, G. & Gallagher-Thompson, D. (1996). *Ethnicity and the dementias.* Bristol, PA: Taylor and Francis.

Reinhard: *Chapter Seven*

Arno, P. S., Levine, C., & Memmott, M. M. (1999). The economic value of informal caregiving. *Health Affairs, 18*(2), 182-188.

Burggraf, V. Nurses can have impact when families assume caregiver role. *The American Nurse, 25(7)*, 25, 30.

Brody, E. (1985). Parent care as a normative family stress. *Gerontologist, 25(1)*, 19-29.

Dellasega, C. (1989). Health in the sandwich generation. *Gerontologist, 10(5)*, 42-3.

Duvall, E. M. (1977). *Marriage and family development* (5th edition). New York: J. B. Lippincott Company.

Families USA Foundation. (1993, April). *The heavy burden of home care.* (Issue No. 5). Washington, DC: Author.

Feinberg, L. F., & Pilisuk, T. L. (1999). *Survey of fifteen states' caregiver support programs* (final report). San Francisco, CA: Family Caregiver Alliance.

Fink, S. (1995). The influence of family resources and family demands on the strains and well-being of caregiving families. *Nursing Research, 44(3)*, 139-146.

General Accounting Office. (1994). *Private sector eldercare.* (Department of Health and Human Services No. 94-60). Washington, DC: Author.

Given, B., & Given, C. (1991). *Family caregiving for the elderly.* In J.J. Fizpatrick, R.I. Tantum, & A.K. Jacox (Eds.), Annual review of nursing research, 9, (pp.77-101). New York: Springer.

Kelley, L. S., Buckwalter, K. C., & Maas, M. L. (1999). Access to health care resources for family caregivers of elderly persons with dementia. *Nursing Outlook, 47(1)*, 814.

Leventhal, H., Leventhal, E., & Van Nguyen, T. (1985). Reactions of families to illness: Theoretical models and perspectives. In D. Turk & R. Kerns (Eds.), *Health, illness, and families: A life-span perspective* (pp. 108-145). New York: John Wiley & Sons.

Levine, C. (1998). *Rough crossings: Family caregivers' odysseys through the health system.* New York, NY: United Hospital Fund.

McConnell, S. (1999). Caregiver support strategies: The state of the states. *Family caregivers: Partners in long-term care.* Proceedings from an invitational state policy conference (pp. 12-17). San Francisco, CA: Family Caregiver Alliance

Melillo, K. D., & Futrell, M. (1995). A guide for assessing caregiver needs: Determining a health history database for family caregivers. *The Nurse Practitioner, 20*(5).

Met-Life Mature Market Group and Alliance for Caregiving. (1997). *The Met-Life study of employer costs for working caregivers.* Westport, CT: Author.

Mezey, M. (1999). Bringing the hospital home. *Nursing Counts, 2*(3), 3.

National Academy on an Aging Society (2000). *Caregiving: Helping the elderly with activity limitations,* Washington, D.C.

National Alliance for Caregiving. (1997). *Family caregiving in the US: Findings from a national survey* (Publication No. D16474). Bethesda, MD: Author.

National Center for Health Statistics. (1994). *Health, United States, 1993.* Hyattsville, MD: Public Health Service.

National Health Council. (1999). *Family caregiving: Agenda for action.* Washington, D.C: Author.

Naylor, M. D., Campbell, R., Jacobsen, B. S., Mezey, M. D., Pauly, M. V., & Schwartz, J. S. (1999). Comprehensive discharge planning and home follow-up of hospitalized elders. *Journal of the American Medical Association, 281*(7), 613-620.

Reinhard, S., & Horwitz, A. (1995). Caregiver burden: Differentiating the content and consequences of family caregiving. *Journal of Marriage and the Family, 57,* 741-750.

Reinhard, S., Rosswurm, M. A., & Robinson, K. M. (2000). Policy recommendations for family caregiver support. *Journal of Gerontological Nursing, 26*(1), 47-49.

Robinson, K. (1989). Predictors of depression among wife caregivers. *Nursing Research, 36*(30), 359-363.

Rosswurm, M., & Lanham, D. (1998). Discharge planning for elderly patients. *Journal of Gerontological Nursing, 24*(5), 14-21.

Wagner, D., Hunt, G., & Reinhard, S. (2000). *Identifying and addressing barriers to workplace eldercare programs.* Paper presented at the Work and Family: Expanding Horizons Conference of The Business and Professional Women's Foundation, The Center for Working Families at the University of California, Berkeley.

Whitlatch, C., Feinberg, L., & Sebesta, D. (1997). Depression and health in family caregivers. *Journal of Aging and Health, 9,* 222-243.

Witrogen McLeod: *Chapter Eight*

Harvey, A. (2000). *The direct path: Creating a journey to the divine through the world's mystical traditions.* New York: Broadway Books.

Myss, C. (1996). *Anatomy of the spirit.* New York: Three Rivers Press. Quote is from her PBS series.

Northrup, C. (1994). *Women's bodies, women's minds.* New York: Bantam.

Doka: *Chapter Nine*

Doka, K. J., & Aber, R. (1989). Psychological loss and grief. In K. Doka (Ed.), *Disenfranchised grief: Recognizing hidden sorrow.* Lexington, MA: Lexington Press.

Doka, K. J. (2001). *Disenfranchised grief: New directions, challenges and strategies for practice.* Champaign, IL: Research Press.

Lazarus, R. J., & Folkman, S. (1984). *Stress, appraisal and coping.* New York: Basic Books.

Lindemann, E. (1944). Symptomatology and the management of grief. *American Journal of Psychiatry, 101,* 141-149.

Martin, T. A., & Doka, K. J. (1999). *Men don't cry, women do: Transcending gender stereotypes of grief.* Philadelphia: Brunner-Mazel.

Papadatou, D. (2000). A proposed model of health professionals' grieving process. *Omega, 41,* 59-77.

Rando, T. A. (2000). *Clinical dimensions of anticipatory mourning: Theory and practice in working with the dying, their loved ones and their caregivers.* Champaign, IL: Research Press.

Vachon, M. (1989). *Occupational stress in the care of the critically ill, the dying and the bereaved.* New York: Hemisphere.

Weisman, A. (1972). *On dying and denying: A psychiatric study of terminality.* New York: Behavioral Publications.

Worden, J. W. (1991). *Grief counseling and grief therapy.* New York: Springer.

Blackwell & Stern: *Chapter Ten*

Benson, H. (1996) *Timeless healing.* New York: Simon and Schuster.

Burton, L. (1998) The spiritual dimension of palliative care. *Seminars in Oncology Nursing, 14:2,* 121-128.

Chichin, E. (1999) *On cultural diversity in end-of-life care: the role of culture in the nursing home.* Ethics Network, December.

Congress, E. (1999) *The diverse culture of the long-term care setting.* Ethics Network, December.

Doka, K. J. (Series Editor). (1997). *Clergy to Clergy: Helping You Minister to Those Confronting Illness, Death and Grief.* Washington, DC: Hospice Foundation of America.

Frank, A. (1952) *The diary of a young girl.* New York: Modern Library.

Goffman, E. (1972) *Asylums.* New York: Doubleday.

Lamm, M. (1984) From an address delivered May 4 at the Jewish Hospice Symposium of the Synagogue Council of America.

Lewis, M. and Butler, R. (1974) *Life-review therapy: putting memories to work in individual and group psychotherapy.* Geriatrics, 29.

Lopez, B. (1990) *Crow and weasel.* San Francisco: North Point Press.

Maugans, T. (1996) *The SPIRITual history.* Archive of Family Medicine 5:11-16.

Sherman: *Chapter Eleven*

Addington-Hall, J., & McCarthy, M. (1995). Dying from cancer: Results of a national population-based investigation. *Palliative Medicine, 4,* 295-305.

Aaronson, N. (1990). Quality of life research in cancer clinical trials: A need for common rules and language. *Oncology, 4,* 59-66.

Andershed, B., & Ternestedt, M. (1999). Involvement of relatives in care of the dying in different care cultures: Development of a theoretical understanding. *Nursing Science Quarterly, 12,* 45-51.

Beacon, H., & Thompson, S. (1996). Multi-level models for repeated measurement data: Application to quality of life data in clinical trials. *Stat Med, 15,* 2717-32.

Beeney, L., Butow, P., & Dunn, S. (1997). Normal adjustment to cancer: Characteristics and assessment. In R. K. Portenoy, & E. Bruera (Eds.), *Topics in palliative care (Vol 1)* 213-244. New York: Oxford University Press.

Berns, R., & Colvin, E. (1998). The final story: Events at the bedside of dying patients as told by survivors. *ANNA Journal, 25,* 583-587.

Blanchard, C., Albrecht, T., & Ruckdeschel, J. (1997). The crisis of cancer: Psychological impact on family caregivers. *Oncology, 11,* 189-194.

Bone, R. (1995). Hospice and palliative care. *Disease-a-Month, 61,* 773-825.

Byock, I. (1997). *Dying well: The prospect for growth at the end of life.* New York: Riverhead Books.

Canadian Palliative Care Association. (1995). *Palliative care: Towards a consensus in standardized principles of practice.* Ontario, Canada: Author.

Cella, D. F. (1992). Quality of life: The concept. *Journal of Palliative Care, 8,* 8-13.

Cella, D. F., & Tulsky, D. S. (1990). Measuring quality of life today: Methodological aspects. *Oncology, 4,* 29-38.

Chapman, C. R., & Gavrin, J. (1993). Suffering and its relationship to pain. *Journal of Palliative Care, 9,* 95-113.

Davies, B., Reimer, J., & Marten, N. (1994). Family functioning and its implications for palliative care. *Journal of Palliative Care, 10,* 35-36.

Davies, B., Reimer, J., Brown, P., & Marten, N. (1995). *Fading away: The experience of transition in families with terminal illness.* New York: Baywood Publishing Company, Inc.

Doyle, D. (1994). *Caring for a dying relative: A guide for families.* New York: Oxford University Press.

Ell, K., Nishimot, R., Mantell, J., & Hamovitch, M. (1998). ongitudinal analysis of psychological adaptation among family members of patients with cancer. *Journal of Psychosomatic Research, 32,* 429.

Emanuel, E., Fairclough, D., Slutsman, J., Alpert, H., Baldwin, D., & Emanuel, L. (1999). Assistance from family members, friends, paid care givers and volunteers in the care of terminally ill patients. *The New England Journal of Medicine, 341,* 956-963.

Ferrans, C., & Powers, M. (1995). Quality of Life Index: Development and psychometric properties. *Advances in Nursing Science, 8*, 15-24.

Ferris, F., Flannery, J., McNeal, H., Morissette, M., Cameron, R., & Bally, G. (1995). *Palliative care: A comprehensive guide for the care of persons with HIV disease*. Ontario, Canada: Mount Sinai Hospital/Casey House Hospice.

Finlay, I. G., & Dunlop, R. (1994). Quality of life assessment in palliative care. Ann *Oncology, 5*, 13-18.

Foley, K. (1995). Pain, physician-assisted suicide, and euthanasia. *Pain Forum, 4*, 163-176.

Hanestad, R. (1990). Errors of measurement affecting the reliability and validity of data acquired from self-assessed quality of life. *Scandinavian Journal of the Caring Sciences, 4*, 29-34.

Hays, J. C. (1986). Patient symptoms and family coping: Predictors of hospice utilization patterns. *Cancer Nursing, 9*, 317-325.

Higginson, I. J. (1998). Introduction: Defining the unit of care: Who are we supporting and how? In E. Bruera, & R. K. Portenoy (Eds.), *Topics in Palliative Care* (Vol 2). New York: Oxford University Press.

Hinton, J. (1994). Can home care maintain an acceptable quality of life for patients with terminal cancer and their relatives? *Palliative Medicine, 8*, 183-196.

Hodgson, C. S., Higginson, I. J., McDonnell, M., & Butters, E. (1997). Family anxiety in advanced cancer. *British Journal of Cancer, 6*, 120-124.

Hoskins, C. N., Baker, S., Budin, W., Ekstrom, D., Maislin, G., Sherman, D.W., Steelman-Bohlander, J., Bookbinder, M., & Knaus, C. (1996). Adjustment among husbands of women with breast cancer. *Journal of Psychosocial Oncology, 14*, 41-69.

Kaye, J., & Gracely, E. J. (1993). Psychological distress in cancer patients and their spouses. *Journal of Cancer Education, 8*, 47-52.

King, C., Haberman, M., Berry, D., Bush, N., Butler, L., Hassey, K., Ferrel, B., Grant, M., Gue, D., Hinds, P., Kreuer, J., Padilla, G., & Underwood, S. (1997). Quality of life and the cancer experience: The state of the knowledge. *Oncology Nursing Forum, 24*, 27-41.

Klein, S.J. (1998). *Heavenly hurts: Surviving AIDS-related deaths and losses.* New York: Baywood Publishing Company.

Kristjanson, L. (1989). Quality of terminal care: Salient indictors identified by families. *Journal of Palliative Care, 5,* 21-28.

Kristjanson, L. J., Sloan, J. A., Dudgeon, D., & Adaskin. E. (1996). Family members' perception of palliative cancer care: Predictors of family functioning and family members' health. *Journal of Palliative Care, 12,* 10-20.

Kruse, A. (1995). Patients in the terminal phase and their caregivers as a dyad: How do they perceive the finite stage of life, how do they cope with it? *Gerontol Geriatr, 28,* 264-72.

Lederberg, M. (1998). The family of the cancer patient. In J. Holland (Ed.), *Psychooncology.* New York: Oxford University Press.

Loscalzo, M., & Zabora, J. (1998). Care of the cancer patient: Response of family and staff. In E. Bruera, & R. K. Portenoy (Eds.), *Topics in Palliative Care,* (Vol 2). New York: Oxford University Press.

Lynn, J., Teno, J. M. & Phillips, R. S. (1997). Perceptions by family members of the dying experience of older and seriously ill patients. *Ann Intern Med, 126,* 97-106.

McMillan, S. C., & Mahon, M. (1994a). A study of quality of life of hospice patients on admission and at week 3. *Cancer Nursing, 17,* 52-60.

McMillan, S. C., & Mahon, M. (1994b). The impact of hospice services on the quality of life of primary caregivers. *Oncology Nursing Forum, 21,* 1189-95.

McSkimming, S., Hodges, M., Super, A., Driever, M., Schoessler, M., Franey, S., & Lee, M. (1999). The experience of life-threatening illness: Patient's and their loved one's perspective. *Journal of Palliative Medicine, 2,* 173-184.

Medalie, J. (1997). The patient and family adjustment to chronic disease in the home. *Disability and rehabilitation, 19,* 163-170.

Meyers, C. (1997). The Blanchard/Albrecht/Ruckdeschel article reviewed. *Oncology, 11,* 201-202.

Miaskowski, C., Zimmer, E., Barrett, K., Dibble, S., & Wallhagen, M. (1997). Differences in patients' and family caregivers' perceptions of the pain experience influence patient and caregiver outcomes. *Pain, 72,* 217-26.

O'Boyle, C. A., & Waldron, D. (1997). Quality of life issues in palliative medicine. *Journal of Neurology, 244,* 18-25.

Omne-Poten, H., Holmberg, L., Bergstrom, R., Sjoden, P., & Burns. T. (1993). Psychosocial adjustment among husbands of women treated for breast cancer: Mastectomy vs. breast conserving surgery. European *Journal of Cancer, 29,* 1393-1397.

Ragsdale, D., Kotarba, J., Morrow, J. (1992). Quality of life of hospitalized persons with AIDS. *Image, 24,* 259-265.

Rando, T. A. (1984). *Grief, dying, and death: Clinical interventions for caregivers.* Champaign, IL: Research Press.

Smeenk, F., de Witte, L., van Haastregt, J., Schipper, R., Biezemans, H., Crebolder, H. (1998). Transmural care of terminal cancer patients: Effects on the quality of life of direct caregivers. *Nursing Research, 47,* 129-136.

Stewart, A., Teno, J., Patrick, D., & Lynn, J. (1998). *The concept of quality of life of dying persons in the context of health care.* Unpublished manuscript.

Szabo, V., & Strang, V. (1999). Experiencing control in caregiving. Image: *Journal of Nursing Scholarship, 31,* 71-75.

Zacharias, D., Gilg, C., & Foxall, M. (1994). Quality of life and coping in patients with gynecologic cancer and their spouses. *Oncology Nursing Forum, 21,* 1699-706.

Price: *Chapter Twelve*

Murphy, P. and Price, D (1995). ACT: Taking a Positive Approach to End-of-Life Care. *American Journal of Nursing, 95,* 3:42-43.

The President's Commission for the Study of Ethical Issues in Medicine and Biomedical and Behavioral Research. *Deciding to Forgo Life-Sustaining Treatment.* Washington, DC: U.S. Government Printing Office, 1983.

Price, D.M. and Murphy, PA. (1994). DNR: Still Crazy After All These Years. *Journal of Nursing Law*, 1, 3:53—61.

Price, D.M. and Murphy, PA. (1994). Tube Feeding and the Ethics of Caring. *Journal of Nursing Law*, 1, 4:53—64.

Solomon, M.Z. (1993). Decisions Near the End of Life: Professional Views on Life-Sustaining Treatments. *American Journal of Public Health*, 83, 1:14—25.

The SUPPORT Principal Investigators. A Controlled Trial to Improve Care for Seriously Ill Hospitalized Patients. *Journal of the American Medical Association*, 274, 20:1591—1598.

Davidson: *Conclusion*

Halling, E. (2000, December) Learning to love Gabriel. *Good Housekeeping* pp. 89-91.

Lamott, A. (1999) *Traveling mercies: some thoughts on faith.* New York: Random House.

Manning, D. (1999) *Share my lonesome valley: the slow grief of long-term care.* Oklahoma City: Insight Books. (800) 658-9262 or *www.insightbooks.com*

· Notes ·